Economics of Planning Policies in China

Fast urbanizing countries like China have experienced rapid – albeit geographically uneven – local and regional economic growth during the past few decades. Notwithstanding this development pattern, China has been investing heavily in targeted coastal and inland regions through planning policies for infrastructure, location and cities. This is a largely place-based investment process that is of great importance for the public, business and policymakers. China's urban and regional transformations provide incentives for spatial agglomeration and will shift the growth of activities within and across cities for decades to come. This spatial differentiation is likely to be driven by government decisions at all levels about where, when and in what to invest, in an institutional context where policy instruments act to constrain or facilitate China's urban and regional development.

Economics of Planning Policies in China looks at the role that the institutional characteristics of the Chinese planning system and market mechanisms play in transforming and shaping the infrastructure, location and cities with the potential for spatial disparity and inclusive growth. The planning and geographical perspective and evidence make this book a reference for international scholars, policymakers and graduates.

Wen-jie Wu is an Associate Professor at Heriot-Watt University, UK.

Regions and Cities

Series Editor in Chief
Susan M. Christopherson, *Cornell University, USA*

Editors
Maryann Feldman, *University of Georgia, USA*
Gernot Grabher, *HafenCity University Hamburg, Germany*
Ron Martin, *University of Cambridge, UK*
Kieran P. Donaghy, *Cornell University, USA*

In today's globalised, knowledge-driven and networked world, regions and cities have assumed heightened significance as the interconnected nodes of economic, social and cultural production, and as sites of new modes of economic and territorial governance and policy experimentation. This book series brings together incisive and critically engaged international and interdisciplinary research on this resurgence of regions and cities, and should be of interest to geographers, economists, sociologists, political scientists and cultural scholars, as well as to policy-makers involved in regional and urban development.

For more information on the Regional Studies Association visit www.regionalstudies.org

There is a **30% discount** available to RSA members on books in the *Regions and Cities* series, and other subject related Taylor and Francis books and e-books including Routledge titles. To order just e-mail Cara.Trevor@tandf.co.uk, or phone on +44 (0)20 701 76186 and declare your RSA membership. You can also visit www.routledge.com and use the discount code: **RSA0901**

113 Economics of Planning Policies in China
Infrastructure, Location and Cities
Wen-jie Wu

112 The Empirical and Institutional Dimensions of Smart Specialisation
Edited by Philip McCann, Frank van Oort and John Goddard

111 EU Cohesion Policy
Reassessing performance and direction
Edited by John Bachtler, Peter Berkowitz, Sally Hardy and Tatjana Muravska

110 Geography of Innovation
Edited by Nadine Massard and Corinne Autant-Bernard

Economics of Planning Policies in China

Infrastructure, Location and Cities

Wen-jie Wu

Routledge
Taylor & Francis Group

LONDON AND NEW YORK

First published 2017 by Routledge

2 Park Square, Milton Park, Abingdon, Oxfordshire OX14 4RN
52 Vanderbilt Avenue, New York, NY 10017

Routledge is an imprint of the Taylor & Francis Group, an informa business

First issued in paperback 2019

British Library Cataloguing in Publication Data
A catalogue record for this book is available from the British Library

Library of Congress Cataloging in Publication Data
Names: Wu, Wenjie, 1985– author.
Title: Economics of planning policies in China : infrastructure, location
    and cities / Wen-jie Wu.
Description: Abingdon, Oxon ; New York, NY : Routledge, 2017.
Identifiers: LCCN 2016034240| ISBN 9781138790452 (hardback) |
    ISBN 9781315764207 (ebook)
Subjects: LCSH: Regional planning—China. | City planning—China. |
    Urban policy—China.
Classification: LCC HT395.C55 W827 2017 | DDC 307.1/2160951—dc23
LC record available at https://lccn.loc.gov/2016034240

ISBN: 978-1-138-79045-2 (hbk)
ISBN: 978-0-367-87046-1 (pbk)

Typeset in Times New Roman
by Swales & Willis Ltd, Exeter, Devon, UK

Contents

PART IV
Conclusions   215

Figures

Tables

Foreword I

The rest of the world has been waking up to China and Chinese development for twenty-five years now, but still remarkably little is really known outside of China. And even less is known about Chinese spatial development and planning policies dating back to the early phases of Mao's People's Republic of China. The non-Chinese world, especially in the Anglo-Saxon West, is fascinated by China but seriously ignorant; two cultures separated by an uncommon language. Unlike India, there is no common history of interrelationship. Neither Britain nor the US has a distinguished history in their relations to China. Britain had one of the most disgraceful episodes of its colonial era, fighting wars to force China to become addicted to opium, then condemning the Chinese in popular culture as opium addicts. The Americans simply ignored China for 150 years and then locked themselves into backing the losing side in the revolutionary struggle against the Japanese and in the post-Second World War era.

There have been individuals in the West who have contributed to understanding Chinese culture and society over the past 150 years but collectively there has been a failure. The English-speaking world has only begun to come to terms with the reality of China in the last twenty years. But even now there is a real problem of language: both of the English-speaking world to Chinese sources; but also of the Chinese to English-language material. China is the largest nation on earth; its economy over the past thirty years has been the fastest growing in the world's history. It has gone through a period of industrialization and urbanization that makes the Industrial Revolution in Britain look like an almost glacial set of changes. In the twenty-five years from 1980 to 2005, the proportion of China's population which was by UN definition 'urban', more than doubled, from 19.6 to 40.4%. According to Bairoch (1988) it took 100 years from 1750 for the urban population of England to grow from some 17 to 19% to 45% of the total population.

So this book is extremely welcome and opportune. If we do not know a lot in the English-speaking world about the facts of China's development, we know even less about the policies which provided the structure, sometimes assisting and sometimes restricting that astonishing growth of the economy and of its cities. The scope of this book covers the whole development of modern China, its cities and its regions, from the start of the Communist era in 1950 to the present.

'Planning' in China means something different from the meaning of the word as used in the UK or the USA. It is not just a passive system of zoning or regulating; it does not just proscribe what development can happen where and when. Over much of the earlier part of the period, planning activity actively built on much more than just infrastructure. It also, of course, proscribed what development could happen where, but it also initiated and coordinated development too. This book has two chapters on the development and influence of two key elements in China's development strategy, as exemplified by the rolling out of airports and high-speed rail networks. It also provides a valuable analysis of the effects these have had on China's uneven – or concentrated – urban development and the emergence of mega-cities. The evolution of spatial economic development patterns in China has been dramatically changed over the past sixty-five years, especially since the '*reform and opening up*' (*gai ge kai fang*) of China in the 1980s.

In this invaluable book Wen-jie Wu provides a window for international students and researchers into the forms and influence of planning, Chinese-style. In the era of central planning, roughly from 1950 to 1990, planning took on the role of the market in allocating resources. Chinese cities developed on a common plan yet, nevertheless, uneven development patterns were typical of industrial development, infrastructure and resource allocations as guided by the planning system.

The period of 'reform and opening up' after 1990 saw market mechanisms begin to play an increasing role in allocating – including spatially allocating – resources of labour and capital. This had the potential to weaken State-owned industries' dependency on municipal authorities. But it also spurred investment in places that had been left behind, leading to new forms of spatial economic disparities. Perhaps unsurprisingly, however, the transition towards a market-orientated economic system, while it has been real and it has been significant, has been only partial; it has been proclaimed more firmly than it has been enacted. This leaves China as a special case in the study of the economic implications of planning policies and their impact on cities, location and infrastructure.

The emerging pattern of spatial agglomeration has been driven significantly by what one might think of as market-generated labour mobility and urban development. The rapidly emerging new urban agglomerations and concentrations of economic activity have also supported an expansion of transport infrastructure to connect them to the peripheral regions. This process is guided by regional planning policies as much as market pressures. But still a considerable share of the old industrial cities is dominated by State-owned enterprises, and the economic transformation of these cities have been relatively unsuccessful. This means that there are at least two types of regional planning policies at work today in China: one is to stimulate and sustain economic growth in vibrant regions; and the other is to regenerate the regions left behind, in the former industrial and economic structure. This has a Chinese dimension – it has all occurred in a period of only sixty-five years or so and the declining regions were largely planned – yet the problem is familiar to old industrial countries such as the UK or the USA.

This book addresses a very important era in Chinese development and the evolution of its planning policies. All economists understand that there are endemic problems of 'market failure' (in the technical sense found in welfare economics) in land markets and in patterns of spatial development. We understand, therefore, that there is a role for spatial planning. However the defects in the patterns of spatial development and land use perceived by politicians and policymakers frequently diverge from this welfare economics analysis of market failure. Planning policies may intervene to provide public good, coordinate development and channel the spatial pattern of development, but the tune is significantly one composed by a political process and set of judgements. Moreover, the actual distribution of urban systems and agglomerations depends more on the inheritance from the past and on incentives produced by markets, working sometimes invisibly under the surface, than it does on the guidance of planning policies.

Planning, even in a country with as strong a central State as China, constantly faces not just an uneven pattern of prosperity but many forces over which it has less than complete control; and sometimes may generate unintended consequences because of the constant operation of market forces under the surface. As is witnessed by the failure to regenerate many of the old industrial regions of Western Europe, effective policies are difficult to find. There are cases of success: some of the German cities suggest themselves as examples, as well as partial successes such as Glasgow or Lille. But there are many cases where interventions seem to make little difference: cases such as Sunderland, Liverpool or Charleroi.

The place-based policies characterizing the era to about the year 2000 gradually gave way, as the market became more active to more people-based policies. Wen-jie tackles this aspect in the second part of the book. It was hard for cities that relied on the power of centralized, non-market forces to grow, to transform their industrial structures and the skills of their labour force as China moved increasingly towards a market-orientated economic system. In March 2014 the Chinese Government launched a new and ambitious 'National New Urbanization Plan'. This marked a shift in its urban development strategy towards a human-centred and more sustainable pathway.

A major source of academic and policy debates focuses on the roles of transport infrastructure improvements in the urban and regional agglomerations. Can such infrastructure transform spatial patterns of development or merely facilitate them? Indeed can such investments be used successfully at all, to change patterns of development? Certainly the Italian experience of the *Autostrada del Sole,* designed to transform the Mezzogiorno region, does not support that conclusion. The debate about the new high-speed railway in the UK (HS2), which it is claimed will bring substantial development benefits to the old industrial regions of the north, is also relevant. The third part of this book explores recent infrastructure investments in China designed with this transformational logic in mind; the new expansions of airport and railway infrastructure.

Planning in China also plays a central role in the process of spatial development at the intra-city level. Reflecting this a focus in the third part of this book is on the economic implications of the introduction of a degree of market power into the allocation of land and housing, and the interaction between land uses and the patterns of human activity that colours many aspects of planning theory. In the context of China is there evidence that land-use configurations affect the structure of human activity? Answers shed light on debates found in the planning literature; for example, the benefits of complex, mixed land use on human activity as proposed by Jane Jacobs (1961). This is a promising topic for China. Indeed, the future success of city planning needs to be evaluated in terms of its contribution to the vibrancy of life in cities, as well as on the basis of its economic effects on individuals or on the economic growth of specific cities.

In the developing (World Bank, 2008) and developed countries (OECD, 2011; Cheshire et al., 2014), a large body of work has looked at the effects of place-based planning and development policies on local economic performance, measured by productivity, employment, wages, housing prices and other outcomes of interest. More sophisticated work has looked also at the extent to which any local gains only represent displacement effects (Einiö and Overman, 2016). I personally judge that the balance of evidence is that people-focused interventions are more likely to yield net gains, but understanding the interactions between people and places is still imperfect, and understanding it better is vital if we are to make effective policy. The themes in this book and the analysis and Wen-jie Wu's account of the Chinese experience provide new information and evidence to bear on this fundamental question in economic geography.

As Wen-jie's supervisor I am delighted to contribute this Foreword. He is an engaging and dedicated scholar and in this book he provides the non-Chinese-speaking world with a rich array of new information, evidence and analysis on one of the most important processes in the history of world development and urbanization: the staggering growth of China's cities and the role – sometimes positive but also at times negative – that planning policies have played in this, and how they have shaped China's development.

Paul Cheshire
Professor of Economic Geography
London School of Economics and Political Science, UK

References

Bairoch, P. (1988) *Cities and Economic Development: From the Dawn of History to the Present*, Chicago, IL: University of Chicago Press.

Cheshire, P., Nathan M. and Overman, H. (2014) *Urban Economics and Urban Policy: Challenging Conventional Policy Wisdom*, London: Edward Elgar.

Einiö, E. and Overman, H.G. (2016) *The (Displacement) Effects of Spatially Targeted Enterprise Initiatives: Evidence from UK LEGI*, SERC Discussion Paper 191, London: LSE.

Jacobs, J. (1961) *The Death and Life of Great American Cities*, London: Pimlico.

OECD (2011) *Regional Outlook*, Paris: OECD.

World Bank (2008) *World Development Report 2009: Reshaping Economic Geography*, Washington, DC: World Bank.

Foreword II

China's urbanization over the last three decades has been unprecedented in human history: 260 million migrants have moved to cities, supporting rapid economic growth and development. China's urbanisation rate has been increasing by about one percentage point per year, from 26% in 1990 to 56.1% in 2015. Over the next 30 years, an additional 300 million Chinese are likely to move to cities. This unprecedented urbanization wave has not only changed the lives of hundreds of millions and contributed to China's amazing 10% annual economic growth rate in the past two decades, but modified the world's political, economic and environmental landscapes.

However, China's growth is spatially uneven. Cities like Beijing and Shanghai show an all-around development, while some cities in the middle and western regions are still backward. Such spatial disparities draw attention to both economists and urban planners. To better understand the spatial dynamics and the underlying mechanisms, this book provides us with an important perspective: the economics of planning policies for cities, location and infrastructure in China. To see how important planning policy is for the configurations of urban and regional development patterns, this book examines the evolution of regional policies in China, aiming to understand the state-of-the-art planning implications shaping recent urban transformations, vibrancy and agglomerations in the spatial context. This is a meaningful topic which has recently emerged as the focal point of policy questions about what works for instrumenting with spatial disparities in China and elsewhere in the developing world.

This book is full of insight about regional and urban policies in contemporaneous China, and will no doubt become a reference for policymakers and scholars interested in economics, urban planning and development policy.

Professor Siqi Zheng
Director, Hang Lung Center for Real Estate, Tsinghua University, China

Acknowledgements

This book attempts to learn useful lessons from an emerging body of literature on China's planning policies, and particularly from my involvement in various research projects at the Chinese Academy of Science, the University of Glasgow and Heriot-Watt University. I am particularly appreciative of my (senior) co-workers in these projects: Jie Fan, Wenzhong Zhang, Jinfeng Jun, Bing Wang, Yutian Liang, Guanpeng Dong, Zhenbin Dong, Jianghao Wang and among others. I thank Qing Zhang, Di Wu, Xin Wang, Chengyu Li and others, who have helped me with materials and given excellent editorial support. I would like to thank the editors at Routledge for their encouragement. I am grateful to Paul Cheshire, Steve Gibbons, Olmo Silva and Henry Overman from the London School of Economics and Political Science, Siqi Zheng from Tsinghua University, and Yaping Wang from the University of Glasgow, for inspiring me with great thoughts over the years.

Part I

Overview

1 Introduction

China has experienced substantial but uneven urban transformation in the past six decades, which has brought great challenges and opportunities for planners and policymakers. This transformation has come alongside massive infrastructure investments, the gradual formation of agglomerations and market integration that are guided by various planning policies. Indeed, the implementation of planning policies has emerged as an important way of re-orientating urban and regional transformations in China. Historically, the introduction of the 'Five-Year-Plan' by the Chinese Government in the early 1950s signified a landmark shift in its development strategy towards a regular five-year planning system. One important focus of the 'Five-Year-Plan' series is to make infrastructure, particularly transport infrastructure, available to both core regions and marginal regions, and integrate a variety of Socialist-based and Capitalism-based regimes into a local and regional economic development tide. However, inherent tension rises as infrastructure, including railway and airport network improvements, help to raise spatial disparities between metropolitan and periphery regions. The planning programmes of infrastructure improvements have profound implications for urban systems and spatial agglomerations. The role of China's planning policies on economic transition and growth, and their spatial implication are therefore crucial to our understanding of what drives success and failure in local and regional agglomeration and development modes.

There has been a growing interest from various disciplines such as economics, political economy, and social policy in the role of place-based planning policies on influencing spatial economic performance (e.g. Glaeser and Redlick, 2008; Neumark and Kolko, 2010; Kline, 2010; Busso et al., 2013; Faggio, 2014; Cheshire et al., 2015). Recent Chinese studies have investigated the macro-level transitions on economic systems. However, lessons are likely to be generalized in the spatial context because of the unique characteristics of the spatial-temporal evolution of uneven development patterns in Communist China. Existing theoretical frameworks – derived from transitional socialist legacies to interpret the roles of the State and market forces in urban and regional transformations – are reflected by the evolution and repositioning of China's planning policies that often lead to differential economic convergence and divergence modes, within and among regions. International mainstream journals have published a growing number of studies using Chinese evidence and data, but much remains to be known about the evolution of planning policies and their spatial economic implications in transitional socialist countries, including China. The scarcity of the literature leaves a gap for spatial policymaking.

The resurgence of China's spatial economic disparities depends, to some extent, on planning policies for cities, locations and infrastructure investments. In this situation, careful evaluation of planning policy interventions is needed. Planning policies, however, do not work simply and effectively because of rules and regulations in policy initiatives. According to Cheshire et al. (2014), reducing spatial disparities through planning policies is challenging, as evidenced in the UK. Planning policies might work because of the non-random way in which they invest in mega-projects within and between cities. These investments can be regarded as a prominent policy tool for reshaping comparative locational advantages and enhancing the agglomeration process of production factors such as amenities, labour force and capital fundamentals in specific cities and regions. This policy channel has played a critical economic role in urban development.

As shown in the following chapters, the role of planning policies in shaping China's spatial development patterns over the past six decades makes understanding the fundamentals and characteristics of the Chinese planning policies essential. Tracking these patterns is a difficult but meaningful task. Take cities, for example: decades of rapid urbanization and infrastructure improvements, as guided by the planning system, have changed the 'faces' of many Chinese cities dramatically. In particular, the constraints on migration and private sector investment in the centrally planned economy era (1950s–1980s) shifted the spatial economic growth towards industrial towns in the north-eastern and 'Third-tier' (*san xian*) regions. With reforms and opening up, large proportions of planning policies have concentrated on promoting spatial economic performance in coastal regions. At the intercity level, expressways, airports and high-speed railways have been built and expanded to strengthen intercity connections, whereas non-randomly distributed infrastructure projects have also affected the economic disparities between cities. At the intra-city level, subways, ring roads and radial roads have developed rapidly to reduce commuting times. However, congestion and pollution problems in mega-cities have increased. This infrastructure expansion is driven by Government planning decisions on where and how to invest, in a context where powerful political and institutional factors act to constrain or facilitate the economic implications of planning policies. This basic viewpoint – that the interaction of cities, location and infrastructure improvement is important for economic growth – has influenced most planners, economists and economic geographers alike, as well as their evaluations of which planning policies work better for local economic development.

The aim of this book is to analyse the role that planning policies play in China's urban and regional transformation when growth, agglomeration and regeneration are the potential objectives; that is, how important planning decisions play a role in influencing urban and regional development. In fact, there are three specific motivations for the focus on cities, location and infrastructure.

The first motivation is to help build a solid evidence base for understanding the economic implications of planning policies on Chinese cities and regions. Although planning policies are frequently championed as a useful instrument, both for growth and for addressing spatial economic disparities, the existing evidence and theoretical arguments are not clear-cut (Gibbons, 2015). The Chinese experience and evidence over the past six decades can inspire those involved in the planning of cities and infrastructure, by shedding light on what outcomes to expect and how regulations enhance or distort the spatial agglomeration process when massive Government investment is allocated in the Third-tier regions, when special economic zones are reinforced by the Central Government in contemporary China, or when transport links that connect cities with each other in the urban system become denser. Such information is critical to good policymaking, yet has so far been relatively deficient in China.

China's urban and regional development in recent decades and its relation with planning policies will be a useful lens to reflect economic transitions from the centrally planned economy era to the market-orientated economy era. Overall, economic growth is enhanced by necessary policy incentives to gain better access to markets in other cities and various ports. In the market-orientated economy era, differential changes in market access affect relative growth rates between cities and regions, whereas such changes don't create so much difference in economic performance in the centrally planned economy era. The range of China's planning policies that will be elaborated in the following chapters include the guiding principles, rationales and philosophy of the Chinese planning system, as well as the economic implications of formulating uneven spatial development over the past six decades.

The second motivation, at least since the works of Johan George Kohl and Alfred Marshall in the nineteenth century, is that transport accessibility has played a pivotal role in urban theories among geographers, planners and economists alike. Transport accessibility determines the spatial layout and structures of core-periphery urban systems and influences how cities of different rank connect with others. Urban and regional agglomerations, as suggested by economic theories, rise with improved transport accessibility. Decades of rapid transport infrastructure expansions, as regulated by the Central Government's planning policies, have provided a good opportunity for paramount scientific value, by creating a foundation for the economic implications of infrastructure investments. A natural question emerges: will the transport infrastructure expansion as guided by the Chinese planning system influence the spatial configuration of urban systems and regional disparities? Using airport and railway networks as case studies, Chapters 6 and 7 examine these elements using a combination of complex network models (Dong et al., 2009; Wang et al., 2011; Lin, 2012) and traditional market potential models, based on the economic geography literature (Harris, 1954; Gibbons et al., 2012). However, a major barrier to the identification of causal effects on outcomes of new infrastructure is that these facilities may not be allocated randomly across fast-growing cities and regenerated regions. Recent works of Faber (2014) and Banerjee et al. (2012) on China's intercity road network have overcome this problem by measuring the local effects of transport accessibility, and have focused on places between cities that were affected incidentally by inter-city road infrastructure expansion.

Third, this book provides insights into, and alternative thoughts on, the vibrant urban space in a spatial context where big data emerge (Batty, 2013; Goodchild, 2013). To some extent, the intensity of human activity at fine geographical scales can be regarded as a proxy indicator in identifying city vibrancy patterns by tracking the temporal distribution of human activity based on mobile phone data (Jacobs-Crisioni et al., 2014). Chapter 8 provides an empirical insight into this topic within the land and housing marketization context, employing Beijing as the case study. In the research, we do not adopt traditional static surveys, but use temporally integrated human activities collected by the positioning system of mobile phones. The underlying ways of thinking adopted in Chapter 8 favour the market-reform and land-development mechanisms that played important roles in shaping the vibrant urban space.

Given this focus, this book touches on many of the priorities identified in the economic geography and planning literature in China, but is centred on three factors: at the regional level, the need for understanding the rationales of planning policies that drive the uneven economic development modes, and the roles planning policies play in affecting the formation and evolution of urban and regional agglomerations; and at the intra-city level, the importance of focusing on geographic uncertainties of urban vibrancy patterns through the interactions between people and places. The book is organized into four parts, starting with the Chinese planning system, with Part IV providing some concluding remarks.

In the rest of Part I, the basic building blocks of Chinese planning policies are developed in Chapter 2. The mix of industries and economic linkages across cities has been altered under the evolution of the Chinese planning system. Cities higher in the administrative and urban hierarchy may gain more than others. Core cities may flourish and peripheral cities decline when facing place-based planning policies such as transport infrastructure improvements. As a result, there will be differential effects from planning policies within and across regions, and spatial inequalities occur. For example, cities by-passed by high-speed railways are likely to be disadvantaged in developing service sectors, and may resort to activities reliant on expressways (Duranton et al., 2014). When this book looks at the role of transport infrastructure improvements in affecting intercity connections and market access, and when it looks at the effects of planning policies on the reallocation of resources and other factors within and between regions, it overlaps with relevant literature and other topics listed in Routledge's *Regions and Cities* and *Advances in Regional Economics, Science and Policy* series.

Chapter 2 also examines the fundamentals of Chinese planning policies with an aim to develop cities in different places in the productive urban system. An ideal planning policy for guiding urban and regional development, as discussed in Chapter 2, needs to consider the economies of agglomeration, comparative location advantages and the optimized usage of infrastructure systems. These economic implications of planning policies (although these policies are less predictable regarding their economic impacts) could affect the degree of city sprawl, overcrowding, exclusion, productive density and vibrancy through the intervention of infrastructure investment and planning regulations.

China's growth is uneven. Unlike engineering-driven infrastructure construction policies, cities and industries tend to respond to regional planning policies differently. In the centrally planned economy, these differences can be affected by planning rules and regulations which reallocate labour, capital and resources from coastal regions towards inland areas. In the market-orientated economy, these differences can be enhanced by planning policies because some cities get better access to infrastructure and other resources. Furthermore, the transition of economic growth in the resurgence of China's geographic economy is a fundamental reason to rethink the importance of planning policy fundamentals – especially regarding cities, location and infrastructure – over the past 65 years.

Part II explores these characteristics in detail. As Chapters 3 to 5 acknowledge, China's planning policies regarding urban and regional development have played an important role in influencing the success of urban and regional transformation. It is expected that the Chinese economic reforms we have observed over the past few decades are going to continue in a more in-depth way. In turn, this makes designing planning initiatives a key policy toolkit for fostering urban and regional transformation.

Chapter 3 examines how the evolution of China's planning policies in the centrally planned economy affected local and regional development (1950s–1980s). This period is characterized by using planning policies to fully control the allocations of industrial projects, infrastructure, skilled labour and all other types of economic activity across regions. This period is also characterized by the emergence of spatial disparities. For example, Jian et al. (1996) found significant evidence for regional economic divergence across provinces during the Cultural Revolution period (1966–1977). In general, cities in the north-eastern region (e.g. Liaoning province) and in the Third-tier regions (e.g. Chongqing, Sichuan, Guizhou) have done well and outperformed those in the coastal regions (e.g. Guangdong province), but the neglect of market channels at work may result in the low efficient resource allocation and the lack of consistent driving force in formulating agglomeration economies over space. After the economic reform and opening up since the 1980s, a market mechanism has been re-established in China. Its establishment has paralleled China's overall economic transition from the centrally planned economic system to the market-orientated economic system. The establishment of market mechanisms has also generated widening spatial disparities of economic integration and agglomeration, leading to the emergence of mega-metropolitan areas and core-periphery urban systems in contemporary China.

Chapter 4 characterizes the spatial disparity patterns in more detail. Cities and infrastructure are typical public investment areas via various planning policies. Since the 1980s, the most rapidly growing cities – for example, Shenzhen – have been greatly affected by planning policies under the umbrella of Deng Xiaoping's politically brave reform. The gain of comparative locational advantage in industrial production in places with the support of planning policies is an important factor in enhancing access to domestic and international markets, and in stimulating regional economic development in coastal regions such as Guangdong province. However, the spatial heterogeneity in agglomeration economies and market integration boost the unevenness of economic growth across provinces. The old industrial cities in the north-eastern region, such as Liaoning province, for example, gradually lost the locational advantage. Furthermore, the decline in demand for many traditional services and declining mining resources have worsened people's quality of life and living environments in these regions. To address these problems, even if it is challenging to reverse economic performance in declining areas, recent planning programmes have tried to regenerate them and stimulate the growth of vibrant regions. As discussed in Chapter 5, the significant spatial disparity in urban agglomeration across regions is a lens to review foregone planning policy outcomes and their future visions: planning policies have provided important incentives and transport infrastructure investment, to allow cities to gain access to a wider range of markets. These planning policies have gradually formulated several major urban agglomeration belts (e.g. the coastal urban agglomeration belt; Beijing–Guangzhou Railway urban agglomeration belt; Yangtze River urban agglomeration belt; and the main land-based Silk Road urban agglomeration belt), and regional agglomeration zones (e.g. Yangtze River Delta Metropolitan Region; Pearl River Delta Metropolitan Region; Beijing-Tianjin-Hebei Region; Shandong Peninsula Metropolitan Region; the West Coast of the Taiwan Strait Metropolitan Regionl and so on) in the country. Analysing such patterns in China, as elsewhere, is important for a more complete understanding of how planning policies, particularly in cities, location and infrastructure, shift regional economic development patterns spatially and drive local trends unevenly; a thorny issue described in detail in Chapters 3 to 5.

A key argument is that the economic implication of planning policies in urban and regional development can be better understood by embedding spatial economic and geographical insights into policy design and public investment. In order to do this effectively, planning policy needs to work together with markets. This means that taking the market mechanism into consideration before making planning policies – especially policies on city planning and infrastructure investment –is important to avoid market failure and inefficiencies of Government interventions. This in turn has serious impacts on the configuration of urban systems and sustainable development.

In Part III, we turn to the investigation of several specific planning policies at both the intercity and intra-city levels, using a combination of traditional census data and newly emerging big-data sources. China, as one of the most centralized planning countries across the globe, is characterized by decentralization trends of cities (Baum-Snow et al., 2015) in a way that helps to shape spatial economic development patterns. In the urban administrative hierarchy, it is useful to ask whether intercity transport links have helped to 'level the playing field' or exacerbate inequalities. Chapter 6 presents the planning policy of civil-aviation infrastructure as an example to show that decentralization trends of urban systems are strong, and the regional disparity pattern is rather muddled. Chapter 7 examines the impacts of railway (including high-speed railways – HSR) network development on local market access (local accessibility). Exposure to railroad network expansion is measured by changes in 'market access'; a reduced-form expression derived from the general equilibrium model of the economic geography literature (Gibbons et al., 2012; Donaldson and Hornbeck, 2013). This chapter provides evidence for the importance of railway network expansions that can reinforce the evolution of local market potential over space. Taking the city vibrancy of Beijing as an example, Chapter 8 looks at the land and housing marketization process, and the spatial distribution of human activities. Based on the availability of mobile phone big-data resources, the evidence clarifies the importance of conceptualizing the contextual channel in the transformation of human activity over time and across space, thus providing direct implications for land-use planning in mega-cities. The conclusion in Chapter 9 is striking. Rigorous evaluations are needed to show if planning programmes in infrastructure and other amenities can, in effect, affect the trajectory of China's local and regional economic development patterns. That is to say, planning policies are powerful tools for fostering the configuration of the spatial economy of individual cities and urban systems. Hence, the fundamental theme of this book is to shed light on the importance of China's planning policy in cities, infrastructure and locations, which will continue to play a significant role in shaping the country's economic geography patterns.

The economics of planning policies would be complex and it would be not easy to simply say yes or no when it comes to the context of urban and regional development. To go further on these conjectures, descriptive evidence might no longer be sufficient. Instead, theoretical models and 'casual-sense' identification strategy will need to be articulated. This, of course, warrants further studies. But as a baseline, China's diverse economic growth patterns as induced by planning policies are likely to be the important evidence for helping economic experts, policymakers and planners to understand how the spatial layout and the structure of cities evolve.

References

Banerjee, A., Duflo, E. and Qian, N. 2012. On the road: Transportation infrastructure and economic development, Working Paper 17897, Cambridge, MA: National Bureau of Economic Research.

Batty, M. 2013. Big data, smart cities and city planning. Dialogues in Human Geography, 3(3), 274–279.

Baum-Snow N., Brandt, L., Henderson, J.V., Turner, M. and Zhang, Q. 2015. Roads, railways, and the decentralization of Chinese cities. London: LSE manuscript.

Busso, M., Gregory, J. and Kline, P. 2013. Assessing the incidence and efficiency of a prominent place based policy. American Economic Review, 103(2), 897–947.

Cheshire, P., Nathan M. and Overman, H.G. 2014. *Urban Economics and Urban Policy: Challenging Conventional Policy Wisdom*. London: Edward Elgar.

Cheshire, P.C., Hilber, C. and Kaplanis, I. 2015. Land use regulation and productivity-land matters: Evidence from a UK supermarket chain. Journal of Economic Geography, 15(1), 43–73.

Donaldson, D. and Hornbeck, R. 2013. Railroads and American economic growth: A market access approach. NBER Working Paper, No. 19213.

Dong, Z., Wu, W., Ma, X., Xie, K. and Jin, F. 2009. Mining the structure and evolution of the airport network of China over the past twenty years, in Proceedings of 5th International Conference on Advanced Data Mining and Applications (ADMA '09). Berlin, Heidelberg: Springer.

Duranton, G., Morrow, P.M. and Turner, M.A. 2014. Roads and trade: Evidence from U.S. cities. Review of Economic Studies, 81(2), 681–724.

Faber, B. 2014. Trade integration, market size, and industrialization: Evidence from China's national trunk highway system. Review of Economic Studies, 81, 1046–1070.

Faggio, G. 2014. Relocation of public sector workers: Evaluating a place-based policy. SERC Discussion Paper No.155. London: London School of Economics and Political Science.

Gibbons, S. 2015. Planes, trains and automobiles: The economic impact of transport infrastructure. Spatial Economics Research Centre Policy Paper No. SERCPP013, London: London School of Economics and Political Science.

Gibbons, S., Lyytikäinen, T., Overman, H.G. and Sanchis-Guarner, R. 2012. New road infrastructure: The effects on firms. SERC Discussion Papers, SERCDP00117. London: Spatial Economics Research Centre (SERC), London School of Economics and Political Science.

Glaeser, E.L. and Gottlieb, J.D. 2008. The economics of place-making policies. Brookings Papers on Economic Activity, Spring.

Goodchild, M. F. 2013. The quality of big (geo)data. Dialogues in Human Geography 3(3), 280–284.

Harris, C., 1954. Market as a factor in the localization of industry in the United States. Annals of the Association of American Geographers, 44(4), 315–348.

Jacobs-Crisioni, C., Rietveld, P., Koomen, E. and Tranos, E. 2014. Evaluating the impact of land-use density and mix on spatiotemporal urban activity patterns: An exploratory study using mobile phone data. Environment and Planning A, 46(11), 2769–2785.

Jian, T., Sachs, J.D. and Warner, A.M. 1996. Trends in regional inequality in China. China Economic Review, 7(1), 1–21.

Kline, P. 2010. Place based policies, heterogeneity, and agglomeration. The American Economic Review, 100, 383–387.

Lin, J. 2012. Network analysis of China's aviation system, statistical and spatial structure. Journal of Transport Geography, 22, 109–117.

Neumark, D. and Kolko, J. 2010. Do enterprise zones create jobs? Evidence from California's enterprise zone program. Journal of Urban Economics, 68(1), 1–19.

Wang, J., Mo, H.H., Wang, F.H. and Jin, J.F. 2011. Exploring the network structure and nodal centrality of China's air transport network: a complex network approach. Journal of Transport Geography, 19 (4), 712–721.

2 Fundamentals of China's planning policies

Introduction

Adopting Adam Smith's idea in his seminal work, *An Inquiry into the Nature and Causes of the Wealth of Nations* (1776), Chinese policymakers have recognized the importance of regulating economic activity through the market mechanism (Yin, 2006; Yang and Wu, 2009).

However, two centuries after the publication of *The Wealth of Nations*, Marxism and Keynesianism emerged from the practices of the market economy and capitalism. Marx saw the inevitability of 'cyclical economic crisis' in a free-market economic system and came up with the idea of resolving the crisis with a planned system. Meanwhile, Keynes proposed a macro-control framework of using policies to intervene in the market mechanism. Over hundreds of years, empirical studies have shown that the 'invisible' market mechanism can work in synergy with 'visible' policies for stimulating economic growth. But it is perfectly valid to question the economic implications of planning policies.

Planning policy is the major way for the Government to coordinate, control and intervene in economic activity. Therefore, for the purpose of analysing and discussing the economic implications of planning policy, this book will first explain the basic building blocks of China's planning policies, including type, target, principle and philosophy, etc. Planning policies in China typically cover the following elements: the current status and feature of economic development, target and orientation; spatial economic layout; planning emphases; major infrastructure construction; and guiding policies etc. These elements affect the leverage of locational advantages, infrastructure provisions and spatial patterns of urban and regional development.

This chapter starts by looking at the main principles of planning policy, which help to understand the evolution of the Chinese planning system (see Chapters 3 and 4), and its significant economic impacts on location, cities and infrastructure. There are three reasons to do so: first, it is important to understand the rationales behind the planning policy objectives that ought to be achieved; second, it is worthwhile to understand the intention to achieve these objectives; and third, it is useful to reflect on how planning can be productive in helping promote spatial economic development. For example, the strategic objectives of city planning must be the planning of urban development – and it must include a bundle of planning policies, such as land-use planning, environmental planning, infrastructure planning and social welfare planning etc. This system can be widely applied in China. However, questions still remain as to the spatial economic consequences of planning policies. Empirically, planning policies have played a role in influencing the natural process of economic development, both locally and nationally. Economic development is a sophisticated concept to be measured. It not only refers to the amount of overall economic growth, but also encompasses economic structural changes and spatial relations between cities and regions. Neoclassical economic theory argued that economic development would depend on specific locational factors, such as the comparative advantages of labour, capital and natural-resource endowments. Under the theoretical prediction, the absolute economic convergence trend across regions with similar factors, regarding technology, resources, infrastructure and policies, are expected to be seen (Barro and Sala-I-Martin, 1995). For example, Barro and Sala-I-Martin (1991) showed empirical evidence in favour of the absolute economic convergence trend across states in the USA during 1880–1988, and across some European regions during 1950–1985. But the absolute economic convergence trend may not be applied to a region with a heterogeneous group of local economies. Thus recent studies suggest the importance of looking at the conditional economic convergence trend by controlling differences in locational factors, such as population across regions (Mankiw et al., 1992; Barro and Sala-I-Martin, 1995).

China is a large developing country with an uneven distribution of economic activity. These uneven distribution patterns have been evolving with and affected by a range of regional planning schemes. The aims of these schemes vary substantially over time between the centrally planned economy era (1950s–1980s) and the market-orientated economy era (1991–present). The connection between economic development and planning policy reflects the visions of various organizations, political groups and Central Government. Dealing with these issues in China increasingly requires a more complete understanding of the characteristics of the evolution of the Chinese Five-Year national planning system; a key policy framework that will be discussed in detail in Chapter 3.

Spatial disparities: institutional contexts, theories and strategies

The transformation from Mao's redistributive planned policies to contemporary spatial disparities, as guided by China's recent planning system, can be attributed to several institutional contexts: the history of regional development from China's perspective; and the prediction of economic theories based on international experience. The first institutional context is related to the viewpoint that Maoist redistributive planned policies attached significant importance to reallocating resources and industrial development, but overlooked market integration and economic agglomerations. This viewpoint is evidenced by the slow economic growth in the first three decades after the establishment of the

People's Republic of China, and the low cost-benefit investment efficiency of the 'Third-tier Region' construction (*san xian jian she*) strategy (Naughton, 1988; Peng, 1991; Tu, 1995).

The second institutional context is related to the reform and opening-up of China since the 1980s. After its reform, China has offered a special case for generating evidence of the conceptual foundations that underlie many neoclassical economic growth theories regarding uneven regional development (Myrdal, 1957; Hirschman, 1958; Williamson, 1965). Theory suggests that the stage of uneven regional development is inevitable, and is the spatial manifestation of agglomerations in specific industrial sectors or geographic locations. For example, theoretical notions of 'growth poles' (*zeng zhang ji*) proposed by Hirschman (1958), 'spread' (*kuo san*) proposed by Myrdal (1957), and the 'inverted-U model' proposed by Williamson (1965) have been used for justifying regional development patterns in developed countries. For example, Mankiw et al. (1992) found evidence for the conditional economic convergence trend during the period 1960–1985 across almost 100 countries, after controlling for population and capital factors. Following this logic, the international experience of developed countries has attempted to justify a conditional convergence trend across places with similar production factors, technological innovations, resources, institutional policies and preferences.

Overall, neoclassical economic growth theories of regional development have predicted that spatial agglomerations are likely to occur in specific cities before spreading to marginal areas. Evidence from empirical studies suggests the rise of regional inequality since the 1980s in China (Lakshmanan and Hua, 1987; Tsui, 1991). Fan (1995a,b) confirmed this by showing the widening gap between coastal provinces in the eastern region, such as Guangdong, and provinces in inland regions, and by showing the spatial disparities within fast-growing coastal provinces. Based on the evidence from the USA and Japan, Yu and Chen (1985) predicted that spatial economic disparities between the core and marginal regions would shrink when China entered into a more advanced development stage.

In addition to neoclassical economic growth theories, the interpretation of different developmental stages is also embodied in Marxism (Brugger and Kelly, 1990), and has been used innovatively to support the ideas of being practical, and theories of the 'primary stage of socialism' and 'socialism with Chinese characteristics' (Su and Feng, 1979; Zhao, 1987; Deng, 1983, 1993a). Deng (1993a) argued that China was a nation at the primary stage of socialism and a relatively low economic development level, and therefore China should focus on building up socialism with its unique characteristics.

In Mao's egalitarian period, the primary goals of planning policies were to promote industrial development and national defence by allocating investment to inland areas (Falkenheim, 1985; Riskin, 1987). The post-Mao economic transition followed the neoclassical economic growth theories by using pragmatism to guide the implementation of planning policies. Deng's famous maxim 'it does not matter if a cat's colour is black or white as long as it can catch mice' provides a vivid summary of the pragmatism in the post-Mao period. In reality, a functional market mechanism has replaced Marxist ideology to guide regional development in China through the national planning system (Hsu, 1991). Rather than following orthodox principles for restricting allocations of labour and production factors, the implementation of the economic reform and opening-up policy is viewed as a new instrument to establish the so-called 'socialist market economy' and stimulate China's economic growth (Ma, 1992).

Deng Xiaoping's public endorsement of prioritizing efficiency over equity has had long-lasting impacts on uneven regional development through the implementation of planning policies regarding location, cities and infrastructure. For example, Deng (1983; 1993b) argued that the country should allow some people and regions to get rich first, and these regions should provide 'demonstrational examples' for other people and regions to follow (Hsu, 1991). During Deng's 'southern tour' (*nan xun*) in 1992, he emphasized the usefulness of letting coastal areas become rich first (Deng, 1993c), and projected that this development process would ultimately lead to overall national wealth.

Deng's pragmatist view has been embedded in the subsequent National Five-Year-Plans by diverting the investment and preferential policy incentives into coastal cities. In addition to the proposition of prioritizing efficiency over equity, Deng suggested that State intervention might be needed for reducing regional inequality, but that early interventions would undermine economic development in those rapidly growing provinces and special economic zones. The appropriate time for State interventions, Deng projected, would be the end of the twentieth century, when Chinese people had achieved moderate prosperity (*xiao kang sheng huo shui ping*) (Deng, 1993c).

Deng's viewpoint about pragmatism also provides the rationale for Chinese planners to adopt comparative locational advantages as a guiding principle of planning policies, regarding local and regional development. This is consistent with Western neoclassical economic growth theories (see Myrdal, 1957; Hirschman, 1958; Friedmann, 1966; Richardson, 1976) and predictions about agglomeration and diffusion effects between the core and peripheral regions (Chen, 1987; Yang and Liang, 1994). Since the Sixth Five-Year-Plan (1981–1985), China's planning policies have tended to foster regional division of labour, capital and other factors, based on differentials in regional endowments and comparative advantages. Specifically, Chinese policymakers implemented various regional planning policies to favour economic development in the eastern region at the expense of development in inland areas (Shu, 1994). The implementation of recent planning strategies shows that China follows in the footsteps of neoclassical economic growth theories and learns from the experience of other countries that have experienced regional inequality and conditional convergence. However, it may be not feasible to address China's uneven regional development based on neoclassical economic growth theories and international experience, owing to its unique historical and geographical contexts (Chen, 1987; Wang and Zeng, 1988; Xu, 1995). For example, China's inland regions are less developed and economic growth is not likely to trickle down from the more developed to the less developed regions without strong, planned interventions.

Criticisms of the uneven regional development appeal for new planning policies rather than the existing coastal-led development policies. Since the early 2000s, the strategies of coastal-led regional development have been complemented by other regional planning policies, in order to coordinate economic growth across regions. Among various planning initiatives, transport infrastructure expansion can be regarded as the key instrument for balancing the economic development among regions (Peng, 1991; Lao, 1993). Along the main railways and roadways, several economic agglomeration belts, stretching from east to west and from north to south, have emerged (see Chapter 5). Proponents argue that transport infrastructure development lays the foundation for urban systems by facilitating the movement of goods and people across regions, and by influencing the spatial distribution of businesses and workers, with different income and different preferences for local amenities. Arguments for public investment are that inadequate infrastructure might constrain China's economic growth by causing increased congestion and more costs to producers and consumers in cities. On the basis of this kind of argument, policymakers should invest more carefully in places with an urgent demand on growth, and try to reduce the regional inequality by building and improving transportation systems between cities.

To summarize, the spatial economic disparities in China are formed within unique institutional contexts, manifesting Maoist's redistributive policies and Deng's uneven regional development philosophy. China has witnessed a significant process of industrialization and urbanization over the past sixty-five years that have affected not only the physical layout of cities but also the intercity connections between locations. There are potentially useful and plausible neoclassical economic growth theories and differential timing of policy reforms to aid the identification of the economic effects of China's planning policies. But as a baseline, institutional contexts, theories and strategies are important to the evolution of China's planning policies that will eventually transform the landscape of Chinese cities for decades to come.

Basic building blocks of China's planning policies

For economists and geographers, industrialization and urbanization are two main drivers for shaping the economic development of a country or a region. Thus, it is of crucial importance for the Government to adapt itself to the acceleration of industrialization and urbanization. Recent economic studies have suggested that, compared with natural resources, human capital is also a key factor in determining local economic growth patterns and their spillover effects (Lucas, 1988; Barro et al., 1991; Glaeser and Mare, 2001). There have been a substantial number of studies addressing this issue. Chen and Fleisher (1997) showed that the human capital significantly affected overall productivity in China. Others have reported the positive significant impacts of human capital on regional growth of GDP per capita using different datasets (see Chen and Fleisher, 1996; Démurger, 2001; Cai et al., 2002) during the initial stages of economic reform. In addition to the traditional factors of production (such as mechanical equipment) that contribute to economic growth, technological innovations have also been an important driving force for influencing the urbanization and productivity (Andersson et al., 2009).

This section describes the fundamental building blocks of planning policies, with a specific focus on the rationales of China's planning policies, and their importance to the uneven spatial economic performance from the perspective of location, cities and infrastructure. There are many ways to decide what the planning policy ought to be and what is the rationale underlying the planning policy. In China, the building blocks of planning policy encompass the policy instruments and intervention measures to promote urban and regional development. The planning system is formulated based on the rational analysis of the current spatial economic conditions. When implementing planning policies, governments at all levels should combine the market mechanism with administrative instruments, to regulate economic development. In this context, the Chinese Government has gradually found an effective way to allocate capital, resources and infrastructure across regions over the past sixty-five years. Considering these guiding principles, the Chinese Government comes up with specific objectives of economic development, together with a package of fiscal, financial and tax policy instruments to guarantee the feasibility of planning policies. Specifically, the principles of the Chinese planning system involve:

- **The weaknesses of relying purely on the market mechanism in regional development:** with the market mechanism, the price signal is used to reflect the scarcity of resources and the cost or utility of goods and labour. But resources could be misallocated in a purely market-dominated environment without Government intervention. In terms of the regional layout, the dispersal of production and other factors has close forward and backward connections. Therefore, spatial agglomeration effects are likely to be strengthened in areas with comparative locational advantages. The market channels may exacerbate such effects and reinforce the uneven spatial development.
- **Economic factors are not equally distributed across regions:** the market regulates the regional development by distributing economic activity over space in China. First, labourers in rural areas have gradually transferred to urban areas to live and for work as a result of industrialization and urbanization. Second, local economic growth has relied on market access, technological innovation and transport infrastructure improvement. In fact, even in the centrally planned economy era (1950s–1980s), without a market mechanism, there is a strong trend of unevenness in economic development across provinces. For example, Jian et al. (1996) found the significant GDP per capita divergence trend across provinces during the Cultural Revolution period (1966–1977). Kanbur and Zhang (2005) also found the income divergence trend in this period. Zhang and Zou (2012) suggested that the distribution of industrial resources in the centrally planned economy era could contribute to uneven regional development in China. Third, market failure and inefficiency are endemic and therefore market forces may not always regulate the resource reallocation across regions effectively. These factors would contribute to regional inequality in China.

- **Spatial multiplier effect enlarges regional inequality:** the market regulates the economic performance mainly through the competitive mechanism so as to improve the efficiency of resource allocation between regions. But the market could also produce spatial multiplier effects that may further intensify the imbalance of regional economic development (Moretti, 2010). Some areas have been better developed than others owing to initial locational characteristics, and these areas could obtain sustained growth as a result of the self-reinforcing agglomeration factors. Over time, these spatial multiplier effects will lead to a widening of the development gap between regions.

In light of these principles, planning policy is often used as means of policy intervention to coordinate the market force between people and places, although it is hard to know whether it works in reality. Under the guidance of the national Five-Year-Plan system, China's planning policies vary differently in topics, content and spatial scales. But these planning policies are all framed within the national Five-Year-Plan system, with the aim of promoting regional economic performance, and improving social welfare. Table 2.1 provides a key summary of the Chinese planning system with respect to regional development. To narrow down the broad inquiry, this book focuses on China's planning policies that are relevant to urban and regional development:

Comprehensive regional planning

A comprehensive regional planning programme means the intervention of the distribution pattern of spatial economy in specific provinces, municipalities, autonomous regions and mega-cities. Comprehensive regional planning falls into various types depending on its spatial impact scales. For example, the comprehensive regional planning for *Yangtze River Delta Regional Planning* covers the economic agglomeration area of the Shanghai Municipality, Jiangsu province and Zhejiang province etc. As a pioneering development region, the future vision of this region is to develop its advanced manufacturing industry, high-tech industry and high value-added service industry sectors. Most economic activity in the region is of national importance. Another example is the *Promotion Plan of the Rise of Central China,* a transregional city agglomeration planning aimed at generating critical growth poles, and driving the rise of the central region, including Shanxi, Anhui, Jiangxi, Henan, Hubei and Hunan provinces. These kinds of planning programmes for specific regions are generally consistent with the administrative jurisdiction or fall under the administrative jurisdiction of the corresponding regulatory agencies. Within the broad planning framework, it can be divided further into the following types. First, governments in specific regions can set up free economic trade zones in a planned way to attract foreign capital investments and technology exchanges. Second, in order to accelerate the economic development of certain regions, the Chinese Government sets aside a piece of land for

Table 2.1 Key summary of the Chinese planning system

Category	Governance	Nature	Spatial coverage	Economic implications
Five-Year-Plan	State Council	Planning for comprehensive set of socioeconomic activities	The whole country	Set up policy incentives, rules and guidance for the allocation of public resources and funds to promote economic development
Regional planning	State Government	Planning for spatial development in a specific region, including one or more provinces	Targeted region(s)	• Implementation of the Five-Year-Plan at regional level • Set up policy incentives, rules and guidance for the entire region's economic development in terms of coordinating productivity layout, infrastructure connections, and spatial agglomeration factors
Urban planning	City Government	Planning for spatial layout, land use, industrial development and social welfare in a single-city context	A single city	• Implementation of the Five-Year-Plan at city level • Set up policy incentives, rules and guidance for urban growth, land-use configurations and intra-city infrastructure constructions
Specialized sector planning (e.g. infrastructure expansion)	State Government	Planning for specialized industrial sector development or infrastructure expansion	A specific industrial sector, or infrastructure system, covering a range of cities and regions	• Implementation of Five-Year-Plan in specialized industrial sector or at infrastructure level • Set up policy incentives, rules and guidance for the spatial layout and structures of specific industrial sectors, or infrastructure systems

development and construction, where governments can provide incentive-based preferential policies for investors so as to develop local businesses. Various types of economic agglomeration zones, economic and technological development zones and high-tech industrial parks fall into this type. Third, some places such as resource-exhausted cities and old industrial towns have been confronted with poor economic performance, high unemployment rates, and environmental degradation. To address these urgent problems, the Chinese Government makes use of regional planning policies for regional revival. Different types of comprehensive regional planning vary in their objectives, development priority and content. But the basic principle of these comprehensive regional planning programmes remains largely unchanged: to promote regional economic development.

Finally, it is worth noting that comprehensive regional planning is usually framed under the guidance of the Five-Year-Plan system. More generally, as an important part of the national Five-Year-Plan system, regional planning should be subordinated to the basic rules and guidelines of the system. It incorporates the consideration of various natural and socioeconomic factors, including production conditions, natural resources, historical basis, transportation, labour, technology, capital and access to domestic and foreign markets. Throughout the history of the People's Republic of China, the formation of comprehensive regional planning policies has played an essential role in influencing the levels and patterns of regional economic disparities.

Urban planning

Urban planning is the specific planning arrangement of the nature, size and spatial layout of a city, in order to achieve economic and social development objectives in a certain period. All types of urban planning strategies should be approved by senior administrative organizations in China. For example, *The Reply of the State Council on the Overall Urban Planning of Zhengzhou City* comes under the State Council's approval of the planning strategy of the urban development in Zhengzhou City. In China, urban planning is the fundamental basis for guiding the construction and administration of a prefecture city or a county, as well as an important way of reallocating resources and the rational use of land. It includes two aspects: urban planning and urban construction. Here, urban planning refers to an appropriate overall development plan regarding the arrangement of city structures, land use and industrial layout, with local characteristics. Urban construction means the implementation of infrastructure construction in a planned way, covering energy, transportation, communications, information network, landscape, environmental protection and so on.

The design of urban planning strategies implies the intervention of spatial and physical development in a single city. The discussion of a specific city's planning strategy is beyond the scope of this book, given that there are more than 2,000 counties and in China. In addition, cities may publish different versions of planning strategies within a certain historical time period, so it would be not very helpful to make use of these city-level planning strategies to understand the spatial economic performance of the whole country. Thus, we will discuss the two most important factors in this book. First, it is likely to be the case that cities and counties might gain or lose differently owing to the implementation of certain regional planning programmes as guided by the national Five-Year-Plan system. This will further exacerbate the economic impacts of the national Five-Year-Plan system and affiliated regional planning programmes on influencing regional inequality. The evidence for these Five-Year-Plans and affiliated regional planning programmes will be discussed in subsequent chapters so that readers can get a full view of the economic implications of planning policies in China over the past sixty-five years. The second is the existence of local externalities and uncertain geographic contextual problems (Kwan, 2012). For example, the building of a new subway line may lead to changes in economic outcomes such as property price rises in nearby areas (see Zheng and Kahn, 2008; 2013; Wu et al., 2015). At the intra-city level, differential human activity patterns have emerged over time and space, probably as a result of the city structure based on historical urban planning. As a typical Chinese mega-city, Beijing is studied extensively in Chapter 8 to show this pattern.

Specialized industry or infrastructure planning

Under the current planning system, industry and infrastructure planning policies focus on industry-related and infrastructure-related policy initiatives, based on the guidance of the national Five-Year-Plan system. That is to say, specialized industry or infrastructure planning programmes can regulate the development of a certain type of industry (such as the development planning of the steel and petroleum industries) or infrastructure (such as planning of transportation or hydropower infrastructure) in the whole country or in certain regions. This type of planning policy has paid specific attention to using public investment in specialized industries and infrastructure as leverage to construct urban systems and influence local economic performance in affected areas.

This book focuses on discussing the economic implication of infrastructure planning. The term 'infrastructure' has been used intensively in the literature, although it doesn't have a unified definition. Fourie (2006) suggested that there are different ways to define the concepts of infrastructure, and these concepts might overlap with each other. Policymakers and practitioners have made a popular and practical justification by dividing it into physical infrastructure and social infrastructure. The social infrastructure, which is beyond the focus of this book, can include a package of institutional services and well-being services (Fourie, 2006). The typical examples of social infrastructure are social housing systems, health-care and educational systems, as well as creative, leisure and cultural facilities. The physical infrastructure refers to infrastructure investments that can be used to spur productivity, trade and economic activity by providing services to households and firms within and across cities. The typical examples of physical infrastructure are transportation (including airports, roadways and railways), telecommunications and hydropower supplies (including dam reservoir facilities) in China.

The provision of physical infrastructure has emerged as an important way to accelerate urban transformation in China and other quickly urbanizing countries. The introduction of various physical infrastructure planning policies by the Chinese Government since the early 1990s has signified a shift in its urban transformation strategy towards a physical infrastructure-orientated development mode. The notion of physical infrastructure is introduced to connect cities in distressed and vibrant regions, support social production and consumption, make fundamental accessibility services available to residents and firms, and integrate a variety of market mechanisms into the urbanization process. However, inherent tension rises as increasing physical infrastructure, especially transport infrastructure development, leads to increased spatial disparities that may have serious implications for urban and regional agglomeration. The role of physical infrastructure in China's new urban transformation processes and their spatial implications are therefore crucial to our understanding of the evolution of local and regional development.

There has been a growing interest from various disciplines including economics, political economy, social policy, planning and geography in the role of physical infrastructure in influencing China's economy. In the broad scope of physical infrastructure, this book only focuses on the economic implications of transport infrastructure. Transport infrastructure investment is treated as a prominent policy tool by the Chinese Government and its importance has been increasingly recognized by recent Five-Year-Plans. Within the context of massive public spending, for example, China's railway network had reached up to 93,000 km by 2011 and ranked as one of the world's largest railway markets, as measured by freight and passenger traffic volumes (Amos and Bullock, 2011). Road network expansion has also experienced fast growth since the mid-1990s, but the regional inequality in terms of highway infrastructure provisions are substantial (Yao, 2009). Faber (2014) quantifies robust evidence on the economic impacts of highway infrastructure development in China during 1996–2007, and finds significantly heterogeneous impacts on GDP and other key economic indicators between core and peripheral regions. As shown in Chapters 6 and 7, the construction and expansion of transport infrastructure systems (e.g. railway networks, airport networks) are important for influencing the evolution of hub urban systems and local market potential between regions. In turn, this makes the prediction of the economic impacts of infrastructure planning policy a promising topic for further studies. There are two reasons for us to focus on the transport infrastructure. First, planning for transport infrastructure construction and expansion is necessary to support China's economic growth that fuels rising demand for infrastructure accessibility. Second, planning for transport infrastructure construction and expansion is necessary to improve the market access of inland regions that are lagging behind, to cope with the ever-widening regional inequality. As a consequence, large-scale infrastructure planning programmes for airports, roadways and railways have been launched successively to accelerate infrastructure construction and expansion throughout the whole country, and such programmes have provided a new way to explore regional disparities in China (Démurger, 2001; Faber, 2014; Baum-Snow et al., 2015).

In sum, the Chinese national Five-Year-Plan system is used to determine strategic priorities for guiding economic development, and thereby forms an important basis for arranging Government investments and infrastructure provisions in specific regions. This planning system can be regarded as a strategic approach to guide all kinds of comprehensive regional planning and specific planning policies. Specifically, the comprehensive regional, infrastructure and other place-based planning policies, are key elements of the Chinese planning system, regarding the spatial layout of cities and infrastructure development. In practice, there are close connections among various types of regional planning policies since they should be approved by the Central Government based on the same planning principle as the corresponding national Five-Year-Plan. The principle that interactions among cities, location and infrastructure, as guided by the Chinese planning system, will help explain spatial economic development patterns is one of the fundamental insights into China's planning policies. Governments at all levels should adhere to the following rules when implementing the planning policies regarding the local and regional development:

Recognizing locational advantages: the spatial economy to be nurtured by the current planning system must have absolute or comparative locational advantages, take a role in the geographical division of labour and resources, and feature a high degree of specialization and economic agglomeration. That is to say, the planning policy sets regulations and incentives to develop the spatial economy with comparative locational advantages. Moreover, when designing the planning policy, governments should try to avoid vicious transregional competition. A crucial implication of this is that differences in economic performance are a basic feature of the country, and therefore, planning policy should be used as leverage to rebalance locational advantages so as to coordinate spatial economic performance.

Recognizing market mechanism: the aim of the planning system is to foster the development of the market mechanism, and the formation of the economic integration and agglomeration at the local or regional level. Even if some cities are not yet core cities in the region, the planning policy should support their growth and transformation. A general analysis of the implementation of China's planning policies for the nature of the market mechanism will be beyond the scope of this chapter. But it is useful to think through serious planning implications of the lack of market mechanism in specific historical periods (e.g. 1953–1980), when the administrative commands and policy rules in the central-planned system (as outlined in Chapter 3) dominated the distribution of labour and resources.

Recognizing ecological and environmental protection: in order to protect land, water resources and urban environment, the Chinese Governments has embedded resource-saving and environmental friendly strategies into the planning policy decision-making process. Increasingly, the Chinese planning system tends to impose energy consumption, level of resource utilization and other indicators to guide the development of industrialization and urbanization. These policy instruments are used to formulate the appropriate thresholds for industrial pollutant emissions and urban energy use. Before the 1990s, the importance of ecological and environmental protection was not fully recognized by senior policymakers, and it is difficult to measure the relative strength of this principle empirically, although one could argue that ecological and environmental protection has helped to determine the industrial structure changes in different locations. In reality, spatial externalities will be at work and the impact of planning policy instruments on firm performance and urban productivity is not clearly studied in Chinese cities. For example, as industrial activity concentrates in city M, the formulated policy thresholds for industrial pollutant emissions and urban energy use can make significant changes in the profits and productivity for firms in city M, compared to other cities that do not apply the same set of policy thresholds. Agglomeration forces affect the diffusion of industrial activities further over space. In the presence of spatial agglomeration economies, the development of city M would be different from other cities, leading to spatial economic disparities. An in-depth empirical evaluation of the linkages between policy instruments, such as industrial pollutant emissions, as well as urban energy use, and spatial economic disparities is not the focus of this book. However, if one focuses on evaluating the causal impacts of place-based environmental policies, it is important to justify these linkages, and confirm the relationships between the spatial concentrations of industrial activity and environmental protection policies.

Transitions of planning policy philosophy

From above, it appears that the philosophy and practical principles of planning policy implementation are effective for a long period of time, at least for Chinese cities and regions. There is, however, some evidence from a number of studies which cast doubt on even the consistency of planning systems regarding local and regional development. In fact, since the 1980s, when China implemented economic reform and opening-up, the country has gradually turned away from the centrally planned economic system to the market-orientated economic system (Kanbur and Zhang, 2005; Zhang and Zou, 2012). The basic philosophy of planning policy regarding local and regional development has also changed within this transitional socioeconomic institutional background. The differences observed are substantial:

A shift of focus from the previous quantity of economic output to the present quality of economic development: the evaluation of China's planning policy effectiveness as guided by the Central Government has been transformed from a simple economic output increase to overall economic development and social welfare. In the centrally planned economy era (the pre-1980s period), regional economic performance was measured by indicators such as regional GDP and the scale of investment, among others. Since the economic reform and opening-up (the post-1980s period), the Central Government has placed more emphasis on the evaluation of quality of life, production efficiency and sustainable growth when designing and implementing the planning policies. More recently, the Central Government has given full consideration to potential economic consequences of planning policies, regarding the allocation of infrastructure and resources to cope with regional inequality.

A transformation from the previous focus on the isolated development mode to the coordinated development mode: at the intercity level, in the centrally planned economy era, the Chinese Government focused mainly on managing specific projects through planning policies to promote industrial development in individual cities and provinces, without considering the potential spillover effects on other places. With the introduction of the market-orientated economic system, the Chinese Government has recognized market channels at work and shifted its planning instruments from managing specific projects to guiding the configuration of the spatial economy. At the intra-city level, as Chinese urban lands are increasingly valuable, land resources have become a constraining factor in the economic development of all localities. Before the 1980s, planning approaches on land-use configuration were designed to meet the requirement of units (*Danwei*), rather than that of private developers. The efficiency of land-use configuration was not well considered in the spatial layout, and implications for human activity were not well studied. The low-density, garden-style factories and other non-mixed land-use development models have caused a serious waste of land resources. Therefore, since price signals became effective in the 1980s, land-use efficiency in Chinese cities has been widely considered. As differential sets of amenities are capitalized into land and housing values (Zheng and Kahn, 2008, 2013; Wu and Dong, 2014; Wu and Wang, 2016), it is expected that variations in human activities over time and space, interacting with heterogeneity in amenities (e.g. subway stations, green space, schools), will lead to changes in city structure and the emergence of marginal towns.

A transformation from previous Government-dominated planning to current Government-led planning with public participation: as the democratization of Government management and decision-making continues, China's planning policies are actively absorbing the opinions of the public, the private sector and NGOs. Furthermore, the Chinese Government has set up the legal supervision of planning policy implementation as an important dimension of socioeconomic transformation. Violation of planning policy will lead to severe consequences in economic development. These consequences may be linked to subjective assumptions by mayors, or errors in administrative decrees. The focus of planning policies tends to cater to the demand of different interest groups, especially when a planning programme is likely to exert spillover effects. Legal supervision and public participation may help avoid subjective bias and ensure the scientific design and implementation of planning policies, in order to formulate urban and regional agglomeration in China. For example, a city's productivity could be significantly affected by the economic performance of its neighbouring areas and how good their productivity and infrastructure accessibility are. Peripheral cities are connected to core cities through transport systems with lower transportation costs, and core cities can attract more valuable resources from peripheral cities. Thus the patterns and incidence of uneven economic growth as guided by planning policies deserve further exploration.

Main content of planning policy

China's planning policies regarding urban and regional development contain the following elements: the justification of current economic conditions and development objectives, layout of spatial economy, and infrastructure construction, etc. As in many scenarios, the content of the Chinese planning system for urban and regional development; and how they provide direct implications for spatial economic configuration rely on careful evaluation. In this section, we examine how the Chinese planning system may affect spatial economic performance. By doing so, we aim to understand the common specifics of the planning system and the institutional context within which the planning system works.

The justification of current economic conditions: analysis and determination of the current status and features of economic development are a prerequisite to design planning policy appropriately. The economic development of a region can be divided into different stages. The issues and driving factors for growth and spatial layout features differ significantly from stage to stage. Therefore, planning policy designs should be based on the examination of the current status of economic development, as well as on issues and features from the perspective of sustainable regional development. Such an examination process will include the analysis of economic development stages at national and regional levels. At the national level, by analysing the development trends and characteristics, policymakers should judge and analyse the overall level of economic development. At the regional level, policymakers should analyse the comparative locational advantages and the drivers of economic development patterns within and across regions. In the current planning system, the various issues assessed in different economic development stages include resource utilization, infrastructure, locational advantages and ecological and environmental protection. By doing so, a micro-foundation for the formulation of effective planning policies can be laid. In practice, planners in China usually carry out an empirical analysis of locational characteristics that may influence the economic conditions. More recently, it is common to see clearly quantitative-based predictions about the trends of the economic growth rate, and quality and structure in planning policy research reports (Zhang et al., 2009; Zhang et al., 2014).

Based on the justification of the current economic conditions, economic development objectives are set up and involved as essential parts of planning policies. In many cases, these objectives are measured by qualitative terms. These qualitative measures are based on the judgements about domestic and foreign macro-development backgrounds, and intra-regional advantages/disadvantages. In addition to qualitative-assessed objectives, quantitative measures have also been used in planning policy implementation. A good case in point is the *Main Functional Areas Planning* (*zhu ti gong neng qu gui hua*) launched in 2011, in which the quantitative indicators regarding economic growth, population growth and the environmental capacity index are applied to regulate the future vision of different functional areas in China.

Box 2.1 Introduction to 'Main Functional Area Planning'

The main functional area planning is a comprehensive consideration of future population distribution, economic layout, land use and urbanization pattern, based on the carrying capacity of resources and the environment, existing development density and development potential. The main functional area planning policy used the quantitative evaluation methods to divide the national geographic space into four types of main functional areas including: *optimized development areas, key development areas, restricted development areas* and *prohibited development areas. Optimized development areas* refer to regions that have priority in limiting the agglomeration of industries with a large consumption of resources and significant emissions of pollutants, and these regions should focus on the agglomeration of high-tech industries and modern service industries, as well as the optimization of the regional economic structure, to lead national economic growth. *Key development areas* refer to regions that need to accelerate industrialization and the agglomeration of advanced manufacturing industries. *Restricted development areas* refer to regions that should strictly limit the development of industries with heavy pollution and a large consumption of resources, and properly develop low-pollutant emission industries. Finally, *prohibited development areas* should not allow the development of industrial activity that may affect the environmental protection. As guided by the State Council, the spatial economic development and layout should be carried out according to the different types of main functional areas.

The key point here is to stress that the Chinese planning system for urban and regional development has intentionally generated profound economic impacts in the configuration of spatial economy. In the next paragraph this point is illustrated with an outline of why the spatial layout is included as a key element of planning policies.

The justification of spatial layout: theory suggests that different levels and scales of economic agglomeration are likely to be concentrated in core cities related to peripheral cities along main transportation lines (Faber, 2014). The spatial layout should therefore be included into the planning policies. Based on regional economic characteristics, the Government can select core cities and/or declining areas in a region as the target for infrastructure provisions through the implementation of place-based planning programmes. These programmes are the concrete implementation of Government interventions and investment for influencing the spatial layout of economic activity within and between regions. This can be achieved mainly by imposing regulations associated with land-supply controls, industrial subsidy, taxation and environmental protection, and by coordinating the relationship between growth and equity among regions. But as originally conceived, the development objectives should be combined with spatial agglomerations, as these spatial layout patterns could be important for forming the hierarchical urban system in China.

Future work for studying the Chinese planning system lies in the evaluation of how to maximize the use of regional resources in accordance with market mechanism and promote the economic agglomeration at different geographical levels. Recently, China's planning policymakers have taken into account the ecological constraints and the requirements of people's quality of life when designing the spatial layout for urban and regional development. This is a good start. Economic geographers and scientific researchers from other disciplines, who are involved into the policy decision-making process, can propose more rigorously assessed opinions that can be included into the content of planning policies in future.

The justification of infrastructure development: infrastructure development is an important building block to consider when making planning policy. The implementation of planning policies involves ambitious investment programmes in transportation, electricity and water-supply systems, and other infrastructure. These infrastructure investment programmes are not likely to be distributed evenly over space. Hence, infrastructure investment programmes are expected to generate differential economic impacts across cities and regions. For instance, when planning and constructing the transportation infrastructure, such as airports, highways and high-speed railways, a key focus is to enhance the links between cities. The transport improvement can be a prerequisite for improving spatial economic performance, but may also lead to territorial polarization across cities and regions at the same time. Chapters 6 and 7 will describe the effects of major transport improvements on intercity connectivity patterns.

Conclusion

This chapter considered fundamentals of China's planning policies regarding local and regional development, with a specific focus on explaining the basic building blocks (that is, the rationale and principle of planning policy), and the transition in the planning policy philosophy (that is, the transformation from a centrally planned system to a market-orientated system). Furthermore, this chapter has also explained why the justification of current economic conditions, spatial layout and infrastructure development is one of the fundamentals of China's planning policies. The focus here is to provide an overview of how the Chinese planning system works; in particular, how multi-layered comprehensive regional planning, urban planning and specialized infrastructure planning policies can help explain both how the overall economic development patterns play out spatially, and the role that the planning system plays in driving urban agglomeration and influencing the configuration of regional inequality.

In addition to the fundamentals of the Chinese planning system regarding regional development, insights reflecting on how the planning system contributes to the evolution of spatial economic configuration over time have been provided. The evidence and experience from Chapters 3 and 4 will show how the fundamental principles, content and other building blocks of planning policies can be used to carefully rethink the economic implications for people and places, when incentive-based policy instruments favour some targeted cities and regions over others. When the Government focuses only on the average economic growth of the whole country, it is likely to neglect the uneven spatial economic development patterns, where the income, housing prices and firms' productivity rise in some grow-ing regions and decline in others. But from the perspective of fighting against regional inequality, the importance of spatial planning policy intervention can be much more subtle. As is the case for the successful transition from the centrally planned system to the market-orientated system in China, regional inequality is likely to occur. As can be seen from the evolution of the Chinese planning system (see Chapters 3 and 4), rethinking the economic implications of spatial planning policy requires policymakers and planners to clearly identify the differences of spatial economic consequences for people and places. To sum up, the 'big picture' of rationale, content and principles of China's planning policy is, on the one hand, closely related to the stages of regional development, and on the other, a reflection of locational characteristics and market mechanisms, including market integration and economic agglomeration. To sustain the economic growth, senior Chinese policymakers have designed a set of Five-Year-Plans as 'roadmaps' for guid-ing local and regional development. Chapters 3 and 4, will discuss how Chinese Governments used these 'Five-Year-Plans' to restructure regional development during the 1950s and the 2010s. These chapters will also show how China's plan-ning history allows us to reflect on differential mechanisms that led to uneven economic development across regions during the centrally planned economy era (1950s–1980s) and the market-orientated economy era (1990s–the present).

This chapter briefly considered the evidence from recent popular spatial plan-ning interventions, such as the *Main Functional Area Planning*. Many instruments of this *Main Functional Area Planning* initiative have proved useful in guiding the prospective National Five-Year-Plans, and promoting sustainable develop-ment. This highlights one of the central focuses in this book: planning policy does matter in influencing the spatial economic performance in China. It is for this reason that Parts II and III of this book examine the economic, geographical implications of China's planning policies. As Chinese policymakers have recog-nized the significant role of planning policy in affecting regional inequality and agglomeration directly, the next step is to pay careful attention to the evaluation of policy implementation effectiveness.

When policymakers become more realistic about the effectiveness of policy implementation and its external effects to counteract market forces, it is expected that more effective policy leverages will be seen for the spatial configuration of the urban system and economic agglomeration. While the policy reform is a work in progress in China, this book stresses the importance of considering the economics of planning policies regarding location, cities and infrastructure. This raises another set of inquiries on the effectiveness of the centralized planning policy design and implementation. On one hand, planning-policy implementation could provide insights into addressing problems at the local level; on the other hand, centralized Five-Year-Plan could deliver uneven benefits over space and may have difficulty in connecting to local strategies depending on the transfer instruments, financial incentives and investment in local prefecture cities. There is a lack of hard evidence confirming if this is really the case, but there are good reasons to believe that in large developing countries like China, the reform of planning-policy design and implementation may generate benefits at the local, regional and national levels.

Some promising research into the implementation of China's planning policy is the potential impact on people's quality of life and skills. Although building bigger and nicer cities is not a bad thing, this raises public inquiries into whether policymakers could also reduce the spatial disparities in terms of quality of life and social welfare for local residents. This will be a controversial research objective for China. Fortunately, Chinese leaders are in favour of 'human-centred' urban and regional planning strategies and there will be strong evidence of what really works for local economic performance, especially for declining cities and regions such as old mining and industrial towns in China.

Urban and regional development planning policies remain a meaningful topic, and China offers a textbook scenario for further studies, given its dramatic transformation from the centrally planned system to the market-orientated system. As this chapter and the following parts of the book suggest, more evidence and experience will be needed to help cope with empirical challenges and to find effective ways to strike a balance in spatial economy through the implementation of planning policy. Economic geographers should do more rather than less.

References

Amos, P. and Bullock, R. 2011. Governance and structure of the railway industry: three pillars, China Transport Note Series 02, World Bank Office, Beijing.

Andersson, R., Quigley, J.M. and Wilhelmsson, M. 2009. Urbanization, productivity, and innovation: Evidence from investment in higher education, Journal of Urban Economics, 66(1), 2–15.

Barro, R.J., Sala-I-Martin, X., Blanchard O.J. and Hall, R.E. 1991. Convergence across states and regions. Brookings Papers on Economic Activity, 1991 (1), 107–182.

Barro, R.J. and Sala-I-Martin, X. 1991. Economic growth in a cross section of countries. The Quarterly Journal of Economics, 106 (2), 407–443.

Barro, R.J. and Sala-I-Martin, X. 1995. *Economic Growth*, New York: McGraw- Hill.

Baum-Snow, N., Brandt, L., Henderson, J.V., Turner, M. and Zhang Q. 2015. Roads, railways, and the decentralization of Chinese cities, London: LSE manuscript.

Brugger, B. and D. Kelly. 1990. *Chinese Marxism in the post-Mao Era*. Stanford, USA: Stanford University Press.

Cai, F., Wang, D. and Yang, D.U. 2002. Regional disparity and economic growth in China: The impact of labor market distortions. China Economic Review, 13, 197–212.

Chen, J. 1987. Study of movement by escalation and development poles-growth points theory. Economic Research, 3, 33–39 [in Chinese].

Chen, J. and Fleisher, B.M. 1996. Regional income inequality and economic growth in China. Journal of Comparative Economics, 22, 141–164.

Chen, J. and Fleisher, B.M. 1997. The coast-noncoast income gap, productivity, and regional economic policy in China. Journal of Comparative Economics, 25, 220–236.

Cheng, Y. 1994. The regional development strategy of China's foreign trade. Economic Geography, 14(2), 75–80 [in Chinese].

Démurger, S. 2001. Infrastructure development and economic growth: An explanation for regional disparities in China. Journal of Comparative Economics, 29, 95–117.

Deng, X. 1983. Liberate ideas, be practical, united toward the future. In: *Selected Works by Deng Xiaoping (1975–1982),* Beijing: People's Publishing House [in Chinese].

Deng, X. 1993a. Develop socialism with Chinese characteristics. Speech on 30 June 1984, in: *Selected Works by Deng Xiaoping,* Vol. III, Beijing: People's Publishing House [in Chinese].

Deng, X. 1993b. Approaching everything according to the realities of the primary stage of socialism. Speech on 29 August 1987, in: *Selected Works by Deng Xiaoping,* Vol. III, Beijing: People's Publishing House [in Chinese].

Deng, X. 1993c. Summary of speeches in Wuchang, Shenzhen, Zhuhai and Shanghai. Speeches 18 January–21 February 1992, in: *Selected Works by Deng Xiaoping,* Vol. III, Beijing: People's Publishing House [in Chinese].

Faber, B. 2014. Trade integration, market size, and industrialization: Evidence from China's national trunk highway system, Review of Economic Studies, 81, 1046–1070.

Falkenheim, V.C. 1985. Spatial inequalities in China's modernization program: some political- administrative determinants. In: C-K. Leung and J.C.H. Chai (eds.), *Development and Distribution in China,* Hong Kong University of Hong Kong.

Fan, C.C. 1995a. Of belts and ladders: State policy and uneven regional development in post-Mao China. Annals of the Association of American Geographers, 85(3), 421–49.

Fan, C.C. 1995b. Developments from above, below and outside: Spatial impacts of China's economic reforms in Jiangsu and Guangdong provinces. Chinese Environment and Development, 6(1/2), 85–116.

Fourie, J. 2006. Economic infrastructure: A review of definitions, theory and empirics, South African Journal of Economics, 74(3), 530–556.

Friedmann, J. 1966. *Regional Development Policy: A Case Study of Venezuela.* Cambridge, MA: MIT Press.

Glaeser, E.L. and Mare, D.C. 2001. Cities and skills. Journal of Labour Economics, 19(2), 316–342.

Hirschman, A.O. 1958. *The Strategy of Economic Development.* New Haven: Yale University Press.

Hsu, R. 1991. *Economic Theories in China, 1979–1988.* Cambridge, UK: Cambridge University Press.

Jian, T., Sachs J. and Warner, A. 1996. Trends in regional inequality in China. China Economic Review, 7, 1–21.

Kanbur, R. and Zhang, X. 2005. Fifty years of regional inequality in China: A journey through central planning, reform, and openness. Review of Development Economics, 9(1), 87–106.

Kwan, M.-P. 2012. The uncertain geographic context problem. Annals of the Association of American Geographers, 102(5),958–968.

Lakshmanan, T.R. and C-I. Hua, 1987. Regional disparities in China. International Regional Science Review, 11, 97–104.

Lao, C. 1993. Recognition on the theory and practice of China's economic regionalization. Economic Geography, 13(3), 9–13.

Lucas, R.E., Jr. 1988. On the mechanics of economic development. Journal of Monetary Economics, 22(1), 3–42.

Ma, H., 1992. Building the new social market system. Economic System, 11, 3–10 [in Chinese].

Mankiw, N.G., Romer, D. and Weil, D. 1992. A contribution to the empirics of economic growth. The Quarterly Journal of Economics, 107(2), 407–437.

Moretti, E., 2010. Local multipliers, American Economic Review: Papers and Proceedings, 100(2), 373–377.

Myrdal, G. 1957. *Rich Lands and Poor: The Road to World Prosperity (Economic Theory and Underdeveloped Regions)*. New York: Harper.

Naughton, B. 1988. The third front: Defense industrialization in the Chinese interior. The China Quarterly, 115, 351–86.

Peng, Q. 1991. Regional development study: New trends of Chinese geography. Economic Geography, 11(4), 1–6 [in Chinese].

Richardson, H.W. 1976. Growth pole spillovers: The dynamics of backwash and spread. Regional Studies, 10, 1–9.

Riskin, C. 1987. *China's Political Economy: The Quest for Development since 1949.* Oxford: Oxford University Press.

Shu, Q. and Huang, M. 1993. Study on economic allocation under the socialist market system. Economic Geography, 13(2), 5–9 [in Chinese].

Shu, W. 1994. Selection of macro regional strategy of China at the turn of the century. Economic Theory and Business Management, 6, 21–5 [in Chinese].

Su, S. and Feng, L. 1979. On the stages of social development after the proletariat has seized power. Economic Research, 5, 14–19 [in Chinese].

Tsui, K.Y. 1991. China's regional inequality, 1952–1985. Journal of Comparative Economics 15, 1–21.

Tu, R. 1995. Analyzing the regional policy in economic theory. Economic Theory and Business Management, 1, 23–8 [in Chinese].

Wang, Z. and Zeng, X. 1988. On the strategy of areal exploring in Chinese industrial distribution. Economic Research, 1, 66– 74 [in Chinese].

Williamson, J.G. 1965. Regional inequality and the process of national development: A description of the pattern. Economic Development and Cultural Change, 13(4), 3–45.

Wu, W. and Dong G. 2014. Valuing 'green' amenities in a spatial context, Journal of Regional Science, 54(4), 569–585.

Wu, W., Dong, G. and Zhang, W. 2015. The puzzling heterogeneity in amenity capitalization effects on land markets, Papers in Regional Science, online version available. DOI: 10.1111/pirs.12186

Xu, F. 1995. Difference in development of local economy and the choice of countermeasure in the future. Inquiry into Economic Problems, 6, 4–6 [in Chinese].

Yang, C. and Wu, L. 2009. National wealth discusses the core thought of our country modern market economy enlightenment. Science and Management (*Ke Xue Yu Guan Li*), 29(1), 5–8.

Yang, W. and Liang, J. 1994. On China's theoretical models for regional development. Geographical Research, 13(3), 1–13 [in Chinese].

Yang, Y. 1994. Current challenge and strategy of helping the development of the poor. Inquiry into Economic Problems, 8, 48–49 [in Chinese].

Yao, Y, 2009. The political economy of government policies toward regional inequality in China, in Yukon Huang, and Alessandro M. Bocchi (eds.), Reshaping Economic Geography in East Asia. Washington, DC: The World Bank.

Yin, B. 2006. Three Stages of the influence of Adam Smith's economic Theory in China: In commemoration of the 230th anniversary of publication of Adam Smith's work *An Inquiry into the Nature and Causes of the Wealth of Nations.* Exploration and Free Views (*Tan Suo Yu Zheng Ming*), 4, 45–47.

Yu, J. and Chen, A. 1985. Discussion of the gap between the East and the West and special policies for developing the West. Journal of Chinese Industrial Economy, 4, 76–81, 89 [in Chinese].

Zhang, Q. and Zou, H. 2012. Regional inequality in contemporary China, Annals of Economics and Finance, 13 (1), 113–137.

Zhang, W. et al. (eds.) 2009. *Theory and Practice of Industrial Development and Planning,* Beijing: Science Press [in Chinese].

Zhang, W., Yu, J., Wang, D., Chen, L. et al., 2014. *Study on Sustainable Development of Resource-Based Cities in China.* Beijing: Science Press [in Chinese].

Zhao, Z. 1987. *Documents of the Thirteenth National Congress of the Communist Party of China.* Beijing: Foreign Languages Press [in Chinese].

Zheng, S, and Kahn, M.E. 2008. Land and residential property markets in a booming economy: new evidence from Beijing. Journal of Urban Economics, 63,743–757.

Zheng, S. and Kahn, M.E. 2013. Does government investment in local public goods spur gentrification? Evidence from Beijing. Real Estate Economics, 41(1), 1–28.

Part II

Spatial evolution of planning policies in China

3 Planning for spatial development in the post-war era

Introduction

Governments in China and perhaps elsewhere in the world are concerned with addressing spatial economic disparities. However, concentrating the limited resources and capital on supporting the prosperity of heavy industrial cities has become a general consensus for policymakers after the establishment of the People's Republic of China in 1949. This is one of the key focuses of China's planning policies during the centrally planned economy era. The consequence is that within and between regions, spatial allocation of public resources plays an essential role in pushing the unevenness of the industrialization process in China during the First and Seventh Five-Year-Plan periods. This has direct impacts on urban and regional agglomeration in modern China. The Five-Year-Plan system is a 'Soviet Union style', comprehensive, socioeconomic development plan for the whole country. To avoid broad inquiries, this book focuses on the planning elements regarding cities, location and infrastructure in the Chinese Five-Year-Plan system, and this chapter looks into the role that the evolution of national Five-Year-Plan polices (1950s–1990) play and the tendency of planning policies in driving economic growth, accelerating economic transitions and enlarging spatial disparities.

There is clear evidence that Government investment promotes industrial development in specific regions of China through various planning policies. The consequence is that rapid industrialization becomes the key driving force to enlarge spatial economic disparities (Jian et al., 1996). Take Liaoning as an example, where a disproportionately large share of centrally allocated asset for industrialization was invested there, thus achieving higher GDP growth than the average and a higher growth rate of fixed-asset investment compared with other provinces during this period (see Tables 3.1 and 3.2). Indeed, with the support of Government investment between the First and the Seventh Five-Year-Plan periods, heavy industry and resource-based cities in the north-eastern region and 'Third-tier' regions were pushed towards rapid industrialization, whereas agricultural provinces such as Henan province were underdeveloped.

Table 3.1 GDP growth by provinces during 1st–7th Five-Year-Plan periods

Region	Provinces		1st Five-Year-Plan (1953–1957)	2nd Five-Year-Plan (1958–1962)	3rd Five-Year-Plan (1966–1970)	4th Five-Year-Plan (1971–1975)	5th Five-Year-Plan (1976–1980)	6th Five-Year-Plan (1981–1985)	7th Five-Year-Plan (1986–1990)
East	Beijing	Mean	24.78	40.90	46.82	74.56	112.18	190.18	395.74
		Growth rate	14.18%	−3.76%	9.31%	10.56%	10.35%	16.58%	15.14%
	Tianjin	Mean	19.30	33.81	40.31	61.65	82.43	133.73	253.72
		Growth rate	8.22%	−7.05%	6.72%	6.05%	12.23%	12.95%	12.42%
	Hebei	Mean	47.82	62.96	86.84	115.48	179.54	297.24	675.80
		Growth rate	5.32%	−6.46%	6.79%	5.40%	13.09%	15.56%	19.69%
	Shanghai	Mean	58.65	113.80	131.41	183.75	261.92	374.25	627.52
		Growth rate	7.71%	−2.98%	5.85%	5.49%	10.64%	9.49%	11.42%
	Jiangsu	Mean	58.44	76.62	110.58	166.46	251.60	469.72	1122.90
		Growth rate	5.58%	−2.09%	4.13%	5.62%	14.20%	16.82%	17.43%
	Zhejiang	Mean	31.44	44.50	60.30	82.52	129.66	288.74	722.26
		Growth rate	8.21%	−0.23%	4.38%	4.58%	19.78%	20.24%	15.76%
	Fujian	Mean	17.72	25.72	30.66	44.16	65.38	141.76	373.08
		Growth rate	11.18%	−2.44%	1.97%	3.20%	16.74%	17.39%	23.87%
	Shandong	Mean	56.22	69.64	106.16	147.50	231.18	492.78	1111.44
		Growth rate	7.60%	−3.09%	6.66%	4.44%	12.93%	18.37%	19.46%
	Guangdong	Mean						407.36	1097.24
		Growth rate						16.85%	24.06%
	Hainan	Mean						37.48	85.92
		Growth rate						20.27%	24.36%
Central	Shanxi	Mean	24.66	40.90	46.90	64.80	88.62	166.48	322.92
		Growth rate	10.06%	−4.83%	3.80%	3.01%	13.92%	15.82%	16.25%
	Anhui	Mean	33.74	50.46	60.54	89.30	119.20	234.04	529.28
		Growth rate	11.28%	−6.33%	4.68%	4.94%	7.43%	18.07%	14.50%
	Jiangxi	Mean	22.40	34.25	49.82	65.71	88.28	155.27	324.93
		Growth rate	8.91%	1.45%	4.79%	2.28%	14.65%	14.43%	16.73%
	Henan	Mean	46.50	56.05	81.04	116.19	170.36	332.54	729.39
		Growth rate	6.21%	−8.27%	6.21%	5.08%	16.24%	15.98%	16.76%
	Hubei	Mean	36.41	58.27	81.06	109.17	158.08	288.70	620.74
		Growth rate	12.04%	−4.43%	1.85%	5.40%	15.85%	15.88%	15.87%
	Hunan	Mean	35.94	55.96	79.26	109.70	152.88	267.38	567.28
		Growth rate	10.52%	−2.17%	6.38%	4.55%	12.78%	13.66%	16.97%

Region	Province		C1	C2	C3	C4	C5	C6	C7
West	Inner Mongolia	Mean	19.70	30.18	35.04	43.40	58.06	113.80	255.34
		Growth rate	8.10%	−2.78%	0.58%	3.96%	9.20%	20.42%	15.15%
	Guangxi	Mean	17.78	25.02	33.20	57.42	78.78	141.72	318.58
		Growth rate	11.06%	−0.72%	5.59%	9.98%	9.65%	12.38%	21.59%
	Chongqing	Mean							
		Growth rate							
	Sichuan	Mean						321.56	656.96
		Growth rate						14.82%	18.09%
	Guizhou	Mean	12.74	20.28	23.93	29.18	45.84	93.37	202.57
		Growth rate	12.96%	−5.09%	3.43%	−0.93%	19.75%	16.23%	16.84%
	Yunnan	Mean	18.82	24.28	33.99	50.72	67.05	125.77	305.42
		Growth rate	10.96%	1.36%	1.43%	5.71%	14.36%	15.06%	25.46%
	Tibet	Mean	1.47	2.16	3.60	4.58	6.77	12.47	20.89
		Growth rate	3.49%	8.80%	1.11%	6.40%	12.46%	14.31%	13.10%
	Shanxi	Mean	22.14	32.68	38.58	60.40	80.68	133.56	306.10
		Growth rate	10.13%	−3.48%	3.68%	2.98%	10.83%	15.37%	18.03%
	Gansu	Mean	17.86	17.74	26.50	46.00	64.26	93.18	190.32
		Growth rate	9.66%	−13.78%	9.27%	10.93%	6.94%	14.86%	14.61%
	Qinghai	Mean	2.96	5.90	7.06	10.96	14.80	23.88	53.44
		Growth rate	23.85%	−1.57%	7.35%	7.24%	9.46%	17.18%	16.20%
	Ningxia	Mean						22.30	49.70
		Growth rate						14.81%	17.05%
	Xinjiang	Mean	12.07	20.53	22.39	25.67	41.08	81.04	192.34
		Growth rate	13.82%	1.19%	−3.65%	1.84%	13.77%	17.24%	20.71%
Northeast	Liaoning	Mean	63.98	110.08	108.70	171.64	232.60	384.90	854.42
		Growth rate	10.44%	−8.48%	4.99%	7.51%	8.34%	15.78%	15.11%
	Jilin	Mean	22.06	34.70	46.96	63.52	82.38	151.56	342.08
		Growth rate	7.32%	0.16%	4.69%	4.38%	10.02%	15.86%	16.97%
	Heilongjiang	Mean	38.70	64.88	96.82	125.54	176.58	285.38	550.64
		Growth rate	8.53%	−2.97%	4.82%	5.18%	11.26%	11.67%	15.58%

Note: GDP figures are reported in 100 million yuan at historical value. Some province data are missing.

Data sources: China Compendium of Statistics, 2004, and regional (*di qu*) statistical yearbooks for the relevant years.

Table 3.2 Fixed-asset investment growth by provinces during 1st–7th Five-Year-Plan periods

Region	Provinces		1st Five-Year-Plan (1953–1957)	2nd Five-Year-Plan (1958–1962)	3rd Five-Year-Plan (1966–1970)	4th Five-Year-Plan (1971–1975)	5th Five-Year-Plan (1976–1980)	6th Five-Year-Plan (1981–1985)	7th Five-Year-Plan (1986–1990)
East	Beijing	Mean	6.94	11.28	5.80	11.62	22.60	57.36	144.82
		Growth rate	13.00%	-30.64%	10.67%	24.84%	25.23%	26.59%	13.97%
	Tianjin	Mean	1.88	4.85	3.55	11.67	19.67	43.69	80.51
		Growth rate	11.02%	-24.94%	12.59%	25.45%	15.20%	24.31%	5.08%
	Hebei	Mean	3.98	11.42	7.30	17.62	34.30	80.22	172.88
		Growth rate	27.42%	-31.63%	8.39%	18.04%	7.85%	20.05%	7.78%
	Shanghai	Mean	3.86	11.12	6.95	19.16	30.29	82.55	204.07
		Growth rate	9.25%	-23.73%	10.81%	30.09%	16.67%	21.39%	11.50%
	Jiangsu	Mean	2.20	8.24	3.90	9.24	21.70	107.58	321.34
		Growth rate	21.46%	-30.07%	9.33%	9.18%	29.34%	33.45%	10.25%
	Zhejiang	Mean	1.04	5.52	2.95	6.20	19.34	57.40	167.82
		Growth rate	31.61%	-25.29%	10.98%	-1.21%	52.85%	31.48%	10.07%
	Fujian	Mean	2.42	3.23	7.21	9.67	12.93	32.02	92.68
		Growth rate					19.08%	31.73%	15.67%
	Shandong	Mean	2.92	9.06	7.34	15.94	42.30	119.12	306.38
		Growth rate	14.11%	-25.30%	5.14%	11.29%	36.78%	24.99%	10.75%
	Guangdong	Mean	2.55	7.93	5.19	13.15	26.43	109.76	309.98
		Growth rate	13.28%	-17.71%	10.72%	16.58%	18.53%	32.22%	15.21%
	Hainan	Mean							
		Growth rate							
Central	Shanxi	Mean	5.32	11.00	7.20	15.02	21.00	53.10	108.46
		Growth rate	28.47%	-24.72%	7.29%	2.89%	16.33%	37.71%	6.20%
	Anhui	Mean	2.62	7.12	3.74	9.14	13.14	47.76	119.18
		Growth rate	13.92%	-24.54%	16.00%	3.28%	10.99%	50.57%	4.41%
	Jiangxi	Mean	1.71	5.84	4.09	6.53	9.04	29.78	66.84
		Growth rate	16.04%	-22.19%	19.33%	-9.74%	41.61%	26.69%	7.27%
	Henan	Mean	4.32	13.15	8.68	18.49	22.85	75.21	180.64
		Growth rate	40.07%	-33.96%	31.78%	5.30%	5.87%	28.03%	9.20%
	Hubei	Mean	4.47	10.48	10.39	20.49	33.45	63.16	136.02
		Growth rate	30.00%	-31.05%	31.92%	-5.85%	5.37%	32.41%	6.70%
	Hunan	Mean	3.70	9.78	9.14	17.84	22.00	54.68	118.86
		Growth rate	2.08%	-26.65%	19.77%	-3.71%	17.66%	25.65%	5.75%

Region	Province								
West	Inner Mongolia	Mean		8.06	4.66	8.46	13.70	26.56	62.90
		Growth rate		−30.26%	2.05%	9.60%	10.39%	43.96%	10.43%
	Guangxi	Mean	1.24	3.92	3.90	6.58	9.78	24.02	66.92
		Growth rate	18.92%	−20.47%	8.87%	6.53%	10.02%	41.59%	5.58%
	Chongqing	Mean							54.04
		Growth rate							13.27%
	Sichuan	Mean	3.34	9.66	21.98	23.16	21.68	63.20	145.32
		Growth rate	22.31%	−28.41%	6.44%	−9.54%	19.11%	28.29%	9.59%
	Guizhou	Mean	0.68	4.59	6.61	9.53	10.10	20.78	43.99
		Growth rate	36.78%	−23.37%	9.30%	−19.55%	21.36%	21.59%	9.38%
	Yunnan	Mean	2.09	6.88	8.46	10.63	14.49	28.23	63.12
		Growth rate	18.11%	−29.53%	−2.52%	1.84%	20.18%	25.88%	10.98%
	Tibet	Mean						3.41	6.15
		Growth rate						57.52%	9.21%
	Shanxi	Mean	4.32	7.18	8.06	18.30	19.22	36.32	87.60
		Growth rate	27.79%	−30.47%	21.68%	−9.79%	21.16%	26.15%	13.04%
	Gansu	Mean	4.86	7.52	7.72	10.68	9.82	21.42	51.66
		Growth rate	39.62%	−37.61%	2.59%	−0.23%	11.00%	24.52%	10.07%
	Qinghai	Mean	1.28	2.86	2.32	3.42	6.54	12.48	21.86
		Growth rate	54.29%	−46.64%	8.95%	7.67%	15.21%	19.27%	5.80%
	Ningxia	Mean	2.93	1.33	1.98	2.41	3.57	7.22	19.01
		Growth rate	17.31%	−19.17%	2.19%	0.01%	14.95%	38.60%	6.07%
	Xinjiang	Mean	2.93	6.29	3.77	4.95	12.36	29.83	66.40
		Growth rate	30.92%	−27.09%	1.98%	6.44%	28.21%	24.69%	16.34%
Northeast	Liaoning	Mean	13.00	16.54	6.68	22.10	33.14	88.96	236.90
		Growth rate	4.78%	−34.05%	18.68%	15.85%	13.85%	23.61%	10.21%
	Jilin	Mean	4.98	7.84	5.94	13.14	16.54	36.18	81.40
		Growth rate	7.03%	−17.45%	10.51%	7.34%	13.94%	31.19%	10.20%
	Heilongjiang	Mean	7.58	13.28	9.82	15.16	24.96	76.42	149.08
		Growth rate	8.45%	−20.40%	−1.72%	15.68%	24.74%	24.19%	7.15%

Note: Fixed-asset investment figures are reported in 100 million yuan at historical value. Some province data are missing.

Data sources: China Compendium of Statistics, 2004, and regional (di qu) statistical yearbooks for relevant years.

This chapter sheds lights on these features. The first half of this chapter examines the characteristics of planning policies from the 1950s to the 1980s – a period before the implementation of the reform and opening-up policy. One of the central focuses is that the uneven spatial development pattern in China is affected largely by place-based planning programmes without considering the market mechanism in allocating resources and infrastructure. A large proportion of the variation in spatial economic performance across cities and regions can be explained by the implementation of Five-Year planning policies regarding cities, location and infrastructure during this period. Better accessed places and places of higher political rank not only tend to grow faster, but also tend to attract more skilled labour, more Government investment, and form denser industrial clusters among other advantages. Realizing this, it is easy to understand the uneven spatial development mode in this period. The central feature of the Chinese planning system in this period is to re-establish a basic industrialization structure in targeted regions, regardless of the supply and demand equilibrium mechanism. As public investment is generous in these targeted regions and transfer of labour force and products is restricted, access to better public resource allocation is thus 'capitalized' into people's quality of life and the economic development in these regions. As a result, the resulting uneven spatial development pattern is not surprising. However, there are some much more suitable places for industrial clusters, because of their locational, social, economic and environmental advantages, which make them attractive to direct foreign investment and investment from the private sector. Thus, if public investment was allocated to these favourable regions, it would be more beneficial for national economic development. However, historical experience demonstrates that the spatial concentration of public investment in heavy industrial bases and Third-tier regions is due primarily to the consideration of national defence. An important insight into the reform and opening-up policy, launched since the early 1980s, provides a possible solution: private firms are allowed to choose their places for business development and get better access to markets. As the relaxation of constraints on human and capital mobility was increasingly applied in most Chinese cities, the planning system after the 1980s gradually shifted its focus to promoting economic growth in the coastal regions, instead of in mountainous areas and old mining towns in the north-eastern and western regions (see the second half of this chapter). Recent evidence suggests that cities with favourable locational advantages grow rapidly in coastal regions with the support of planning policies in the Sixth and the Seventh Five-Year-Plan periods. Coupled with comparable locational advantages, urban and regional agglomerations are concentrated mostly in the coastal regions. Whereas this may explain why skilled labour and firms with high value-added output transfer to coastal regions, the uneven spatial economic performance hereinafter would suggest that recent policies try to achieve the coordinated spatial development before regional inequality becomes much worse. The characteristics of the planning implications in affecting the formation of the 'new' uneven spatial development pattern will be the focus of the second half of this chapter and subsequent chapters (Chapters 4 and 5).

Planning for growth: the power of centralized institutional forces (1953–1980)

The foundation of the People's Republic of China in 1949 marks the beginning of some sixty-five years of independent economic development for China. In the first thirty years after 1949, China achieved significant progress in shaping spatial development through the planning system. Between the 1950s and the 1980s, Government investments were allocated mostly to the poorer inland areas, for the purpose of being close to raw materials and resources for national defence (Falkenheim, 1985; Yang, 1990).

From 1949 to 1952, China experienced a three-year recovery period after China's War of Liberation. During this time, national economic structure featured the coexistence of State-owned, private and individual businesses. On one hand, a number of State-owned enterprises were set up under the direct management of the State, so that the Government gradually controlled private businesses. On the other hand, the market mechanism still played a role in resource allocation for the private sector. However, from 1953 to 1980, China basically copied the planning system of the Soviet Union and prioritized heavy industrial development by administrative command, to distribute resources and guide local economic development. Within this context, China placed all economic activities under the control of the national mandatory planning system (thereafter, the 'Five-Year-Plan'). Since 1953, the Five-Year-Plan has been used to guide national short- and medium-term economic and social development. For example, the First Five-Year-Plan set rules and guidelines for allocating resources, labour and capital to support economic development in this period (1953–1957).

We try to look at the overall evolution process that emerges from historical planning policies, which aimed to support the development of targeted industries but led to increasing spatial disparities. Overall, Maoist regional distributive policies were aimed at narrowing regional disparities, however, some studies argue that allocation of resources during the Maoist period did not fully achieve even regional development (Zhou, 1993; Zhao, 1996). It is perhaps for this reason that much of the subsequent planning policies focus on stimulating coordinated regional development, where policy interventions are strong. The urban and regional economic agglomerations will be considered in more detail in Chapter 5. Place-based planning interventions in this period involve direct Government investment and resource allocation through administrative orders, rather than indirect incentives. Owing to the impacts of the 'Great Leap Forward' (*da yue jin*) movement, the 'Great Cultural Revolution' movement, and the 'Third-tier' construction strategy[1] from the 1950s to the 1980s, the Five-Year-Plans since the 1960s have focused on the formation of industrial structures in inland areas and mega-cities, leading to the emergence of spatial economic disparities.

First Five-Year-Plan period

During the First Five-Year-Plan period, the Chinese Government focused on developing heavy industry in the north-eastern region, centring on Liaoning

Province. During this period, the Chinese Government put forward a guideline to distribute industries in a planned way and clearly stated: '*industrial productivities should be appropriately distributed in regions so as to make them close to raw materials and fuel production areas*'. The priority of Government investment at this time period was the north-eastern region because it already had some heavy industrial bases. This region enjoyed more than one-quarter of total capital construction investment in the country, including new factory constructions centring on metallurgy, coal, machinery and other heavy-industry sectors. Among the 156 construction projects aided by the Soviet Union, 17 started between 1950 and 1952 for the whole country, and 13 out of 17 projects were allocated in the north-eastern region. Meanwhile, Government investment was also heavily concentrated in other old mining towns and industrial cities, such as Wuhan, Baotou, Lanzhou, Xi'an, Taiyuan, Zhengzhou, Luoyang, and Chengdu etc. Furthermore, China began to relocate some enterprises in light industry from the north-eastern region to other regions. It is said that during the First Five-Year-Plan period, industries in China were redistributed in a planned way in order to consolidate national defence (as the top priority of planning policies), and to adjust the productivity layout across cities and regions. Tables 3.1 and 3.2 help explain the economic implications. The simplified growth rate calculation of these tables is formulated as: $g = \sqrt[4]{end\ year\ /\ initial\ year} - 1$, where 'end year' means the last year value of a given Five-Year-Plan period, and 'initial year' means the first year value of a given Five-Year-Plan period. Results from Table 3.1 and Table 3.2 show the growth rate for GDP and fixed-asset investment across provinces. Just taking the growth of four typical provinces in four strategic regions[2] as an example: Liaoning (in the north-eastern region) and Guizhou (in the western region) greatly outperformed Zhejiang (in the eastern region) and Henan (in the central region), in terms of GDP and fixed-asset investment growth rate during this period. Tables 3.1 and 3.2 also show that although provinces in the north-eastern region and some provinces in the western region developed faster than others, there were not so many spatial differences in economic performance and people's quality of life across provinces, compared to the period after the 1990s. One credible explanation is that the connection among GDP growth, fixed-asset investment growth and regional economic divergence is complicated because of the socialist nature of labour markets, industrial markets and property markets; and price signals cannot influence both supply and demand, as well as spatial sorting for houses, wages and other amenities since all resources including land and labour are controlled by governments. As such, China was identified as one of the world's most egalitarian societies with respect to income inequality across regions during this period (Zhang and Zou, 2012). This expectation is also consistent with recent findings that the regional divergence was not obvious before 1967. For example, Yao and Zhang (2001) used the Gini coefficient based on data of GDP per capita between 1952 and 1997, to evaluate the economic divergence across provinces in the eastern, central and western regions. Their results suggest a clear divergence across regions after 1967, and such divergence has become more obvious since the late 1980s.

In terms of transport infrastructure development, 33 new railways, including the Baoji-Chengdu railway and the Yingtan and Xiamen railway, were built during this period. The Wuhan Yangtze river bridge was also built then, which has played a role in linking the north to the south. By the end of 1957, national railway mileage had reached approximately 29,000 km, and road mileage had expanded to approximately 250,000 km. These figures are almost double those of 1950. The gross output value of industry and agriculture also increased substantially compared with that of the early 1950s. Overall, the Government re-established the industrial bases and major transportation lines in specific regions during the First Five-Year-Plan.

Second Five-Year-Plan period

Owing to the lack of industrial resource allocation in coastal regions during the First Five-Year-Plan period, the Chinese Government proposed a more balanced economic development strategy between inland regions and coastal regions during the Second Five-Year-Plan (1958–1962). In the Second Five-Year-Plan (1958–1962), the Chinese Government proposed to appropriately develop existing industrial clusters in coastal regions, while carrying out large-scale industrial constructions in inland regions. However, the beginning of the 'Great Leap Forward' (*da yue jin*) movement[3] since 1958 stimulated an unrealistic industrial development mode, as implemented by governments at all levels, regardless of the quality of industrial output. Take the steel production as an example: perhaps surprisingly, it was once proposed by the Government that national steel production in 1958 had to double that of 1957, and steel production in 1959 was required to double that of 1958. In general, it was common to find the proposition of unrealistic economic goals by local government, such as a doubled or even several dozen times of growth rate in terms of industrial and agricultural products so as to realize 'a great leap forward' in national economic growth. The 'Great Leap Forward' (*da yue jin*) had serious implications for the original implementation of the Second Five-Year-Plan, regarding infrastructure and industry construction projects. The demanding targets and overestimated production quotas during the period of the Great Leap Forward triggered heavy losses in the spatial economy. In addition, the 'natural disaster' (*zi ran zai hai*) that lasted for three consecutive years from 1959 to 1961, resulted in a sharp decline in agricultural production and workers' productivity. Generally speaking, the industrial output growth was much lower than that of the First Five-Year-Plan. The first time after the foundation of the People's Republic of China, there was a serious decline in national economic development. To the end of 1962, key industrial and agricultural outputs, such as steel, cement, grain and cotton failed the development targets that had been proposed at the beginning of the Second Five-Year-Plan. As can been seen from Tables 3.1 and 3.2, most provinces experienced a negative growth rate in terms of GDP and fixed-asset investment during this period.

Owing to the Great Leap Forward movement, the Second Five-Year-Plan was forced to be adjusted, so in general this five-year-plan was suspended.

The Chinese Government proposed taking 'agriculture as the basis and forerunner for national economic development', and a series of urgent measures to address the urgent national crisis including food shortages and famine were also taken (Ashton et al., 1984; Banister, 1987; Peng, 1987; Yang, 2010). An effective system of food rationing and payment mechanism, as well as assistance to rural areas, re-opened the free rural market. In addition, the Government adjusted the industry by reducing the scale of production and by promoting economic recovery. This buffered the failure in achieving a more balanced layout of productivity in places within the institutional background of the Great Leap Forward (*da yue jin*) movement.

Third Five-Year-Plan to Fifth Five-Year-Plan

Between 1963 and 1964, the Chinese Government proposed the Third Five-Year-Plan (1965–1970), based on the planning principle of 'adjustment, consolidation, enrichment and improvement', in order to adjust the spatial economy. Specifically, the aims of this period included the following. First, this period should vigorously develop agriculture to solve the food and clothing problems of the people. Second, this period must strive to strengthen industry for national defence and associated infrastructure construction projects. Third, this period should develop transportation, culture, education, scientific research and other sectors. The implementation of the Third Five-Year-Plan had the following features: first, small State-owned enterprises with low-quality output were suspended to avoid competitive disadvantages and oversupply; second, industrial projects built by local government with improper layout were suspended. The spatial concentration of industries in the inland regions were strengthened further compared with that of the coastal regions. In addition, under the principle of preparing for the possibility of war, the Chinese Government proposed speeding up urban and industrial construction in the Third-tier'(*san xian*) regions during this period. Figure 3.1 shows the distribution of the main Third-tier regions.

This so-called 'Third-tier' concept initially divided the whole country into three regions, from the coastal areas to the inland areas. The First-tier region means the front areas (*qian xian di qu*), including coastal and national bordering areas; the Third-tier region covers 13 provinces and other relevant areas, including most provinces in the western region, such as Sichuan, Guizhou, Yunnan, Shaanxi, Gansu, Ningxia, Qinghai, as well as some mountainous areas in the central region, such as Shanxi, Henan, Hunan, Hubei, Guangdong and Guangxi provinces; The Second tier region refers to the other areas.

In the Third Five-Year-Plan period (1965–1970), the Chinese Government shifted its focus to promoting the Third-tier region, with regard to city, infrastructure and industrial development. During this period, Government investment was largely allocated to the Third-tier region, and a large number of established State-owned enterprises and skilled workers in coastal areas were relocated to the Third-tier region in a planned way. Urban and industrial construction projects in this region were carried out in accordance with the planning principle of

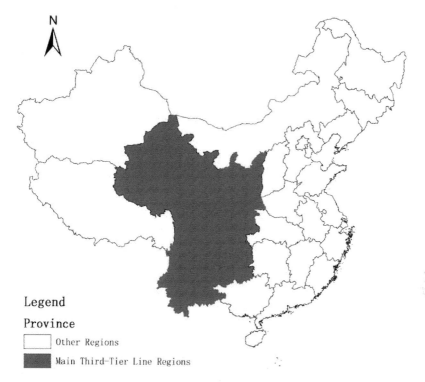

N

Legend

Province

☐ Other Regions

■ Main Third-Tier Line Regions

Figure 3.1 Distribution of main Third-tier regions

'dispersion, mountainous backing and concealing' (*fen san, kao shan, yin bi*). This Third-tier planning programme can be regarded as a way of setting up special economic zones in the country and lasted until the 1980s, exerting direct impacts on the distribution of industrial clusters.

The year 1966 witnessed the beginning of the 'Great Cultural Revolution'.[4] The 'Great Cultural Revolution', from May 1966 to October 1976, was a political movement initiated and led by the Chinese leader Mao Zedong and several other policymakers. This political movement seriously affected the implementation of the Third Five-Year-Plan, as well as other aspects of the Chinese society (MacFarquhar and Schoenhals, 2006). In this period, China's economic development was heavily influenced by this political movement, as evidenced by the dramatic decline in gross output and production. In addition, a large proportion of Government investment was allocated to support the development of steel and heavy industry, leading to a serious imbalance of industrial structure in specific regions.

The adjustment of planning policies was reflected in many aspects during the Fourth Five-Year-Plan period (1971–1975). To improve the policy implementation efficiency, the Central Government divided the country into ten economic regions, to be specific: the south-western, north-western, central, southern, eastern, northern and north-eastern regions, plus Shandong, Fujian-Jiangxi and Xinjiang. The Central Government required these regions to establish their own industrial system and build their own small Third-tier areas within each region, in preparation for possible wars. The Fifth Five-Year-Plan followed this relatively decentralized planning strategy and proposed the establishment of an independent industrial system within each region. Different regions had heterogeneous financial capacities, and thus investment in factories and infrastructure dominated by the Government was not distributed evenly across regions during this period. Jian et al. (1996) found a clear economic divergence measured by GDP per capita across provinces during this period. Kanbur and Zhang (2005) found similar results and suggested the emergence of regional inequality during the Great Cultural Revolution period in China.

From the First to the Fifth Five-Year-Plan period, the Chinese Government invested heavily in urban and industrial construction in the inland areas, including the Third-tier region, under the guidance of the centrally planned economic system. As suggested by Naughton (1988), two-thirds of industrial investment had been allocated to the Third-tier region during the construction peak, and millions of skilled workers had been relocated to work in the newly built factories there. One implication from this is that although provinces in the eastern region, such as Zhejiang, had relatively good locational advantages, provinces in the north-eastern region, such as Liaoning and Jilin provinces and provinces in the mountainous inland provinces, such as Guizhou, experienced even a higher economic growth rate than many other provinces (see Tables 3.1 and 3.2). However, people's quality of life between cities and regions were quite similar given that Government controlled the housing and output pricing systems. To some extent, the uneven industrial development that emerged during this period reflected the spatially heterogeneous priorities of planning policies and political aspirations to develop specific cities and regions.

In this context, the locational layout had the following features. First, the Chinese Government endowed the western region and inland areas with scientific and technological strength by establishing satellite R&D institutions, aircraft-manufacturing clusters and electronic industrial clusters in Sichuan, Shanxi and Guizhou provinces, among others. Major railway infrastructure main lines, such as the Chengdu–Kunming, Hunan–Guizhou, Xiangyang–Chongqing and Qinghai–Tibet railways (the Xige railway section) were built in the western region and inland areas. The supply of transport infrastructure improved the accessibility of the western region and inland areas, drove economic development and enlarged the uneven layout of the regional economy between the east and west.

Second, the industrial development of the Third-tier regions was a response to war preparations under specific historical conditions. On the positive side, many industrial clusters and transport infrastructure projects that had been constructed in the western region and other inland areas improved the economic performance of these regions. On the flip side, the allocation of industry and infrastructure construction projects in these regions neglected the economic and opportunity costs, as well as other market channels at work. During this period, national plans and executive orders served as a regulatory mechanism, and the Chinese Government was the main investment body given the lack of the private sector in the market. As a result, the industrial structure and layout were not suitable for sustaining long-term regional development in these places. With regard to the war preparation and national security purposes, the reallocation of labour and modern industrial technology resources from the coastal regions to remote inland areas was a very costly process, and hindered the economic development of coastal regions during this time. This situation changed dramatically in the 1980s, after the country entered into the early stage of reform and opening-up (*gai ge kai fang*). For example, most State-owned factories built during this period underwent a significant production adjustment and conversion process from the 1980s, to meet the requirement of the national economic transition towards a market-orientated system, and to achieve heavy industrial modernization (Gurtov, 1993; Frankenstein and Gill, 1996; Chai, 1997; Ding, 1997). Table 3.3 summarizes the key characteristics of regional development policy during the First and Seventh Five-Year-Plan periods.

Planning for uneven regional development (1980–1990)

The period from 1953 to 1980 witnessed almost thirty years of China's overly tight, centrally planned economic framework for growth. This period was also characterized by approximately sixteen years of spatial development of Third-tier regions in remote inland areas. Given that planning rules restrict the redistribution of labour, capital and infrastructure resources, it is essential to rethink the economic implications of planning policies on location, cities and infrastructure in this period.

In terms of locational advantages, the Chinese Government invested heavily into developing the industrial bases and associated infrastructure in inland areas and gave priority to promoting industrial development in cities of these areas. In particular, the Third-tier region becomes the first set of 'experimental fields' for industrial agglomeration, and formed the basis for attracting skilled labour and other production factors from the coastal regions. Since the mid-1960s, cities in the Third-tier region and industrial towns in the north-eastern region experienced fast economic growth. As locational advantages of these areas were strengthened by incentives of planning policies, spatial disparities emerged between coastal regions and inland areas. More broadly speaking, the construction of industries and cities in the Third-tier region could be viewed as an overall restructuring process and spatial layout of specific cities in the urban system of China. For example, a large number of industrial cities, such as Shenyang, Chongqing and Chengdu, had been allocated mega-factories. A considerable part of the planning policies for the Third-tier region was to further develop industrial cities in the inland areas that were built originally during the First and Second Five-Year-Plan periods. In addition to existing industrial cities such as Shenyang, Chongqing and Chengdu, new industrial towns emerged close to the existing industrial cities. As suggested by Government reports, the number of cities increased from 167 to 223 during this period. Of course, not all newly built cities were industrial towns,

Table 3.3 Regional development planning policy characteristics during 1st and 7th Five-Year-Plan periods

Period	Regional planning policy guidance	Spatial development priority areas	Economic implications
War recovery period (1949–1952)	• Recovered economic activity after Second World War and the Civil War • Established the State-owned economy system	• Prioritized the development of heavy-industry bases	• Recovered the foundation of the national economy system
1st Five-Year period (1953–1957)	• Established the centralized planning system • Using the allocated industrial projects to re-establish industrial structures	• Prioritized the development of the north-eastern region and inland areas	• Achieved rapid economic growth as compared to the war period
2nd Five-Year period (1958–1962)	• Featured by the 'Great Leap Movement' – targeting the promotion of rapid economic development in all cities and regions in a fast-tracked pathway	• Further prioritized the development of the north-eastern region and inland areas	• Reduced agricultural and industrial outputs owing to the Great Leap political movement and natural disasters
3rd Five-Year period (1966–1970)	• Parallel with the 'Cultural Revolution Movement' • Shifted the focus to the industrial development in the Third-tier Line regions	• Prioritized the development of the Third-tier Line regions, particularly the south-western provinces such as Guizhou, Sichuan	• Reallocated a heavy proportion of skilled labour, factories and capital factors from the coastal regions to the Third-tier Line regions
4th Five-Year period (1971–1975)	• Continued to prioritize the development Third-tier Line regions; and fully utilize the resources in coastal regions	• Further prioritized the development of the Third-tier Line regions, particularly the south-western provinces such as Guizhou, Sichuan	• Reallocated a heavy proportion of skilled labour, factories and capital factors from the coastal regions to the Third-tier Line regions

Period			
5th Five-Year period (1976–1980)	• Planned for adjusting the industrial structure between regions • Entered into the early stage of economic reform and opening-up transition	• Under the framework of inland region and coastal region, 10 subregions were set up by the Central Government: south-western, north-western, central, north-eastern, *hua dong, hua bei, hua nan, shan dong, min gan* and *xin jiang* • Each subregion could establish its own industrial structures	• Adjusted towards a relatively independent subregional development structure; each subregion could begin to make use of its own resources to promote economic growth
6th Five-Year period (1981–1985)	• Public investment as guided by the planning system began to shift the focus towards the coastal regions • 'Dual track system' (*shuang gui zhi*) was allowed to promote the distribution of industrial products and resources	• The classification of regional development system was slightly changed – 3 broad regions were emphasized by the Central Government: inland, coastal and minority ethical group regions (although most minority ethical groups were distributed in inland areas) • In order to attract foreign capital investment, 5 key special economic zones (Shengzhen, Hainan, Zhuhai, Shantou, Xiamen) were established in the coastal regions, particularly in Guangdong province	• Stimulated economic growth in specific coastal regions, particularly in Guangdong province
7th Five-Year period (1986–1990)	• Private capital and foreign capital investments increasingly encouraged in specific regions • Market mechanisms began to assist in distributing labour, capital and resources between regions	• The idea of establishing 'Regional economic agglomeration zones' surrounding Shanghai, Beijing and other mega-cities initially proposed • Additional special economic zones and ports established in the coastal regions, including: the Yangtze River Delta region, Pearl River Delta region, among others	• Broader coastal regions continued to experience rapid economic growth

owing to planning policies in the Third-tier region, but we cannot deny the important role of the policies in forming comprehensive industrial agglomeration hubs in inland areas. Against the background of the Third-tier region development, there is also evidence of rapid transport infrastructure expansion in inland areas. For example, three major railways were built in inland mountainous areas, specifically, the Sichuan–Guizhou, Chengdu–Kunming and Xiangfan–Chongqing railways. The renovated water-transportation system of the Yangtze River was also designed to improve the connection between the hinterland of the Yangtze River and other places. This infrastructure investment strengthened the development of inland cities along the main transport lines. In sum, the rise of economic performance of cities in inland areas was closely linked to the uneven allocation of resources, technology, capital, infrastructure, skilled labour and other factors across places, as guided by the historical planning system.

Empirical evaluation of redistributive planning policies in this centrally planned period neglected the market mechanism, and failed to stimulate rapid economic growth (Fan, 1997). In the 1980s, China began to implement the policy of reform and opening-up. Coupled with economic transitions, senior policymakers adjusted the regional development mode to meet the need of the market mechanism: this mode was the one to combine the centrally planned economy with the market mechanism, to support the rational distribution of locational resources and other production factors across regions. During this period, China's five-year-plans, by allocating public investment projects and offering policy incentives, gave top priority to promoting the economic development of coastal regions. Tables 3.1 and 3.2 support these claims. Some provinces from the eastern region (Guangdong, Zhejiang and Fujian etc.) experienced faster economic growth than provinces from the north-eastern region (Liaoning, Helongjiang and Jilin etc.), in terms of GDP and fixed-asset investment. Figures 3.2 to 3.5 show the distributional trends of key economic growth indicators across provinces, from 1978 to 2012. As can be seen, spatial disparities of provincial economic performance were not obvious in the 1980s within each region.[5] However, the disparities were strengthened across regions. These descriptive statistical results are consistent with findings from empirical modelling evaluations, indicating the conditional economic convergence across regions. For example, Chen and Fleisher (1996) found a clear conditional convergence of per-capita production in the early stage of the reform era (1978–1993), with employment, physical capital, human capital and other socioeconomic characteristics. Gundlach (1997) and Raiser (1998) showed evidence of conditional convergence trends of output per worker in the early stage of the reform era. Using data in a longer time span, Cai et al. (2002) found the conditional convergence of GDP per capita between 1978 and 1998, after controlling for the investment rate, initial human capital, market distortion and other factors. Yao and Zhang (2001) critically summarized this line of research by showing the existence of geo-economic clubs in China, and suggested that output per capita within each club would converge, while output per capita between clubs would diverge. As a result, it is reasonable to assume that wealthy provinces will become wealthier and poor provinces are likely to become poorer.

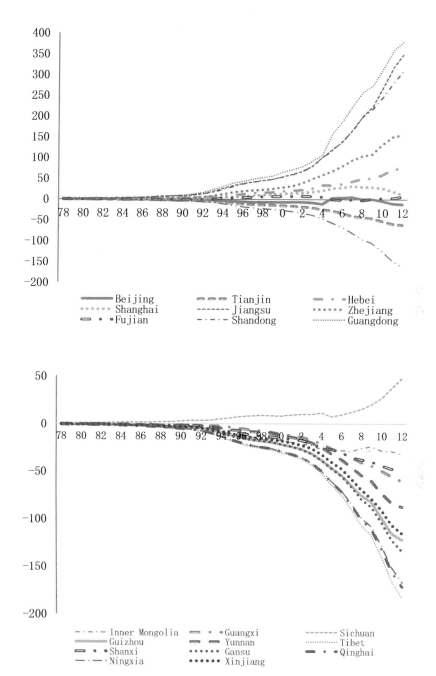

Figure 3.2 GDP growth trend across provinces in north-eastern, eastern, western and central regions

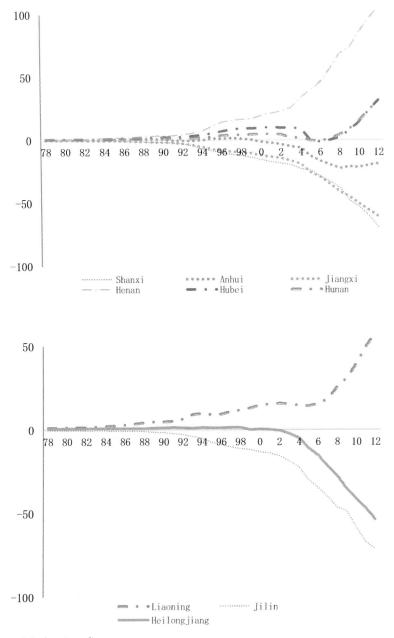

Figure 3.2 (continued)

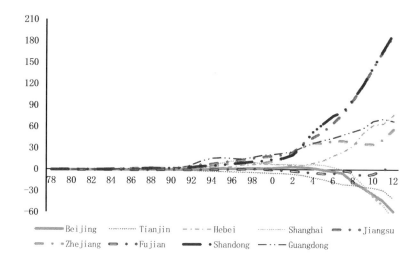

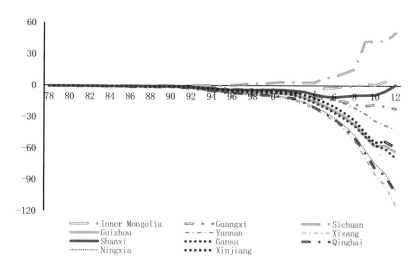

Figure 3.3 Fixed-asset investment growth trend across provinces in north-eastern, eastern, western and central regions

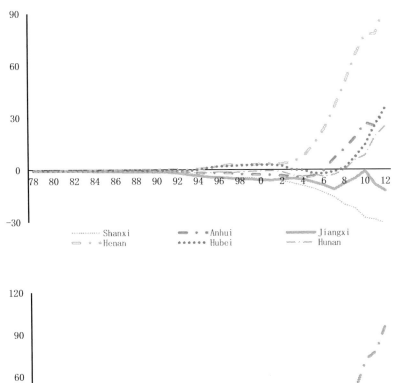

Figure 3.3 (continued)

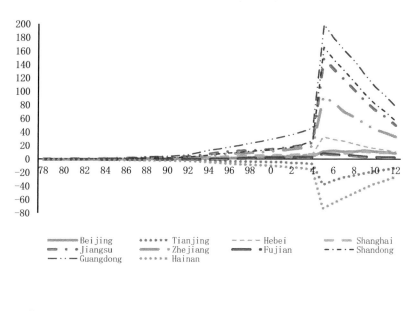

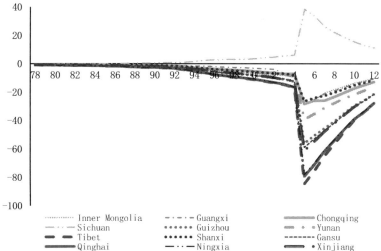

Figure 3.4 Total society retail consumption growth trend across provinces in north-eastern, eastern, western and central regions

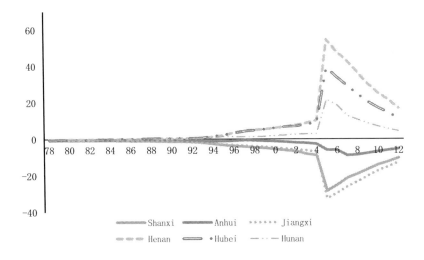

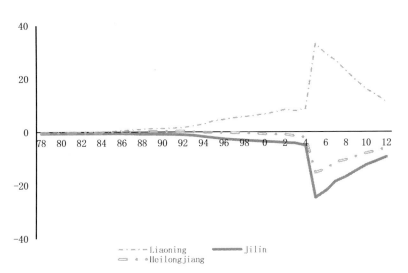

Figure 3.4 (continued)

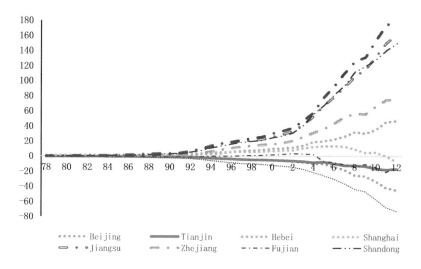

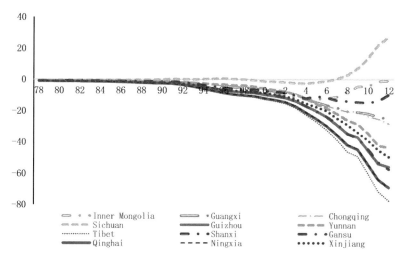

Figure 3.5 Total industrial output growth trend across provinces in north-eastern, eastern, western and central regions

Note for Figures 3.2–3.5: Y-axis denotes the deviation to the national average level. Unit: 10 billion yuan.

Data sources for Figures 3.2–3.5: China Compendium of Statistics 2004 and regional statistical yearbooks for relevant years.

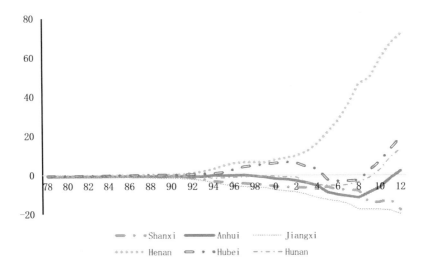

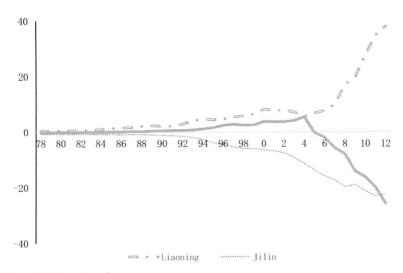

Figure 3.5 (continued)

In addition, significant changes in the planning system included the application of joint ventures between the public and private sectors, to facilitate infrastructure investment and land-market reforms. These transitions were well prepared for deepening the uneven spatial development between coastal regions and inland areas, contradicting the previous planning efforts to restrict spatial differences in quality of life between regions. Instead, people in coastal regions were encouraged to become rich, and cities there were supported to develop first, with a host of special economic zones set up for foreign investment and rapid economic growth (Yang, 1990; 1991). Yet a policy adjustment addressing regional inequality emerged. Since the Ninth Five-Year-Plan in the late 1980s, debates on the appropriateness of uneven development planning policies have attracted increasing public attention, and there have been arguments about shifting the planning focus to inland areas once again, to coordinate regional development.

Sixth Five-Year-Plan

During the Sixth Five-Year-Plan (1981–1985), China's planning policies experienced three major changes. First, the historical planning system tended to pursue industrial growth, particularly growth in heavy industrial output. From the Sixth Five-Year-Plan period, planning policies focused on improving economic efficiency and coordinating the development of agriculture, light industry and heavy industry. Second, historical economic development had been controlled strictly by the Chinese Government using the 'Soviet Union style', centrally planned system. However, after the reform and opening-up, the Chinese Government gradually turned a centrally planned system into a market-orientated system to coordinate price signals and resource allocation across regions. Third, the Chinese Government gradually allowed foreign and private investors to establish their businesses in specific cities, such as the Shenzhen Special Economic Zone, among others.

During the Sixth Five-Year-Plan, a large proportion of production factors, resources and public expenditure were allocated to the coastal region through the planning system. In 1980, the Chinese Government set up special economic zones in Shenzhen, Zhuhai, Shantou and Xiamen, respectively. These zones were all located in coastal region. For these special economic zones, preferential planning policies and tax incentives were implemented to stimulate the economic growth of these 'experimental' zones. After 1984, the Chinese Government decided to open a further 14 coastal port cities, including Dalian and Qinhuangdao, among others, as economic and technological development zones. Similar to the special economic zones, port cities were also given favourable planning polices for stimulating their economic growth. Meanwhile, the Yangtze River Delta, the Pearl River Delta, the Fujian-Zhangzhou-Quanzhou Delta Region and the Liaodong and Shandong Peninsulas were opened successively as economic open zones in the coastal regions. In 1990, the Central Government formally approved the establishment of Shanghai Pudong New Area, allowing it to implement preferential planning policies to attract foreign direct investment (FDI) and stimulate local economic growth. Table 3.4 shows the strong spatial differentiation of FDI performance across provinces. This is not a surprising pattern since only a few provinces (Guangdong and Fujian etc.) were allowed to open their markets to foreign direct investment during the Sixth Five-Year-Plan period.

From the spatial perspective, a belt of special economic zones, stretching from the south to the north along the coastline, was set up in this period. The fact that the sample of special economic zones was confined to cities in the coastal region was associated with the rising trend of uneven spatial development: on one hand, cities in inland areas still largely followed the traditional centrally planned economic development pathway and the market mechanism was mostly underdeveloped during this period; on the other hand, cities in the coastal region enjoyed preferential planning policies for stimulating local economic growth, and could attract foreign and private investment to engage in the local labour market.

Seventh Five-Year-Plan period

Governments at all levels gradually relaxed the direct control of labour, capital, land and all other resources. According to this five-year-plan, the planning system had been reformed by reducing the proportion of mandatory plans and by highlighting the importance of market mechanism in coordinating the distribution of production factors through price signals and other policy incentives. During the Seventh Five-Year-Plan (1986–1990), the Chinese Government proposed 'speed[ing] up the development of the eastern coastal regions, focus[ing] on energy and raw material development in central regions, and actively prepar[ing] for further development of the western regions'. Under this ideology of planning policies, three major regions were set up, namely, the eastern, central and western regions.

In this period, the Chinese Government introduced a series of 'special economic zone' policies to further stimulate the economic growth of special economic zones. These policies achieved a lot by cultivating skilled labour, attracting private and foreign capital, and accelerating economic growth in targeted cities. These policies sought to accomplish these goals by providing State-owned land parcels and by offering a variety of tax and financial incentives to businesses located in targeted cities. These policies were designed to encourage the hiring of skilled workers and to spur local economic development. In addition, private businesses, especially businesses of foreign direct investment in special economic zones, could also receive preferential policies regarding the provision of infrastructure. All these incentives were intended to reduce the start-up costs for businesses located in these zones. In this context, the Chinese Government decided to expand the originally approved four special economic zones, specifically, Shenzhen, Zhuhai, Shantou and Xiamen Economic Zones, and eventually approved the establishment of the Hainan Special Economic Zone in 1987. Since 1988, the Chinese Government decided to further build around 140 new economic zones and technological development zones in cities and counties in the coastal regions including Hangzhou, Nanjing, and so on. Table 3.5 shows that this made sense. Most provinces in the eastern region experienced higher FDI growth than provinces

Table 3.4 Foreign direct investment (FDI) distribution across provinces during 1979–1985

Region	Provinces	1979	1980	1981	1982	1983	1984	1985
East	Tianjin		271	40	578	40	1,190	4,409
	Shanghai			300	333	1,066	2,827	6,242
	Jiangsu			257	257	257	258	1,191
	Zhejiang						252	1,634
	Fujian	83	363	150	121	1,438	4,828	11,782
	Shandong			10			40	559
	Guangdong	3,100	12,300	17,300	17,100	24,500	54,200	51,500
	Hainan		10	109	83	192	1,162	2,095
Central	Shanxi							43
	Anhui							163
	Jiangxi						80	517
	Henan							1,208
	Hunan					26	342	1,761
West	Guangxi						385	1,251
	Chongqing							427
	Sichuan							267
	Guizhou						61	286
	Yunnan							156
	Shanxi						1807	1,374
	Gansu							247
	Qinghai							318
	Ningxia							293
	Xinjiang			392				157
Northeast	Liaoning				38	278	391	1,569
	Jilin						215	488
	Heilongjiang					1,714	8,317	1,747

Note: Monetary figures are reported in US$10,000 at historical value. Some province data are missing.
Data source: China Compendium of Statistics, 2004.

in inland areas. Recent studies also confirm the regional inequality by showing that coastal cities and cities in special economic zones had significant advantages regarding income or GDP growth (Song et al., 2003; Jones et al., 2003). These results are also in line with the geo-economic club predictions proposed by Yao and Zhang (2001).

Regarding infrastructure construction, transport infrastructure developed rapidly in this period, because the Chinese Government adopted a series of reform measures and marketization policies to promote infrastructure development. For example, the separation of the administration and operation organizations in various ports, including highways, railways and the civil-aviation system, had diversified the investment channels, and public–private joint venture structures were gradually allowed to facilitate the expansion and construction of infrastructure projects.

Another important reform of planning policies in this period was the re-establishment of land and housing markets in some cities. By the end of 1987,

Table 3.5 Foreign direct investment (FDI) performance across provinces during 7th–11th Five-Year-Plan periods

Region	Provinces		7th Five-Year-Plan (1986–1990)	8th Five-Year-Plan (1991–1995)	9th Five-Year-Plan (1996–2000)	10th Five-Year-Plan (2001–2005)	11th Five-Year-Plan (2006–2010)
East	Beijing	Mean		82,179.20	197,992.80	246,348.00	563,677.40
		Growth rate		54.72%	12.17%	18.84%	8.74%
	Tianjin	Mean	5,724.40	68,041.80	242,545.60	289,208.80	733,937.60
		Growth rate	18.01%	100.61%	6.29%	0.83%	27.30%
	Hebei	Mean	2,259.25	38,280.40	136,763.80	124,654.00	305,564.20
		Growth rate		78.93%	−4.61%	26.09%	17.43%
	Shanghai	Mean	25,458.40	204,656.00	387,396.20	573,260.00	935,400.00
		Growth rate	16.11%	107.51%	−9.52%	11.75%	11.84%
	Jiangsu	Mean	8,130.40	271,906.00	606,786.60	1,172,231.00	2,365,284.40
		Growth rate	67.07%	112.77%	6.08%	16.64%	13.08%
	Zhejiang	Mean	3,434.40	76,411.00	149,739.20	504,499.80	1,005,390.80
		Growth rate	27.15%	92.49%	1.49%	36.70%	5.47%
	Fujian	Mean	17,237.40	253,581.60	406,308.40	493,182.80	914,434.20
		Growth rate	47.37%	58.22%	−1.73%	12.29%	9.46%
	Shandong	Mean	7,288.80	162,777.80	255,068.80	720,314.40	980,790.33
		Growth rate	67.01%	95.22%	3.49%	32.06%	−100.00%
	Guangdong	Mean	95,460.00	649,000.00	1,195,900.00	1,336,940.00	2,000,120.00
		Growth rate	22.71%	53.72%	1.29%	4.00%	4.24%
	Hainan	Mean	7,222.60	72098.40	62667.60	57735.00	112047.00
		Growth rate	34.89%	56.46%	−14.06%	10.02%	19.21%
Central	Shanxi	Mean	380.80	4,479.20	25,289.20	21,376.20	80,900.00
		Growth rate	118.20%	97.33%	12.96%	4.14%	10.91%
	Anhui	Mean	624.00	23,399.00	37,951.20	46,752.00	335,619.20
		Growth rate	4.89%	166.69%	−10.96%	19.58%	37.73%
	Jiangxi	Mean	524.60	1,7481.00	35,826.60	151,406.00	372,764.20
		Growth rate	7.91%	96.09%	−6.76%	57.29%	16.11%
	Henan	Mean	4,512.60	58,201.80	115,414.20	95,613.60	399,696.40
		Growth rate	11.42%	63.40%	−3.65%	9.25%	35.64%
	Hubei	Mean	13,079.40	66,628.00	130,843.40	168,489.40	323,347.40
		Growth rate	30.53%	43.00%	−7.88%	15.92%	13.41%
	Hunan	Mean	742.60	27,942.00	75,483.60	127,702.60	393,025.80
		Growth rate	4.16%	115.19%	−0.78%	19.23%	18.91%

Region	Province						
West	Inner Mongolia	Mean	337.60	6,204.00	8,725.00	50,360.40	258,174.00
		Growth rate	67.24%	213.35%	19.97%	81.71%	18.09%
	Guangxi	Mean	3,870.20	51,511.60	71,882.60	38,641.00	80,997.60
		Growth rate	-4.91%	103.93%	-5.80%	-0.36%	19.49%
	Chongqing	Mean	1,174.20	24003.60	30356.00	39156.20	310300.00
		Growth rate	-19.48%	149.61%	2.80%	28.72%	64.18%
	Sichuan	Mean	1,734.40	25,654.80	37,365.80	72,531.40	359,397.60
		Growth rate	0.74%	84.56%	18.03%	17.31%	47.68%
	Guizhou	Mean	1,629.00	5,868.20	16,329.20	14,016.80	20,635.60
		Growth rate	23.65%	35.66%	16.45%	8.71%	16.59%
	Yunnan	Mean	428.80	11,022.20	15,453.00	13,175.80	74,257.40
		Growth rate	-7.43%	195.27%	-8.15%	28.04%	44.80%
	Tibet	Mean	7,215.60	17,478.00	36,480.80	47,668.60	136,403.60
		Growth rate	3.05%	78.97%	-2.33%	15.61%	18.44%
	Shanxi	Mean	375.00	6,179.00	5,699.00	6,388.80	21,240.40
		Growth rate		54.53%	-8.77%	15.84%	22.10%
	Gansu	Mean		1,217.80	5,401.60	26,902.20	24,786.00
		Growth rate		236.88%	59.59%	7.61%	-5.50%
	Qinghai	Mean	1,097.40	3,669.20	5,754.80	8,416.00	16,043.60
		Growth rate	59.12%	50.99%	15.14%	29.05%	13.85%
	Ningxia	Mean	850.60	3,646.60	3,124.00	3,941.80	17,429.20
		Growth rate	-16.45%	101.26%	-26.64%	23.60%	23.02%
	Xinjiang	Mean	10,901.60	96,160.00	214,128.80	432,167.40	1,265,910.40
		Growth rate	65.66%	45.46%	11.16%	3.63%	36.45%
Northeast	Liaoning	Mean	4,212.60	48,178.80	69,915.00	66,234.80	293,204.20
		Growth rate	23.88%	53.72%	-16.25%	21.23%	26.04%
	Jilin	Mean	9,305.80	34,199.00	86,850.20	110,394.20	227,280.40
		Growth rate	23.96%	84.57%	1.36%	13.85%	11.73%
	Heilongjiang	Mean	3,465.60	3,639.20	3,770.20	3,815.16	3,826.20
		Growth rate	1.15%	0.87%	0.53%	0.06%	0.07%

Note: Monetary figures are reported in US$10,000 at historical value. Some province data are missing.

Data sources: China Compendium of Statistics, 2004, and regional (*di qu*) statistical yearbooks for relevant years.

Shenzhen held a public auction of land-use rights. This means that the Chinese Government started to establish an open, fair and impartial system for land-asset allocation in accordance with the requirements of the market economy. This was also an endeavour to promote the re-establishment of a standardized, unified, open and orderly land market. Since then, most Chinese cities have experienced a fundamental change from a free land-allocation system towards a land leasehold system. Early in 1988, the Chinese Government promulgated the *Implementation Plan of Urban Housing System Reform by Stages and in Groups throughout the Country.* According to the reform, houses, which had been considered as a fixed-asset investment in the former centrally planned economy era, could become a commodity for trade in the market-orientated economy era. The effective implementation of these policies accelerated urbanization in coastal cities with booming property markets. As shown in the substantial literature, planning policies regarding land and housing market reforms had profound implications on the speed, pattern and structure of urban growth across regions.

In the decade from 1981 to 1990, China entered the early stage of reform and opening-up. Overall, as can be seen from Table 3.3, there had been dramatic changes in planning-policy transitions regarding urban and regional development during the Sixth and Seventh Five-Year-Plan periods. Considering the comparative locational advantages of coastal regions in attracting foreign direct investment, the Chinese Government prioritized the economic development of these areas. Preferential policies related to local and regional development were also implemented to stimulate the creation of businesses and jobs. As a result, there is clear evidence of the rapid economic development for cities and provinces in coastal regions, in terms of GDP, industrial output, fixed-asset investment and retail consumption compared to other places in the country (see Figures 3.2–3.5).

With regard to locational development, important changes occurred in the guiding ideology of the planning policies, with respect to urban development and infrastructure construction. To be specific, support for economic development was given to the eastern region and portal cities rather than to industrial cities in inland areas and the Third-tier region. On the whole, the main theme of the country's planning policies shifted from preparing for industrial output against war and natural disasters towards stimulating economic growth in coastal regions. From the Sixth to the Seventh Five-Year-Plan, there was an obvious increase in the Government investment ratio into the eastern region and portal cities. With the 'visible' support of planning policies, new spatial disparities emerged.

Concerning infrastructure construction, the Chinese Government began to make use of long-term planning policies to promote the development of transport infrastructure in a sustainable way. Several features emerged. First, in this transitional period, infrastructure funding was mainly from the Government, whereas shortages were encouraged to be filled by private capital and/or through investment subsidies, guaranteed subsidies and loans with discounted interest. Second, infrastructure institutions were required to apply modern enterprise management mechanisms, to improve operation and construction efficiency. In addition, social capital was also encouraged in construction and operation in a variety of ways. With the equal treatment for all kinds of investors, a fair competition system was gradually created. In the field of public service, resources and the environment, ecological protection, and infrastructure improvement, cooperation between governmental and social capital was also proposed, to improve the efficiency of the investment and operation mechanism. Finally, in the centrally planned economy era when the price adjustment was not in place, the Chinese Government had to arrange financial funds to compensate for the construction and operation of infrastructure. But in this transitional period, a pricing mechanism was gradually developed in the infrastructure investment process. Operators and builders could be compensated at a reasonable cost and got a reasonable return. Taken together, these market-orientated reforms sustained rapid infrastructure expansion and strengthened interregional connections.

For urban development, in this transitional period, the Chinese Government actively promoted the construction of various economic zones and districts. In particular, 5 special economic zones, 14 coastal opening cities, and 260 coastal opening counties were set up in the eastern region, under preferential policies and in favourable geographic conditions. Actually, 25 of the country's 30 State-level economic and technological development zones were in the eastern region; and 13 tariff-free zones (*bao shui qu*) were all located in the eastern coastal region. The allocation of these zones and districts effectively enhanced the economic performance of this region and promoted the agglomeration of small- and medium-sized cities surrounding mega-cities. This agglomeration process was strengthened further by a series of policy incentives covering finance, banking, land and taxation. Under the influence of the market mechanism, differences in economic performance between cities along main transportation routes were strengthened. Furthermore, there is clear evidence of the spatial concentration of foreign direct investment in provinces in the eastern region, which may have eventually contributed to technological innovations in the cities. These innovations were crucial to reinforce the agglomeration in this region. In contrast, the central and western regions gained much less from foreign direct investment in the early stages of economic reform and opening-up, which led to the widening gap between regions. In addition, as technology transfer and product cycle proceeded, it was expected that cities in the eastern region would become more expensive locations for labour-intensive manufacturing (Duranton and Puga, 2001), and consequently the manufacturing industry would seek to decentralize its operation to the western and central regions, where land and labour costs were cheaper. In the theoretical spatial economic agglomeration framework (Rosenthal and Strange, 2003), regional inequality would continue to grow.

Conclusion

There has been considerable debate about whether the strictly centralized 'Soviet Union style' planning system for cities can optimize the distribution of production factors in order to enhance spatial economic development. For example, planning restrictions that control labour, industry and resource allocation could evidently exert friction on economic activities and trade between cities of differential locational advantages. By investing heavily in infrastructure in mountainous areas and other places in the Third-tier region, the Chinese Government delayed investment and hindered urban agglomeration in coastal areas. Little is known about comparable evidence for what would have happened with regard to spatial economic performance if policymakers had adopted the market economic system from the 1950s. But from the fact that industrial investment tended to be allocated to the north-eastern and Third-tier regions, one could speculate that the economic impacts might have been more substantial if the historical planning system during the first three decades of the People's Republic of China had recognized the effect of the market. This does not mean that the historical planning system is not important for enhancing economic growth and shaping spatial disparities. Growth in terms of industrial and agricultural output over time certainly suggested that the Chinese planning system was not entirely inefficient in promoting economic development. Evidence from the industrial development in the north-eastern and Third-tier regions further suggests that places allocated more resources, skilled labour and capital would generate more economic output. In fact, old industrial cities and cities in the Third-tier region can be regarded as a sort of historical and institutional 'special economic zone' in the centrally planned economy era.

There is also evidence that the emergence of the 'special economic zones' unintentionally transformed the evenly distributed development mode, as guided by the historical 'Soviet Union style' planning system, into an uneven structure (Zhou, 1993; Zhao, 1996; Fan, 1997). The most important effect on the spatial variation in industrial productivity and output, however, was from the Third-tier planning policies. The application of the Third-tier planning policies since the mid-1960s enhanced the spatial disparities between the inland and coastal regions. The reinforcement of Third-tier planning policies gradually decreased in the 1980s, allowing for the reallocation of public investment and resources among cities, and infrastructure construction in coastal regions. The centralized planning allocation, along with a lack of financial incentives to local businesses for the development of the private sector, also led to economic disparities between Chinese provinces (Jian et al., 1996; Zhang and Zou, 2012). Arguments have been made that centralized planning allocation for infrastructure and factories across cities, and the resulting economic performance differentials, are the manifestation of uneven regional development. The rationale behind this is that, if all else were equal, places with more State resources and investment would grow faster than other places. While this viewpoint is not conclusive, the Chinese case – that planning policies would improve both quality of life and real industrial output for targeted cities – is pretty impressive and effective as outlined in detail in this chapter.

Other potential external effects of the planning system in this historical period are not well investigated (for example, the direct and indirect external effects from the Great Leap Movement and the Cultural Revolution Movement on manufacturing and infrastructure distribution, or the dynamic effects from these political movements on people's quality of life and economic growth). Subsequent planning policies have attempted to solve the problems left by these political movements by changing the focus. But local and regional government constrained industrial market activities and restricted the use of price mechanism to coordinate the market supply and demand during this period. Therefore, reforms in planning system did not lift the fundamental barriers and allow the market mechanism to work together with the planning system in shaping urban and regional development.

Given the lack of market mechanism, it is reasonable that the coastal regions lagged behind the economic performance of business productivity and output, since skilled labour and industrial equipment were relocated from cities in coastal regions to support the development of the Third-tier region. This awkwardly shaped spatial economic disparity tended to be reversed after the implementation of the economic reform and opening-up since the 1980s. Evidence from the Sixth and Seventh Five-Year-Plan periods shows overwhelmingly that cities – especially those newly established special economic zones which are able to supply land for businesses and provide tax and financial incentives to attract private-sector investment and foreign direct investment – have accumulated more and more locational advantages for their growth. One should therefore stress the implications of the market-orientated economic transitions on spatial economic performance. There might be even broader social and environmental implications associated with Chinese market-orientated economic transitions, and recent evidence suggests that the overheated economic development pushed by local and regional government is associated with social and residential segregation, environmental pollution, congestion and other side effects. These issues are beyond the scope of this book but are worth careful evaluation when micro data and policy information are available. In essence, this chapter makes it clear that the Chinese planning system in the centrally planned economy era plays an important role in driving urban and regional economic development. From the 1990s, emerging special economic zones and massive private and foreign capital investment have been likely to accelerate economic development in coastal regions. The relaxation of the labour and industrial markets, coupled with the establishment of land and housing markets, will be even more important than that of the 1980s, and spatial economic agglomeration for cities will be even more obvious. Dealing with these characteristics in China will require the adjustment of planning policies; a new feature that Chapters 4 and 5 will describe in detail.

Notes

1 The Third-Tier Line Region strategy can also be referred to as the 'Third-Front Movement'. See https://en.wikipedia.org/wiki/Third_Front_(China)
2 The classification of strategic regions in the Chinese planning system has experienced changes over different Five-Year-Plan periods. Some studies have divided China into two broad geographical clubs: coastal region and inland region. The coastal region usually includes all provinces in the eastern region (e.g., Chen and Fleisher, 1996; Jian et al., 1996). For the purpose of the consistency with recent Five-Year-Plans, the whole county is divided into four regions: north-eastern, eastern, western and central regions.

The north-eastern region includes Heilongjiang, Liaoning and Jilin. The western region includes Sichuan, Shannxi, Guizhou, Xinjiang, Tibet, Yunan, Gansu, Qinghai, Ningxia, Guangxi and Inner Mongolia. The eastern region includes Beijing, Tianjin, Liaoning, Shanghai, Hebei, Shandong, Zhejiang, Jiangsu, Fujian, Guangdong and Hainan. The central region includes Shanxi, Henan, Anhui, Jiangxi, Hubei and Hunan.

3 https://en.wikipedia.org/wiki/Great_Leap_Forward
4 https://en.wikipedia.org/wiki/Cultural_Revolution
5 For the purpose of consistency, this book tries to use four strategic regions (namely the western, central, north-eastern and eastern regions) for empirical investigations.

References

Ashton, B., Hill, K., Piazza, A. and Zeitz, R. 1984. Famine in China, 1958–61. Population and Development Review, 10(4), 613–645.

Banister, J. 1987. *China's Changing Population.* Stanford, CA: Stanford University Press.

Cai, F., Wang, D. and Yang, D.U. 2002. Regional disparity and economic growth in China: The impact of labour market distortions. China Economic Review 13, 197–212.

Chai, B. 1997. Conversion and restructuring of China's defense industry, in J. Brommelhorster and J. Frankenstein (eds.) *Mixed Motives, Uncertain Outcomes: Defense Conversion in China,* Boulder, CO: Lynne Rienner.

Chen, J. and Fleisher, B.M. 1996. Regional income inequality and economic growth in China. Journal of Comparative Economics, 22, 141–164.

Ding, A.S. 1997. The regional implications of defense conversion: The case of the 'Third Line' and Guizhou, in J. Brommelhorster and J. Frankenstein (eds.) *Mixed Motives, Uncertain Outcomes: Defense Conversion in China,* Boulder, CO: Lynne Rienner.

Duranton G. and Puga, D. 2001. Nursery cities: Urban diversity, process innovation, and the life cycle of products, American Economic Review, 91, 1454–1477.

Falkenheim, V.C. 1985. Spatial inequalities in China's modernization programme: some political-administrative determinants. In C-K. Leung and J.C.H. Chai (eds.), *Development and distribution in China*, Hong Kong: University of Hong Kong.

Fan, C.C. 1997. Uneven development and beyond: Regional development theory in post-Mao China. International Journal of Urban and Regional Research, 21(4), 620–639.

Frankenstein, J. and Gill, B. 1996. Current and future challenges facing Chinese defense industries, The China Quarterly, 146, 394–427.

Gundlach, E. 1997. Regional convergence of output per worker in China: A neo-classical interpretation. Asian Economic Journal, 11 (4), 423–442.

Gurtov, M. 1993. Swords into market shares: China's conversion of military industry to civilian production, The China Quarterly, 134, 213–241.

Jian, T., Sachs, J. and Warner, A. 1996. Trends in regional inequality in China. China Economic Review, 7, 1–21.

Jones, D., Li, C. and Owen, A.L. 2003. Growth and regional inequality in China during the reform era. China Economic Review, 14, 186–200.

Kanbur, R. and Zhang, X. 2005. Fifty years of regional inequality in China: A journey through central planning, reform, and openness. Review of Development Economics, 9(1), 87–106.

MacFarquhar, R. and Schoenhals, M. 2006. *Mao's Last Revolution.* Cambridge, MA: Harvard University Press.

Naughton, B. 1988. The third front: Defense industrialization in Chinese interior, The China Quarterly, 115, 351–386.

Peng, X. 1987. Demographic consequences of the Great Leap Forward in China's provinces. Population and Development Review, 13(4), 648–649.

Raiser, M. 1998. Subsidizing inequality: Economic reforms, fiscal transfers and convergence across Chinese Provinces. Journal of Development Studies, 34(3), 1–26.

Rosenthal, S.S. and Strange, W.C. 2003. Geography, industrial organization, and agglomeration, Review of Economics and Statistics, 85(2), 377–393.

Song, S., Chu, G.S.F. and Cao, R. 2003. Intercity regional disparity in China. China Economic Review, 11, 246–261.

Yang, D. 1990. Patterns of China's regional development strategy. The China Quarterly 122, 230–257.

Yang, D. 1991. China adjusts to the world economy: The political economy of China's coastal development strategy. Pacific Affairs 64(1), 42–64.

Yang, J. 2010. The fatal politics of the PRC's Great Leap famine: The preface to tombstone, Journal of Contemporary China, 19(66), 755–776.

Yao, S. and Zhang, Z. 2001. On regional inequality and diverging clubs: A case study of contemporary China. Journal of Comparative Economics, 29, 466–484.

Zhang, Q. and Zou, H. 2012. Regional inequality in contemporary China. Annals of Economics and Finance, 13(1), 113–117.

Zhao, S.X. 1996. Spatial disparities and economic development in China, 1953–92: A comparative study. Development and Change, 27(1), 131–163.

Zhou, Q. 1993. Capital construction investment and its regional distribution in China. International Journal of Urban and Regional Research, 17(2), 159–171.

4 Planning for transformation

Spatial economic prosperity and disparity

Introduction

Chapter 3 showed how the Chinese planning system affects the infrastructure allocation, and how this generated the volatility of industrial markets and economic growth during the centrally planned economy era and the early stage of economic reforms. But of course since national Five-Year-Plan systems allocate public resources, not only to support national defence but also to guide other types of economic activities across regions, they have direct impacts on shaping the spatial development of cities and regions. Based on Chapter 3, this chapter focuses on the implementation and adjustment of Deng's uneven regional development ideology since the Eighth Five-Year-Plan period. It aims to shed light on how the configuration of planning policies has influenced the evolution of four major spatial development 'plates' (*ban kuai*) in the country, specifically, the western, north-eastern, central and eastern regions. It is arguable that if planning policies are used appropriately for intervention, they might be helpful in achieving the balanced development of the country. From the strategic perspective, Chinese Five-Year-Plans between 1991 and 2014 paid great attention not only to maximizing locational advantages, but also to generating multiplier effects between core regions and peripheral regions. Table 4.1 provides a brief summary of regional characteristics of Five-Year-Plans during this period.

In the context of marketization, planning systems regarding cities, location and infrastructure have direct and indirect impacts on shaping the level and pattern of spatial economic development. The lack of a well-performed market mechanism during the centrally planned economy era allowed the planning systems to play a dominant role in determining the economic activities of units *(Danwei)* in Chinese urban society (Björklund, 1986; Chai, 1996; Bray, 2005). Since the early 1990s, the market mechanism has been re-established by the Chinese Government, and various 'new' planning policies have been implemented in guiding the uneven regional development. The market mechanism has irreplaceable functional advantages over direct institutional commands, in terms of economic restructuring. There is strong evidence of the vitality of the market mechanism in China over the past few decades (1991–2014): the market mechanism has been recognized as the hybrid organizational mechanism for stimulating economic integration and optimizing

Table 4.1 Regional development planning policy characteristics during 8th and 12th Five-Year-Plan periods

Period	Regional planning-policy guidance	Spatial development priority areas	Economic implications
8th Five-Year period (1991–1995)	• Promoted the development of coastal regions • Further strengthened the economic reform process	• The classification of regional development system was changed – 4 broad regions were emphasized by the Central Government: inland, coastal, minority ethical group, and poor regions • Prioritized the mining industry development in Shanxi, Inner Mongolia, Heilongjiang and Anhui provinces • Established major agricultural production bases in provinces of Henan, Hubei, Sichuan, Inner Mongolia and Ningxia	• Policy incentives to support the development of local businesses in coastal regions • Transport infrastructure improvements further strengthened urban exchanges in coastal regions
9th Five-Year period (1996–2000)	• Regional planning principles were changed from the uneven development pathway to a coordinated development pathway • Formulated a stable economic reform transition mode	• The classification of regional development system was further changed – 7 broad regions were emphasized by the Central Government: Yangtze River Delta and associated region, Huan Bo Hai region, south-eastern coastal region, south-western region, central region, southern region and the western region (although the classification principle and objectives are not clearly defined) • Prioritized the allocation of infrastructure investment projects in central and western parts of China	• Trying to coordinate regional development patterns • Accelerated public expenditure in infrastructure projects in central and western parts of China
10th Five-Year period (2001–2005)	• The Chinese Government shifted its development focus towards improving the economic performance of the western region	• Prioritized the allocation of infrastructure investment projects in the western region of China • Prioritized the provision of financial incentives to attract private and foreign investment in the western region of China	• Tried to stimulate overall economic growth in the western region of China

(continued)

Table 4.1 (continued)

Period	Regional planning-policy guidance	Spatial development priority areas	Economic implications
11th Five-Year period (2006–2010)	• Based on the coordinated development pathway, policymakers formulated the so-called four-plate regional development strategy, including *'the development of the Western region, the rise of the Central region, the revitalization of old industrial towns in the North-eastern region and the pioneering development of the Eastern region'*	• Emphasized the differential development priorities for different regions so as to match their regional locational advantages • Stimulated the formation of major regional economic agglomeration zones to lead the coordinated regional development pathway	• Achieved a more relatively coordinated regional economic growth pattern compared to before
12th Five-Year period (2011–2015)	• The idea of Main Functional Area (*zhu ti gong neng qu*) was formulated as the regional planning guidance to coordinate economic growth and environmental protection	• Prioritized the shift in regional development strategy towards a human-centred and sustainable pathway • Prioritized the coordination of spatial development in distressed and vibrant regions • Prioritized the urban and regional agglomerations in suitable regions	• Integrated the varieties of infrastructure investment and other public expenditure to make fundamental social services available to support the growth of core metropolitan and peripheral regions

resource allocation (see Nee, 1992, and Naughton, 1995, about economic reforms). In the market-orientated system, workers and firms can respond in a timely manner to the changes in market supply and demand and choose where to maximize their utilities. But the market mechanism has its own limitation: the reallocation of resources in the market is achieved by supply and demand equilibrium and therefore the market-orientated system might bear a certain degree of blindness and spontaneity. In addition, the effectiveness of the market mechanism relies on competitions. In reality, market competition often leads to a monopoly in production and price manipulation. Thus, the complete abandon of Government intervention in the market-orientated system may result in so-called 'market failure' scenarios. In addition, conflicts between provinces and regions occurred, owing to the existence of a 'scissors gap' (*jian dao cha*) in production prices (Zhu, 1992). On one hand, coastal provinces competed to produce high value-added light industrial and consumer goods, so as to make use of the 'scissors gap' price structure to promote their own economic development (Sai and Zhu, 1990). On the other hand, inland provinces tended to set up institutional barriers (*guan ka*) to constrain flows of raw materials, resources and products for their own benefit (Zhang, 1992; Huang, 1993; Liao, 1993). Meanwhile, inland mega-cities and provinces lobbied the Central Government to give preferential planning policies to them, and promote economic growth in inland provinces (Li, 1988; Zhang, 1989; Yang, 1991). To some extent, the national market system remained spatially segregated during the early stage of the economic reform. The consequence is that, although China maintained rapid economic growth during the early 1990s, uneven spatial development between regions increased. To address this concern, a coordinated development pathway was proposed by the Chinese Government through the implementation of a series of planning policies.

This chapter considers the forms of guiding ideology and development pathways that have embedded market mechanisms into the planning-policy decision-making process. The focus here is to highlight the fundamental changes between 1991 and 2000, relative to the previous planning policies during the centrally planned economy era and the early stage of economic reform (1949–1990). More recently, as shown in the second half of this chapter, several large-scale regional planning programmes have been implemented over the past few years (2001–2014), namely, *the Development of the Western Region, the Rise of the Central Region, the Revitalization of Old Industrial Towns in the North-eastern Region, and the Pioneering Development of the Eastern Region*. Of course, senior policymakers want to use these strategies to regenerate declining cities and guide the configuration of the spatial economy. But it is not clear what forms of planning policies would be more effective in intervening in the uneven spatial development in the long term. There are observable and unobservable links between planning policies and their effects on benefiting society and the spatial economy, which must be considered when evaluating the dynamic economic impacts of specific urban and regional planning programmes. Chapter 5 will try to describe the formation of urban and regional economic agglomerations, as guided by planning policies.

Role that market-orientated planning system plays spatially (1991–2000)

During the last decade of the twentieth century, China kept pushing ahead with the implementation of economic reforms and improving its national economic performance. An uneven development pattern emerged; in particular, spatial economic disparities between the east and west, and between rural and urban areas, increased. To this end, the Chinese Government gradually prioritized the coordinated development of the regional economy and set up planning guidelines for this. As a result, since the early 1990s, a fundamental shift from the centrally planned economy towards the market orientated economy has been achieved by the Chinese Government. Correspondingly, the comprehensive and coordinated development has been highlighted by planning policies during the Eighth Five-Year-Plan period (1991–1995) and the Ninth Five-Year-Plan period (1996–2000). For example, the Eighth Five-Year-Plan proposed 'promot[ing] the rational division of labour and coordinated development of regional economy' and considered that 'the rational distribution of productivity and the coordinated development of regional economy were extremely critical to China's economic construction and social development'. In the same vein, the Ninth Five-Year-Plan clearly pointed out that it was necessary, in the next fifteen years to 'adhere to the coordinated development of regional economy and gradually narrow the development gap between regions' for future economic development, and indicated that 'more attention should be paid to supporting the development of inland areas, implementing policies to alleviate the widening gap between regions, and working hard to narrow the gap'.

The first half of Table 4.1 summarizes the transformation of the development pathway and the characteristics of planning policies during the Eighth and Ninth Five-Year-Plan periods. The first characteristic is the change in the guiding ideology of the regional development policies. Given that spatial disparities increased across regions from 1991 to 2000, an important guideline was to use planning instruments to change regional economic structure towards a more harmonious pattern (see Table 4.1). The second and more meaningful difference between planning policies in the centrally planned economy era and those in this transitional period was the obligation to apply both mandatory means and market mechanism to guide the labour, capital and resource distribution. This transition is designed to intervene more effectively in urban agglomeration and infrastructure layout. These characteristics can be summarized as follows:

In terms of spatial development, the unevenness of economic performance between regions widened during the Eighth and Ninth Five-Year-Plan periods. This is not surprising, because the Chinese Government focused on prioritizing efficiency over equity so as to make a small proportion of areas and people become wealthy first. As a 'pioneering development' region, the eastern region attracted all the necessary production factors to stimulate its regional economic growth. As can be seen from Tables 4.2 and 4.3, GDP and fixed-asset investment in provinces in the eastern region increased much faster than those in the western region during the Eighth and Ninth Five-Year-Plan periods (especially during the Ninth). Although some provinces outside the eastern region, such as Sichuan

Table 4.2 GDP growth by province during 8th–11th Five-Year-Plan periods

Region	Province		8th Five-Year-Plan (1991–1995)	9th Five-Year-Plan (1996–2000)	10th Five-Year-Plan (2001–2005)	11th Five-Year-Plan (2006–2010)
East	Beijing	Mean	930.08	2,018.08	4,194.86	11,069.24
		Growth rate	23.54%	11.29%	25.10%	14.83%
	Tianjin	Mean	586.58	1,352.11	2,635.29	6,636.16
		Growth rate	27.92%	10.50%	20.70%	19.90%
	Hebei	Mean	1,815.68	4,264.20	7,529.58	15,743.33
		Growth rate	27.68%	10.18%	15.75%	15.48%
	Shanghai	Mean	1,590.84	3,707.34	6,661.67	13,869.71
		Growth rate	28.84%	11.90%	16.91%	12.88%
	Jiangsu	Mean	3,189.66	7,233.00	13,343.12	30,925.06
		Growth rate	33.95%	9.34%	18.25%	17.49%
	Zhejiang	Mean	2,118.50	5,033.88	9,720.18	21,329.51
		Growth rate	34.77%	9.74%	18.74%	15.24%
	Fujian	Mean	1,273.46	3,275.26	5,305.90	10,925.81
		Growth rate	36.52%	10.55%	11.65%	18.07%
	Shandong	Mean	3,089.60	7,177.32	13,256.77	30,335.39
		Growth rate	28.23%	9.72%	18.11%	15.64%
	Guangdong	Mean	3,593.28	7,976.04	14,921.21	36,131.42
		Growth rate	32.72%	10.34%	20.64%	14.70%
	Hainan	Mean	289.64	444.48	702.01	1,508.32
		Growth rate	30.66%	7.37%	13.86%	17.98%
Central	Shanxi	Mean	706.62	1,443.16	2,743.15	6,955.53
		Growth rate	21.84%	7.62%	24.03%	17.19%
	Anhui	Mean	1,205.34	2,752.86	4,196.31	8,949.45
		Growth rate	31.82%	6.78%	12.92%	19.25%
	Jiangxi	Mean	779.39	1708.54	3004.35	6939.65
		Growth rate	25.18%	8.82%	17.04%	18.33%
	Henan	Mean	1,843.08	4,362.16	7,651.99	17,593.32
		Growth rate	30.17%	8.84%	17.05%	16.91%
	Hubei	Mean	1,554.32	3,576.81	5,562.62	11,441.70
		Growth rate	27.79%	9.09%	9.66%	20.33%
	Hunan	Mean	1,379.58	3,128.12	5,034.20	11,556.18
		Growth rate	26.76%	9.32%	13.44%	20.18%

(continued)

Table 4.2 (continued)

Region	Province		8th Five-Year-Plan (1991–1995)	9th Five-Year-Plan (1996–2000)	10th Five-Year-Plan (2001–2005)	11th Five-Year-Plan (2006–2010)
West	Inner Mongolia	Mean	565.78	1,176.74	2,419.55	8,255.18
		Growth rate	23.36%	9.03%	26.07%	23.95%
	Guangxi	Mean	946.56	1,884.34	2,945.18	6,983.92
		Growth rate	30.36%	4.83%	15.60%	19.16%
	Chongqing	Mean		1,407.00	2,466.08	5,766.52
		Growth rate		7.89%	18.31%	19.34%
	Sichuan	Mean	1,637.22	3,521.50	5,738.86	12,638.12
		Growth rate	25.30%	7.66%	13.68%	18.59%
	Guizhou	Mean	443.64	863.46	1,444.67	3,459.90
		Growth rate	21.66%	8.09%	16.60%	18.44%
	Yunnan	Mean	819.19	1,748.12	2,638.91	5,569.34
		Growth rate	23.58%	7.00%	13.66%	16.01%
	Tibet	Mean	40.58	91.20	189.00	395.17
		Growth rate	16.37%	16.05%	15.72%	14.94%
	Shanxi	Mean	696.64	1401.18	2,632.34	7,221.75
		Growth rate	20.98%	9.02%	20.85%	20.87%
	Gansu	Mean	393.30	856.52	1,408.98	3,131.29
		Growth rate	19.50%	8.40%	15.64%	15.98%
	Qinghai	Mean	115.14	222.94	406.28	979.23
		Growth rate	21.80%	7.77%	16.52%	20.13%
	Ningxia	Mean	112.49	227.81	417.19	1,178.38
		Growth rate	24.01%	8.22%	19.70%	23.52%
	Xinjiang	Mean	548.53	1,122.37	1,953.14	4,093.23
		Growth rate	25.19%	10.59%	15.07%	15.60%
Northeast	Liaoning	Mean	1,987.82	3,890.64	6,282.75	13,561.43
		Growth rate	23.52%	10.36%	12.45%	18.68%
	Jilin	Mean	769.56	1,587.38	2,759.07	6,386.45
		Growth rate	25.22%	8.38%	14.75%	19.33%
	Heilongjiang	Mean	1,323.14	2,779.72	4,399.18	8,117.15
		Growth rate	24.91%	8.20%	11.91%	13.66%

Note: GDP figures are reported in 100 million yuan at historical value. Some province data are missing.

Data sources: China Compendium of Statistics, 2004, and regional (*di qu*) statistical yearbooks for relevant years.

Table 4.3 Fixed-asset investment growth by provinces during 8th–11th Five-Year-Plan periods

Region	Province		8th Five-Year-Plan (1991–1995)	9th Five-Year-Plan (1996–2000)	10th Five-Year-Plan (2001–2005)	11th Five-Year-Plan (2006–2010)
East	Beijing	Mean	471.74	1,092.34	2,171.49	4,207.64
		Growth rate	44.69%	10.29%	16.58%	13.15%
	Tianjin	Mean	246.91	537.30	1,063.44	3,715.95
		Growth rate	32.14%	8.72%	20.67%	36.27%
	Hebei	Mean	553.00	1,590.82	2,779.18	9,714.93
		Growth rate	40.58%	11.67%	20.83%	28.86%
	Shanghai	Mean	798.93	1,924.17	2,645.64	4,659.24
		Growth rate	57.80%	-1.07%	15.17%	6.98%
	Jiangsu	Mean	1,061.44	2,485.24	5,536.20	15,954.40
		Growth rate	39.79%	11.34%	25.39%	23.18%
	Zhejiang	Mean	729.82	1,862.64	4,789.29	9,690.40
		Growth rate	54.26%	8.81%	23.79%	13.00%
	Fujian	Mean	392.33	971.89	1,617.79	5381.51
		Growth rate	47.06%	8.19%	19.54%	28.77%
	Shandong	Mean	872.56	2,034.42	5,716.36	16,280.02
		Growth rate	31.65%	13.03%	34.93%	20.31%
	Guangdong	Mean	1,499.64	2,711.03	5,108.23	11,338.62
		Growth rate	48.53%	8.57%	18.52%	18.31%
	Hainan	Mean				787.41
		Growth rate				32.77%
Central	Shanxi	Mean	232.02	493.44	1,189.60	3,930.94
		Growth rate	18.58%	17.01%	26.72%	28.04%
	Anhui	Mean	321.02	734.24	1,602.88	7,180.34
		Growth rate	40.33%	8.99%	27.22%	34.44%
	Jiangxi	Mean	184.71	446.92	1,392.26	5,229.27
		Growth rate	32.91%	11.41%	34.73%	34.46%
	Henan	Mean	491.76	1,244.18	2,634.00	10,939.16
		Growth rate	33.11%	10.12%	27.57%	29.46%
	Hubei	Mean	442.33	1,204.56	2,032.70	6,290.09
		Growth rate	48.89%	9.62%	14.60%	32.36%
	Hunan	Mean	331.12	847.44	1,746.77	6,046.26
		Growth rate	35.14%	11.97%	21.39%	32.08%

(continued)

Table 4.3 (continued)

Region	Province		8th Five-Year-Plan (1991–1995)	9th Five-Year-Plan (1996–2000)	10th Five-Year-Plan (2001–2005)	11th Five-Year-Plan (2006–2010)
West	Inner Mongolia	Mean	198.28	351.40	1,374.68	5,894.95
		Growth rate	28.33%	11.80%	51.91%	27.64%
	Guangxi	Mean	262.96	561.62	1,093.93	4,237.92
		Growth rate	47.40%	8.49%	22.77%	33.85%
	Chongqing	Mean	164.12	481.68	1,324.39	4,283.58
		Growth rate	33.55%	19.58%	24.61%	29.11%
	Sichuan	Mean	443.84	1,112.50	2,354.18	8,333.82
		Growth rate	34.94%	14.96%	22.85%	31.30%
	Guizhou	Mean	111.63	299.13	757.56	2,013.52
		Growth rate	31.29%	18.07%	16.94%	26.90%
	Yunnan	Mean	238.54	615.26	1,138.57	3,691.73
		Growth rate	40.26%	11.72%	24.71%	25.78%
	Tibet	Mean	20.03	46.15	136.64	330.47
		Growth rate	36.75%	21.66%	20.59%	18.95%
	Shanxi	Mean	220.64	541.22	1,306.08	4,944.14
		Growth rate	26.94%	18.99%	21.96%	33.86%
	Gansu	Mean	125.92	327.14	672.53	1,912.17
		Growth rate	29.80%	19.73%	14.56%	32.57%
	Qinghai	Mean	39.95	114.94	275.92	657.94
		Growth rate	23.45%	18.81%	13.09%	25.61%
	Ningxia	Mean	50.14	113.10	313.79	889.49
		Growth rate	24.90%	20.09%	22.66%	21.24%
	Xinjiang	Mean	232.44	499.89	1,004.35	2,365.31
		Growth rate	27.81%	12.00%	17.35%	21.57%
Northeast	Liaoning	Mean	649.22	1,050.48	2,461.97	10,295.89
		Growth rate	29.16%	9.68%	31.12%	29.58%
	Jilin	Mean	232.62	453.14	1,073.88	5,113.32
		Growth rate	31.60%	10.43%	26.51%	31.98%
	Heilongjiang	Mean	331.04	737.04	1,308.35	4,113.37
		Growth rate	26.63%	10.87%	15.40%	32.12%

Note: Fixed-asset investment figures are reported in 100 million yuan at historical value. Some province data are missing.

Data sources: China Compendium of Statistics, 2004, and regional (*di qu*) statistical yearbooks for relevant years.

province, had reasonably good economic performance, the general gap in regional economic performance between the eastern and western regions increased during the Eighth and Ninth Five-Year-Plan periods. In light of the widening spatial disparities, the Chinese Government started to implement a series of planning policies to support the development of the central and western regions during the Ninth Five-Year-Plan.

In terms of city development, urbanization in China during this period undertook a 'leapfrog development' (*kua yue fa zhan*), based on massive public investment in urban construction. This development mode, for example, holds that land resources in cities should be given top priority for development, in order to stimulate the transformation of urban structures (Wu and Yeh, 1999). This process is also paralleled by the relaxation of migration rules and traditional household registration policy (*Hukou*) in the labour market, allowing for a rapid increase in the urban population and labour exchanges between cities. For example, Fan (1996) found that 3.5 million people migrated from the central and western regions to the eastern region between 1985 and 1990, according to the 1990 census data. In particular, there was a large migration flow from Guangxi, Sichuan and other inland provinces to Guangdong and other coastal provinces during this period. This migration trend benefited the urbanization process in the eastern region and reflected skilled workers' preference to seek a higher salary and more business opportunities in these provinces. However, the uneven concentration of human capital further strengthened the uneven regional development. Some Chinese scholars attempted to use the old Chinese proverb 'peacocks flying to the south and east' (*kong que dong nan fei*) to reflect the uneven migration and spatial economic disparities across regions in this period (Fan, 1992; Lin, 1993; Yang, 1994). However, several problems emerged. First, at the interregional level, 'administrative borders' (*guan ka*) had become a key obstacle to the economic agglomeration and integration between provinces and regions. The rationale behind this is that, in order to protect 'self-inclusive development', some provincial authorities tended to discourage raw-resource exchanges between regions (Zhang, 1992; Huang, 1993; Liao, 1993). Second, at the intra-regional level, the economic ties and industrial division of labour between special economic zones were basically independent and isolated. Individual cities, for the sake of their own interests, competed for limited State investment and preferential policies, and thus harmed the regional economic agglomeration to some extent. In addition, urban agglomeration within each region neglected the importance of industrial collaboration and clustering, resulting in inefficient market competition within the region.

The lack of close industrial coordination and clustering between developed and undeveloped regions led to further difficulties in industrial upgrading, on one hand, and gave impetus to the development of less developed areas, on the other. More importantly, urban agglomeration in the eastern region had not shown enough spillover effects for promoting innovation in surrounding areas. The underlying reasons would include the fact that the eastern region had got both cheap labour and raw materials from the central and western regions, resulting in the coexistence of both creative industries and traditional industries in this region, whereas there was no effective channel for transferring traditional industries to the central and western regions. On the other hand, the immature urban agglomeration in the central and western regions had given investors less confidence to relocate their businesses there.

In terms of infrastructure development, the Chinese Government implemented a proactive fiscal policy by issuing Government bonds to support the infrastructure construction and improvement. The Government investment was used mainly for physical infrastructure (including water conservancy, transportation, telecommunications, urban and rural power grid facilities) and other infrastructure projects. The massive amount of capital investment by the Chinese Government in infrastructure also stimulated a large sum of social capital investment to promote steady national economic growth. During this period, some key infrastructure construction projects, such as Three Gorges Dam, and major roads and railroads, extending from the eastern coast to inland regions, were put into operation and started to generate socioeconomic benefits.

Relying on the transportation lines, a T-model regional development pattern was suggested by Chinese scholars (Peng, 1991; Lao, 1993; Chen, 1994), with the vertical line including cities on the north–south coastline and the horizontal line including cities along the east–west Yangtze River (see Figure 4.1). This T-model formulated the backbone of urban agglomeration in China (see Chapter 5), but owing to the institutional constraints of 'administrative borders', there was no sharing mechanism in infrastructure construction between the core cities and their peripheral towns, leading to a large number of repeated constructions and a huge waste of infrastructure investment in metropolitan regions.

During the Eighth and Ninth Five-Year-Plan periods, the Chinese Government implemented further incentive-based policies for reallocating industries between regions, offering preferential initiative policies to attract foreign capital investment to inland provinces. The following parts of this section consider planning-policy implications on the formation of spatial development:

1 **The overall spatial pattern of China's opening-up** (*kai fang*) **policy was basically formed:** the Chinese Government opened up the cities along the Yangtze River, inland border cities and provincial capital cities successively, decided to accelerate the development of township enterprises in central and western regions and implemented the National Poverty Alleviation Programme (Morduch, 2000; Ravallion, 2008; Meng, 2013). Planning policies began to guide the coordinated development of spatial economy from an uneven one. In particular, the development and opening-up of cities along the Yangtze River, led by the Shanghai Pudong New Area, was an important step for attracting foreign direct investment and upgrading the industrial market structure. Since then, the Chinese Government has successively set up various types of special trade and economic zones in the eastern region, including the Shanghai Waigaoqiao, Tianjin Port and Shenzhen Futian Free Trade Zones etc. This period also featured the fact that the Chinese Government further

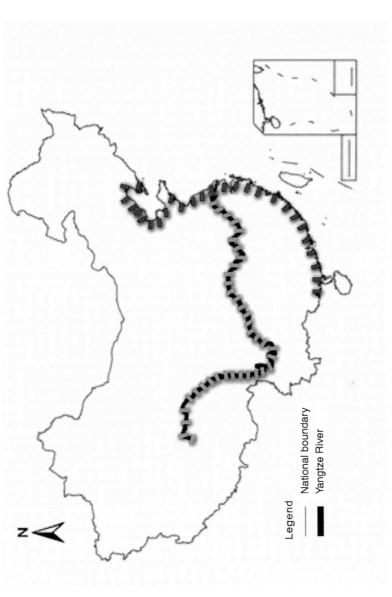

Legend

— National boundary

■ Yangtze River

Figure 4.1 Sketch map of T-model development pattern

expanded the scope and scale of opening-up over space, extending from the eastern region to inland regions, including a number of portal cities, along the Yangtze River and provincial capital cities. In the central and western regions, a set of State-level economic and technological development zones were established in peripheral towns to promote local economic development. Overall, a multilayered opening-up pattern, covering coastal cities, border cities, provincial capital cities and key peripheral towns, was set up as 'growth poles' (*zeng zhang ji*) during the Eighth and Ninth Five-Year-Plan periods.

2   **The reallocation strategy of public investment and industrial layout was gradually adjusted:** to speed up the economic development of inland regions, the Chinese Government increased the proportion of public investment, and actively drove some manufacturing industrial clusters to relocate to central and western regions. For example, the Chinese Government gave priority to investment in industrial markets, including defence industrial conversion (see Naughton, 1988; Chai, 1997) in central and western regions, through incentives during the Eighth and Ninth Five-Year-Plan periods. Specifically, a series of planning policies, including the national level planning initiative of '*demonstration projects of township enterprise cooperation between the eastern region and the western region*', were issued to support the development of township enterprises in the central and western regions. Investors from eastern regions, who were willing to establish township enterprises or enterprises associated with towns or villages in western regions, would enjoy preferential tax and financial incentives. Investors from the central and western regions would enjoy the incentive policies as well, if they set up township enterprises there. Industrial cooperation activities between urban and rural areas were encouraged with incentives. Large- and medium-sized State-owned enterprises and military factories located in China's Third-tier (*san xian*) mountainous areas were also advocated, by incentives to set up joint ventures to promote industrial development, with respect to the manufacturing and processing of raw materials, among other sectors. In addition, the State Council increased the proportion of Government investment in transport infrastructure in the western region under the implementation of *the development of western region programme* (*xi bu da kai fa ji hua*). The transport infrastructure improvements gradually shifted the dynamics of local market potentials over space, although the increase in Government investment did not reverse the uneven regional development pattern in the short term.

In sum, features of this transitional period are as follows: first, the market played a fundamental role in adjusting price and leveraging the competitive mechanism under the guidance of planning policies to coordinate the allocation of resources; second, the Chinese Government allowed various ownership types to coexist in the economic system, with the public ownership economy as the main body, and individual, private and foreign economies as important supplements. Since the Eighth Five-Year-Plan, the Chinese Government has made innovative use of the market-orientated planning system to guide and regulate the spatial economy. Coupled with rising problems such as pollution and ecological destruction in metropolitan regions, the Chinese Government, during the Ninth Five-Year-Plan, put forward a transformation of economic development towards a more sustainable mode, with specific emphasis on improving the quality of life and the environmental efficiency of economic growth over space. It is also worthwhile noting that during the Ninth Five-Year-Plan period, China completed its transformation from a centrally planned economy to a market-orientated economy. Non-public sectors of the economy were developed further, whereas the reform of State-owned enterprises made significant progress. Overall, the regional planning policies in this period focused on the adjustment of industrial layout and the reallocation of public investment between regions, so as to promote economic development through the market integration of domestic demand and foreign direct investment.

Spatial economic implications of contemporary planning policies (2001–2014)

During the early stage of the reform and opening-up, the widening gap between coastal regions and inland areas attracted increased public and political concern. As can be seen from the second half of Table 4.1, the Chinese planning system had shifted its focus to implementing policies to guide the coordinated regional development. In this context, since the Tenth Five-Year-Plan period (2001–2005), the Chinese Government specifically designed four large-scale regional planning programmes, including *the development of the western region, the revitalization of north-eastern region and other old industrial bases, the rise of the central region, and the pioneering development of the eastern region*, aimed at narrowing the development gap between regions. Table 4.4 provides a key summary of the economic geographical conditions of these four strategic regions.

From the Eleventh Five-Year-Plan period (2006–2010), the Chinese Government also changed the term of the 'Five-Year-Plan' into 'Five-Year-*Planning*'. The difference here is beyond the change of names; it marks a transformation from previous institutionally controlled development policies towards market-orientated planning programmes, with careful policy designs for coordinating spatial economic performance. During the Twelfth Five-Year-Planning period, the Chinese Government actively pushed forward the evaluation of the effectiveness of regional planning programmes, and implemented a series of planning policies with incentives to promote the new urbanization, resource-based city transformation and the 'One Belt and One Road' plan.[1] Tables 4.5–4.8 report key regional planning programmes at national level, as implemented in the four strategic regions – western, north-eastern, central and eastern – during this period. The more specific planning implications on shaping urban and regional agglomerations will be discussed in Chapter 5.

In practice, as discussed at the beginning of this section, the implementation of planning policies was intended to reduce spatial economic disparities across provinces. But the descriptive statistics from Tables 4.2 and 4.3 show the unevenness

Table 4.4 Summary of economic-geographical conditions of four strategic regions

	Eastern region	Central region	North-eastern region	Western region
Planning guidance	The pioneering development of the eastern region	The rise of the central region	The revitalization of old industrial towns in the north-eastern region	The development of the western region
Spatial coverage (provinces)	Beijing, Tianjin, Shanghai, Hebei, Jiangsu, Shandong, Zhejiang, Guangdong, Fujian, Hainan	Shanxi, Henan, Hubei, Hunan, Jiangxi, Anhui	Heilongjiang, Jilin, Liaoning	Inner Mongolia,Guangxi, Chongqing,Sichuan, Yunnan,Guizhou,Shanxi,Qinghai, Ningxia,Gansu,Tibet,Xinjiang
Land size	91.6 (10,000 square km), accounting for 9.5% of the national total land area	102.8 (10,000 square km), accounting for 10.7% of the national total land area	78.79 (10,000 square km), accounting for 8.2% of the national total land area	686.7(10,000 square km), accounting for 71.5% of the national total land area
Population(proportional to the national level)	38.2%	26.7%	8.1%	27.0%
FDI (proportional to the national level)	53.71%	17.67%	14.99%	13.63%
Industrial output(100 million yuan)	211,094.28	53,768.8	47,811.94	22,428.28
GDP (proportional to the national level)	51.3%	20.2%	8.8 %	19.8%

Data sources: Population and Gross Domestic Product (GDP) are collected from 2013 China Statistical Yearbook for Regional Economy; FDI and Industrial Output are collected from 2013 regional statistical yearbook.

Table 4.5 Key regional planning policies implemented in eastern region

Month/Year	Policy	Planning implications		
		Guidance	Spatial coverage	Infrastructure
09/2008	State Council: Guiding opinions of further promoting the reform, opening-up and economic development in the Yangtze River Delta area	Taking advantage of the reform and opening-up, promoted regional economic integration and enhanced regional innovation capability and economic development quality. Based on the guiding opinions issued in 2008, the State Council formally approved the Yangtze River Delta Regional Development Plan in 2010.	Shanghai municipality, and 15 cities from Zhejiang, and Jiangsu provinces.	Promoted the integration of major infrastructure construction so as to enhance its ability to support the quality and levels of urbanization and industrialization. Key priority areas include the development of intercity transport infrastructure systems (including highways, waterways and railways) between urban and rural areas along the Longhai railway region, Yangtze River region, Hangzhou Bay area and Jiangsu coastal region. Focused on promoting the construction of national transportation hub cities in Shanghai, Nanjing, Lianyungang, Xuzhou, Hangzhou, Ningbo, and promoting the construction of regional transportation hub cities in Suzhou, Wuxi, Changzhou, Zhenjiang, Yangzhou, Taizhou, Nantong, Yancheng, Huzhou, Jiaxing, Jinhua, Wenzhou, and Quzhou by enhancing rail, water, air and road infrastructure connections.
01/2009	The development and reform plan of the Pearl River Delta region	Promoted strategic economic restructuring process; enhanced the vibrancy of economic development and international competitiveness of industries; promoted the formation of complementary advantages in the Pan-Pearl River Delta region, including Hong Kong and Macao.	Guangdong province, with a specific focus on Guangzhou, Shengzhen, Zhuhai, Foshan, Jiangmen, Dongwan, Zhongshan, Huizhou and Zhaoqing.	Targeted at establishing a fast intercity railway network between all cities in this region, and enhancing the highway transportation capacity in this region. Key projects include the construction of the Pearl River Delta highway network, Gang-zhu-ao bridge, Guang-shen high-speed rail line, Zhongshan-Shenzhen expressway, Nanning-Guangzhou railway line, Guizhou-Guangzhou railway line, and intra-city subway networks in Guangzhou, Shenzhen and other cities.

(continued)

Table 4.5 (continued)

Month/ Year	Policy	Planning implications		
		Guidance	Spatial coverage	Infrastructure
04/2009	*State Council: Opinions on promoting the development of modern service industry and advanced manufacturing industry, and building an international financial centre and an international shipping centre in Shanghai*	To better consolidate and give full play to the comparative locational advantages of Shanghai. To promote international competitiveness and upgrade industrial structure in Shanghai.	Shanghai	Focused on enhancing the capacity of Shanghai's shipping port facilities, and associated infrastructure construction.
05/2009	*State Council: Opinions on promoting the construction of the Western Taiwan Strait economic zone*	Guidance on promoting cross-strait economic exchanges and cooperation, as well as the development of advanced manufacturing, cultural and tourism industries in the pilot zones. Based on the guiding opinions issued in 2009, the State Council formally approved the *Planning for Development of Western Taiwan Strait Economic Zone* in March 2011.	Fujian province	Promoted the development and expansion of highway networks such as Beijing–Fuzhou line and railway networks in cities of Fuzhou, Xiamen, Quanzhou.

(continued)

Table 4.5 (continued)

Month/ Year	Policy	Planning implications		
		Guidance	Spatial coverage	Infrastructure
06/2009	*Jiangsu coastal region development plan*	Focused on accelerating the industrial upgrading and productivity layout of cities in the coastal areas of Jiangsu province.	Jiangsu province, centring on Lianyungang, Yancheng, Nantong cities	Accelerated the development of transportation, coastal ports and energy grids and other major infrastructure construction in Lianyungang, Yancheng and Nantong Cities, to enhance the agglomeration of industries and production factors in this region.
01/2010	*State Council: Opinions on promoting the development of the international tourism island in Hainan province*	Guidance on the construction of the internationally competitive tourist destination, and the development of tourism, culture, sports, property, modern service industries in Hainan.	Hainan province	Provided policy incentives and special funds to promote the construction of the comprehensive transportation systems within the island (including Haikou–Wuzhishan–Sanya highway section, Wanning–Zhanzhou–Yangpu highway section, high-speed rail lines surrounding the island, and other expressways for connecting various ports and tourism locations); and promote the development of transportation links (Qiongzhou Strait) between the Hainan island and the mainland China.

Table 4.6 Key regional planning policies implemented in western region

Month/Year	Policy	Planning implications		Infrastructure
		Guidance	Spatial coverage	
09/1999	Decision on Some Major Issues Concerning the Reform and Development of State-owned Enterprises	Proposed the 'western region development strategy'.	The Western region covers Shanxi, Gansu, Ningxia, Qinghai, Xinjiang, Sichuan, Chongqing, Yunnan, Tibet, Inner Mongolia, Guangxi.	Prioritized infrastructure construction in the western region. These projects are supported by financial transfer payments and other incentives.
03/2001	10th Five-Year-Plan	Initial implementation of the 'western region development strategy'.	The Western region covers Shanxi, Gansu, Ningxia, Qinghai, Xinjiang, Sichuan, Chongqing, Yunnan, Tibet, Inner Mongolia, Guangxi.	Accelerated transportation, natural gas and urban infrastructure construction, and promoted ecological environment protection in this region.
10/2005	Plan of circular economy pilot zone in the Qaidam Basin	Targeted at improving the low-efficiency use of resources, and promoting the sustainable development and efficient allocation of resources through recycling economy.	Qaidam Basin in Qinghai Province.	Stimulated the infrastructure expansion for improving the efficiency of resource uses in the Qaidam Basin areas.
12/2006	Western regional development plan	This was a long-term comprehensive regional planning policy for guiding the western regional economic development. It aimed to promote agglomeration effects of core cities, fostering industrial development, with specific emphasis on utilizing energy, mineral and agricultural resources.	The western region covers Shanxi, Gansu, Ningxia, Qinghai, Xinjiang, Sichuan, Chongqing, Yunnan, Tibet, Inner Mongolia, Guangxi.	Focused on the improvements in roadway, railway, and airports in this region. Focused on the optimal use of natural resources to promote agricultural development and industrial development.

(continued)

Table 4.6 (continued)

Month/Year	Policy	Planning implications		
		Guidance	Spatial coverage	Infrastructure
06/2007	*The establishment of urban and rural comprehensive reform pilot areas*	The planning of pilot areas aimed to foster the integration of urban–rural development.	Sichuan, Chongqing.	Invested in urban and rural infrastructure and promoted the connections between urban and rural areas.
02/2008	*Guangxi Beibu Gulf economic zone development plan*	Targeted at the improvement of industrial layout and infrastructure expansion in the Guangxi coastal areas, to foster economic cooperation with countries in South-east Asia.	Guangxi.	Focused on the improvement of capacities of various ports in the Beibu Gulf Bay Area, and the improvement of port-affiliated industrial development in this region.
11/2008	*Special trade zone in Chongqing*	The first special trade zone in inland areas (*liang lu cun tan*).	Chongqing.	Focused on the improvement of trading businesses, based on international airport and the Yangtze River water port in Chongqing.
06/2009	*Guanzhong-Tianshui regional development plan*	As guided by the 11th Five-Year-Plan, this is a key metropolitan area to be developed in the western region.	Shanxi, Gansu.	Focused on the construction and improvement of highways, including Lian-Huo route, Pingliang-Baoji-Hanzhong, Tongguan-Xi'an-Baoji,Xi'an-Tongchuan-Huangling, and others; Focused on the improvements of airports in Xi'an, Tianshui, Baoji; and on the improvement of railway systems such as Zhengzhou–Xi'an–Lanzhou.

(continued)

Table 4.6 (continued)

Month/Year	Policy	Planning implications		
		Guidance	Spatial coverage	Infrastructure
12/2009	Several opinions on further promoting economic and social development in Guangxi	Targeted at building industrial agglomeration advantages in the West River and Beibu Gulf Economic Zones, and promoting the formation of a new growth pole of coastal economic development in the western region.	Guangxi.	Focused on the improvements of railway systems such as Yun–Gui line, Huangyong–Baise line, Hechi–Nanning line; on the improvement of highway systems such as Wenshan–Napo–Chongzuo–Xinzhou line; and on the improvement of comprehensive transportation systems in core cities, such as Nanning, Liuzhou, Wuzhou.
12/2009	The overall plan of circular economy in Gansu	Targeted at fostering industrial agglomerations so as to change the situation of scattered distributions of cities and large factories in Gansu Province. Targeted at the development of circular economy and the optimization of industrial structures in Gansu Province.	Gansu.	Key projects include: the establishment of Lanzhou Petrochemical metallurgical silver-coloured circular economy base, Pingliang–Qingyang coal-chemical- petrochemical and non-ferrous metal industry base, Jinchang–Jiayuguan–Jiuquan clean energy and equipment manufacturing industry base; and the formation of agricultural circular economy bases in Tianshui, Dingxi, Wuwei, Zhangye, Gannan–Linxia–Longnan areas.

(continued)

Table 4.6 (continued)

Month/Year	Policy	Planning implications		
		Guidance	Spatial coverage	Infrastructure
07/2010	*Plan of key projects of national western regional development*	Targeted at promoting the coordinated regional development across provinces in the western region.	The western region.	Proposed package of 23 key infrastructure construction projects in the western region, with a total predicted investment of over 600 billion yuan. This package includes: Changsha–Kunming passenger railway section, Leshan–Guiyang railway section, Xi'an–Jiangyou passenger railway section, Baoji–Lanzhou passenger railway section, Chongqing–Chengdu passenger railway section, Dali to Lijiang road section, Aksu–Kuqa highway, Leijiajiao–Xifeng highway, Guiyang airport expansion, the construction of various regional airports and other major projects.

Table 4.7 Key regional planning policies implemented in north-eastern region

Month/Year	Policy	Guidance	Spatial coverage	Planning implications
				Infrastructure
03/2003	Government working report	The Chinese Government initially proposed the regional development strategy of the north-eastern region and old industrial bases.	Liaoning, Jilin, Helongjiang provinces and some parts of Inner Mongolia including Chifeng, Tongliao, Xilingol, Hulunbuir areas.	Not specified.
09/2003	State Council: Opinions on the implementation of the northeast region and other old industrial bases	Strategic guidance for promoting the development of the north-eastern region and old industrial bases.	Liaoning, Jilin, Helongjiang provinces and some parts of Inner Mongolia including Chifeng, Tongliao, Xilingol, Hulunbuir areas.	Not specified.
06/2005	State Council: Opinions on promoting the opening-up of old industrial bases in the northeast region	Further encouraged foreign investment, and promoted the restructuring and transformation process of State-owned industries and enterprises in this region.	Liaoning, Jilin, Helongjiang provinces and some parts of Inner Mongolia, including Chifeng, Tongliao, Xilingol, Hulunbuir areas.	Emphasized the necessity of providing transport infrastructure links between cities so as to promote the urban and regional exchange and economic cooperation.

(continued)

Table 4.7 (continued)

Month/Year	Policy	Guidance	Spatial coverage	Planning implications	
				Infrastructure	
08/2007	*The revitalization plan of the north-eastern region*	This was the most important and comprehensive regional plan. It aimed to promote urban, rural and regional development, with a specific focus on resource-exhausted cities, and enhanced the capacity for sustainable development in the whole region. It also aimed to promote the development of three key urban agglomeration areas in this region, including Liao-zhong-nan, Ha-da-qi, and central Jilin.	Liaoning, Jilin, Helongjiang provinces and some parts of Inner Mongolia including Chifeng, Tongliao, Xilingol, Hulunbuir areas.	Six planned comprehensive transport infrastructure systems (including roadways, railways, ports and gas pipelines) for connecting Tongjiang–Dalian, Heihe–Beijing, Suifenhe–Manzhouli, Huichun–A'ershan, Dandong–Xilingol, and the eastern areas of the north-eastern region. Focused on building fast transport systems within and between key urban agglomeration areas, including Liao-zhong-nan, Ha-da-qi, and central Jilin.	
12/2007	*State council: Opinions on promoting the sustainable development of resource-based cities*	Promoted the establishment of institutional mechanisms and planning interventions for supporting the growth of declining industries in resource-based cities.	Old resource-based cities, including many cities in the north-eastern region.	Provided State funds and financial transfer incentives to support the industrial development and associated infrastructure constructions in targeted resource-based cities, including Qitaihe, Fushun, Beipiao, Shulan, Jiutai, Wudalianchi, Dunhua, Huludao, Liaoyang etc.	
07/2009	*Liaoning Coastal Economic Zone Development Plan*	Promoted the economic development and spatial layout of urban agglomerations in the coastal areas of Liaoning province.	Liaoning province.	Targeted at promoting the improvement of transport infrastructure systems across cities in this region, including Dalian, Dandong, Jinzhou, Yingkou, Panjin, Huludao.	

(continued)

Table 4.7 (continued)

Month/Year	Policy	Guidance	Spatial coverage	Planning implications
				Infrastructure
09/2009	State Council on the further implementation of the north-east region and other old industrial base development strategy	Further emphasized the importance of promoting the revitalization of the north-eastern region, with a specific focus on promoting the development of key urban agglomeration areas, such as Liaoning coastal area, Ha-da-qi, and Chang-ji-tu.	Liaoning, Jilin, Helongjiang provinces and some parts of Inner Mongolia including Chifeng, Tongliao, Xilingol, Hulunbuir areas.	Accelerated the construction of Jing-shen, Shen-dan, Ha-qi passenger-dedicated railway lines, and Ji-tu, Da-dan, Ha-du, Ha-jia railway lines; promoted the upgrading of existing railway lines in this region, including Du-sui, Chifeng-jinzhou, among others; accelerated the development of spatial layout of airport allocations and the development of highway systems between cities in this region.
11/2009	The Tumen River area development plan, using Chang-ji-tu metropolitan area as the pilot zone	Promoted the quality of opening-up and international economic cooperation between this region and neighbouring countries, like Russia and North Korea.	Jilin province.	Provided the allocated State funds to promote the transport infrastructure construction and expansion in this region that could promote the levels of international economic cooperation with neighbouring countries.

Table 4.8 Key regional planning policies implemented in central region

Month/Year	Policy	Planning implications		
		Guidance	Spatial coverage	Infrastructure
03/2004	Government working report	For the first time, the Chinese Government clearly stated the importance of promoting the rise of the central region as a key step to accelerate coordinated regional development.	Shanxi, Henan, Hubei, Hunan, Jiangxi, Anhui provinces.	Supported the central region to exploit its locational advantages and promote infrastructure construction between cities in this region.
03/2006	Several opinions on promoting the rise of the central region by the CPC Central Committee and the State Council	Targeted at constructing the central region as an important grain-production, energy and raw materials, modern equipment manufacturing and high-tech industrial base, and an integrated transport hub.	Shanxi, Henan, Hubei, Hunan, Jiangxi, Anhui provinces.	Promoted the rise of the central region through building enhanced intercity infrastructure connection systems.
01/2008	Guidance on setting up the inter-ministerial joint conference system for promoting the rise of the central region	This was not a regional plan but it formed as an important policy guidance to promote the interdepartmental communication of major issues regarding the development of the central region.	Shanxi, Henan, Hubei, Hunan, Jiangxi, Anhui provinces.	Not specified.

(continued)

Table 4.8 (continued)

Month/Year	Policy	Planning implications		
		Guidance	Spatial coverage	Infrastructure
09/2009	*The plan of the rise of the central region*	A comprehensive regional planning policy for guiding the spatial layout of key development areas in the central region.	Shanxi, Henan, Hubei, Hunan, Jiangxi, Anhui provinces.	Supported the construction of national transportation hub cities in Wuhan, Zhengzhou; accelerated the construction of passenger-dedicated railway lines, intercity railway and road networks between cities in this region; built more airports in peripheral cities and expanded existing airports in core cities in this region; altogether, focused on improving comprehensive transportation systems so as to raise the level of industrialization and urbanization.
10/2009	*The plan of Wuhan urban agglomeration circle*	Targeted at promoting the spatial layout of urban agglomerations in the Wuhan metropolitan region.	Hubei province.	Supported the development of intercity railway network between Wuhan and neighbouring cities such as Huanggang, Xiaogan, Xiantao; the construction of city ring roads in Wuhan, and the construction of affiliated expressways to link to the national main highway system, such as Da-Guang highway line, among others.
12/2009	*The plan of Poyang lake ecological economic zone*	Targeted at promoting the spatial layout of urban agglomerations in the Poyang lake metropolitan region, centring on Nanchang, Yingtan, Jingdezhen cities.	Jiangxi province.	Supported the transport infrastructure improvements in core cities such as Jiangdezhen, Jiujiang, Nanchang, Yangtan, and supported the intercity connections between core cities and peripheral cities, such as Xinyu, Fuzhou, Shangrao, Yichun.

(continued)

Table 4.8 (continued)

Month/Year	Policy	Planning implications		
		Guidance	Spatial coverage	Infrastructure
01/2010	The plan of industrial transfer demonstration zone in the Wan River urban agglomeration belt	Targeted at promoting industrial transfer from the Yangtze River Delta metropolitan region to the Wan River urban agglomeration area.	Centred on Hefei city in the Anhui province, but covered surrounding cities in other provinces along the Wan River.	Focused on intra-city transport infrastructure improvements in core cities such as Hefei, Wuhu, and on intercity connections between core cities and peripheral cities, such as Tongling, Anqing, Chizhou, Xuancheng, to support the industrial transfer from the Yangtze River Delta metropolitan region to the Wan River urban agglomeration area.
11/2012	The plan of the central plain economic zone	Targeted at promoting the spatial layout of urban agglomerations in the central plain economic zone, centred on Zhengzhou, Luoyang, Kaifeng cities.	Henan province	Focused on the construction and expansion of airport, subway, highway and railway infrastructure systems in the core city, Zhengzhou, and supported the intercity connections between Zhengzhou and neighbouring cities, such as Luoyang, Kaifeng. Key projects include the construction of intercity railway lines: Zhengzhou–Kaifeng, Luoyang–Pingdingshan, Zhengzhou–Jiaozuo, Zhengzhou–Xinzheng airport, among others.

(continued)

Table 4.8 (continued)

Month/Year	Policy	Planning implications		
		Guidance	Spatial coverage	Infrastructure
12/2008	The plan of Chang-zhu-tan urban agglomeration areas	Targeted at promoting the spatial layout of urban agglomerations in the Chang-zhu-tan region, centred on Changsha, Zhuzhou, Xiangtan cities.	Hunan province	Focused on the development of new Changsha rail station, and a number of railway lines to connect Changsha, Zhuzhou, Xiangtan with other places; the development of expressway systems in Changsha–Zhouzhou, Changshan–Xiangtan, Xiangtan–Zhuzhou sections; and the development of waterway systems and ports in the Xiang River, to raise the agglomeration patterns of industrialization and urbanization in this region.
01/2009	The plan of Taiyuan urban agglomeration area	Targeted at promoting the spatial layout of urban agglomerations in the Taiyuan-Yuci metropolitan area, centred on Taiyuan.	Shanxi province.	Focused on the agglomeration of Taiyuan-Yuci metropolitan area by developing roadway and railway infrastructure connections between Taiyuan and Yuci, and improving the connections with Jiaocheng, Xinzhou and other local cities and counties.
09/2010	State Council guidance on the central and western regions to undertake industrial transfer	Guidance on improving the cooperation mechanism between western and central regions in terms of industrial transfer.	Shanxi, Henan, Hubei, Hunan, Jiangxi, Anhui provinces.	Emphasis on promoting the industrial transfer from the coastal region to the central region, with the support of good transport infrastructure accessibility in the central region.

Table 4.9 Comparison of economic performance between western region and national level during 11th Five-Year-Plan period

Indicators	2006		2010		Annual growth rate (%)	
	Western	National	Western	National	Western	National
Population (10,000 persons)	36,993	131,448	36,937.81	134,091	0.04%	0.50%
GDP (100 million yuan)	39,527.1	210,871.0	81,408.5	401,202	19.80%	17.45%
Local government revenue (100 million yuan)	3,059.4	18,303.58	7,873.4	40,613.04	26.66%	22.05%
International trade volume (US$100 million)	576.7	17,603.9647	1,283.9	29,739.98	22.15%	14.01%
Total fixed-asset investment (100 million yuan)	21,996.9	118,957.0	61,892.2	310,964.2	29.51%	27.15%
Per capita disposal income in urban areas (yuan)	9,728	11,759.5	15,806	19,109.44	12.90%	12.91%
Per capita net income in rural areas (yuan)	2,588	3,587.0	4,418	5,919.01	14.31%	13.34%
Total railway operational mileages (10,000 km)	2.9062	7.71	3.5965	9.12	5.47%	4.29%
Total roadway mileages (10,000 km)	126.0964	345.70	156.83	400.82	5.61%	3.77%
Total highway mileage (10,000 km)	1.1717	4.53	2.1252	7.41	16.05%	13.09%

Data source: China Statistical Yearbook for Regional Economy, 2007 and 2011.

of provincial economic performance in terms of key indicators, such as GDP and fixed-asset investment within and between regions, implying that spatial agglomeration of production factors continues to grow. Nevertheless, Table 4.9 shows that the economic growth in provinces of the western region was more rapid than that of the national average during the Eleventh Five-Year-Plan (2006–2010). There are several possible reasons.

First, the cost of production factors has increased significantly in the eastern region since 2000, and the carrying capacity of resources and environment (*zi yuan huan jing cheng zai li*) has worsened in the eastern region. As such, labour and resource-intensive industries have tended to transfer to the central and western regions. This helps to optimize the industrial structure between regions. Second, with the deepening of the coordinated regional development strategy and a series of preferential planning policies (see Tables 4.5–4.8), a large proportion of Government investment has been allocated to support infrastructure improvement and promote the economic agglomeration in the north-eastern, central and western regions. From the statistics, it appears that the planning system then influenced the spatial development patterns, although rigorous assessments are needed to identify the causal relationship.

Turning the focus to potential consequences at the regional level, there is strong evidence that the eastern region, as the pioneering development region supported by recent planning programmes, has given top priority to the development of high value-added tertiary industries and services, including modern logistics, finance, technology services, information technology and cultural and creative industries. During the Eleventh Five-Year-Plan (2006–2010) and the most recent Five-Year-Planning periods, the eastern region has further upgraded industrial clusters regarding the research and development (R&D) of technology, international marketing and financial services. Furthermore, recent planning programmes have placed the central region as the key area to develop industries such as manufacturing industry, energy industry and the raw-material industry, including iron, steel and non-ferrous metals etc. Shanxi, Henan, Anhui and other provinces in this region have actively constructed large-scale coal bases, and accelerated the economic integration between provinces. Finally, utilizing its advantages in space and mining resources, the Chinese Government has made use of regional planning programmes to formulate industrial chains and clusters in the western region. It has also placed great emphasis on improving the competitiveness of the large-scale equipment manufacturing industry, especially those super-enterprises such as Shenyang Machine Tool Group Corporation.

As an important part of spatial development, the construction of new urbanized areas in existing mega-cities has also been a bright spot in China's contemporary planning practices. In accordance with the planning guidance of 'core-periphery axial expansion' and the 'integration of industry, people and city', some major urban agglomeration belts have been strengthened in a spatial context (see Chapter 5 for details). It has shown the following characteristics: first, new urbanized areas were built as an effective hinterland to link with the core urbanized areas. These linkages were also supported by the transport infrastructure network, such as the expansion of ring roads, subways and high-speed rail between cities or counties. Second, land was used in a more economical and intensive way, to shape the harmonious coexistence of industrial clusters and living environments.

Finally, planning policies in transport infrastructure development acted as a key driving force for reshaping spatial development. From 2000 to the end of 2012, national highway systems were improved substantially, surpassing the United States and ranking first in the world in terms of total mileage. A basic network, made up of 'five radial, two vertical and seven horizontal' national highways and twelve national main lines, including 'five vertical and seven horizontal' ones, was set up. As suggested by Government reports, approximately 40,000 kilometres of railways were built during the same period, and the railway operation mileage of the whole country reached up to approximately 98,000 kilometres. Meanwhile, the operation mileage of high-speed railways amounted to 9,356 kilometres, ranking first in the world and basically forming a 'four vertical and four horizontal' fast railway network. There is also strong evidence of the significant improvement of the civil-aviation system for passengers (Wang et al., 2014). Taken together, the comprehensive transport system has strengthened the connection between regions, promoted the flow of production factors and improved the market integration between regions.[2]

Spatial economic disparities trigger adjustment to the contemporary planning policies to focus on regenerating declining areas, coordinating regional development and promoting the evolution of major economic agglomeration zones (*qu*) and belts (*dai*). This type of adjustment also applies to the context of a single city, as featured mostly by the development of new urbanized areas, used as the spatial manifestation of agglomeration economies on a fine geographic scale. If one can add this adjustment to the empirical evidence that all manners of specific planning programmes regarding cities, location and infrastructure are capitalized into differing people's living costs and urban productivity over space, then it is natural to understand the variations in economic performance, housing prices and total factor productivity across areas. This leads further to the specific spatial layout and economic agglomeration with locational planning interventions. Studies that employ economic theories and empirical evidence from the USA and other countries have produced specific implications for locational policies, spillover effects and agglomerations (see Rosenthal and Strange, 2004; Arzaghi and Henderson, 2008; Ellison et al., 2010; Greenstone et al., 2010; Faggio and Overman, 2014; Faggio et al., 2016). Their general conclusion is that the agglomeration is very likely self-reinforcing, as wealthier cities and regions may benefit more from these planning programmes in order to make their areas even more attractive to industrial businesses and skilled workers. Criticisms on the role of locational policies in influencing local and regional growth also point out that those locational policies may or may not generate higher net economic growth in designated areas, compared to other controlled areas (Neumark and Kolko 2010; Busso et al., 2013; Kline and Moretti 2013). Therefore, the uneven spatial economic development is crucial to both senior policymakers in the country and mayors of cities when implementing planning programmes. If social welfare is significantly affected by regional inequality, the specialized planning programmes should allow more options for targeted regions to find an effective way to achieve economic agglomeration and market integration, and should focus more on helping people there to enhance their skills and quality of life, rather than simply provide incentives for building bigger cities. But of course addressing the problem of spatial differences in economic performance is a big challenge for China and other countries in the world. Therefore, it is essential for policymakers in China to learn from history and international experience, in order to rigorously evaluate the effectiveness of contemporary planning programmes and decide what works better for local economic development.

Conclusion

The main conclusion is that when the uneven spatial development arises in many ways, how to formulate spatial agglomerations is perhaps much more important for policymakers than how to reverse the unevenness of spatial development. The main cause of spatial economic disparities is the trade-off between the diffusion forces and agglomeration forces across regions, as well as policy incentives for guiding the spatial agglomeration process. This process is also paralleled with the transition from a centrally planned economic system towards a market-orientated economic system, and suggests that regional inequality, as guided by Chinese planning policies, is very important in shaping the structure of the Chinese urban system and spatial agglomerations.

As outlined in this and previous chapters, there has been a differential spatial economic disparity in the centrally planned economy era and the market-orientated economy era, and it is this gap that reflects the economic integration and other market channels at stake in the market-orientated economy era. The reallocation of resources, labour and capital from wealthy places to poor places seemed to receive less attention before the 1990s, but recent Chinese planning policies have regulations to promote the more coordinated economic development between regions. From 1991 to 2014, in the transformation from the centrally planned system to the market-orientated planning system, the Chinese Government gradually deepened the understanding of the market economy and showed a tendency to incorporate the market mechanism into its implementation of planning policies. In this context, a series of regional planning programmes have been formulated to stimulate large-scale, transport infrastructure construction and expansion in central, western and north-eastern regions. In addition, the implementation of planning policies has fostered the development of urban and regional agglomerations, and has promoted the regeneration of declining cities. More recently, coupled with the implementation of the 'One Belt and One Road Initiative' in 2015, this has had serious implications for restructuring and coordinating industrial and economic activities across regions.

These planning-policy implications include two aspects: first, uneven economic development is a commonly observed spatial phenomenon; and second, it is the uniqueness of China's transitional process, and the strong power of the Chinese Government at all levels, that can implement these planning policies effectively and that has successfully generated heterogeneous spatial development over the past six decades. This is arguably the most beautiful and challenging part of understanding the Chinese planning system. The interpretation presented in this chapter is that unequal spatial development is largely shaped by the market mechanism under the guidance of policymakers. Wealthier places do not only have more policy incentives, but also have better access to markets and resources, thus the growth patterns of these places are less likely to be suspended, even when the Central Government shifts its focus to providing policy incentives in other places. There might also be a lack of sorting channels and incentives for people and firms to relocate from places with high living and production costs to places with lower costs. As such, bigger differences in economic performance between places are likely to continue.

Policies of more investment in transport infrastructure projects and of financial incentives to coordinate spatial economic development would be effective to raise social mobility, and to generate the displacement of economic activities among metropolitan and peripheral regions. But these policies would probably be a more effective approach to help people in the peripheral areas, given the scarcity of empirical evidence that people-based policies also matter, in addition to locational policies. Indeed, even for places which continue to grow, it is hard to know whether, and to what extent, people's quality of life can be improved through the implementation of contemporary locational planning programmes. Future planning policies should focus on comparing the spatial disparities before and after the policy implementation, and evaluating what really works for local economic development.

The answer to what policies work, however, would further provide implications for why spatial disparities occur. The interpretation provided in this chapter, and supported by recent experience and evidence, is that a spatial variation of the market mechanism between cities and regions, and variations in local market potential, lead to spatial disparities, although there is still much more to learn about the underlying driving forces. Effective planning programmes are designed rigorously and are less likely to make the uneven pattern worse. Generally speaking, people and cities from both wealthy and poor regions are desirable assets for the country.

Overall, Chapters 3 and 4 describe the temporal evaluation and characteristics of China's planning policies, with a specific focus on location, cities and infrastructure. Chapter 5 will explain the significant spatial implications of China's planning policies on urban and regional agglomeration, in order to obtain a more comprehensive understanding of the economic effects of planning policies on location, city and infrastructure development. There are good reasons to believe that current locational planning programmes are useful for influencing spatial economic performance in China, and should consider the lack of opportunities in revitalizing the declining areas in the short term. But the causal link between the implementation of various planning programmes and the likely economic outcomes is not at all clear. However, at least in the current period, it is reasonable to say that urban and regional agglomeration as guided by the planning system has played a critical role in affecting national economic growth.

Notes

1 http://www.chinausfocus.com/finance-economy/one-belt-and-one-road-far-reaching-initiative/
2 In addition to transport infrastructure, the investment of State funds eased the capital shortage in infrastructure construction in the central and western regions so that a large number of super-projects were completed, such as the Three Gorges Project, Guizhou Qianxi Power Plant, Inner Mongolia Ximeng Husbandry Infrastructure Project, the Pipeline Infrastructure Project of West-East Natural Gas Transmission, West-East Electricity Transmission Power Project, and so on.

References

Arzaghi, M. and Henderson, J.V. 2008. Networking off Madison Avenue, The Review of Economic Studies, 75(4), 1011–1038.
Björklund, E.M. 1986. The Danwei: Sociospatial characteristics of work units in China's urban society. Economic Geography, 62(1), 19–29.
Bray, D. 2005. *Social Space and Governance in Urban China: The Danwei System from Origins to Reform*. Stanford, CA: Stanford University Press.
Busso, M., Gregory, J. and Kline, P. 2013. Assessing the incidence and efficiency of a prominent place based policy, American Economic Review, 103(2), 897–947.
Chai, B. 1997. Conversion and restructuring of China's defense industry, in J. Brommelhorster and J. Frankenstein (eds.) *Mixed Motives, Uncertain Outcomes: Defense Conversion in China*, Boulder, CO: Lynne Rienner.
Chai, Y. 1996. Danwei-centered activity space in Chinese cities: A case study of Lanzhou. Geography Research, 15(1), 30–38 [in Chinese].
Chen, H. 1994. Basic strategy of regional economic development in China in the 1990s. Economic Theory and Business Management, 2, 1–6 [in Chinese].
Ellison, G., Glaeser, E.L. and Kerr, W.R. 2010. What causes industry agglomeration? Evidence from coagglomeration patterns, American Economic Review, 100, 1195–1213.
Faggio, G., Olmo S. and Strange, W.C. 2016 (forthcoming). Heterogeneous agglomeration, Review of Economics and Statistics.
Faggio, G. and Overman, H. 2014. The effect of public sector employment on local labour markets, Journal of Urban Economics 79, 91–107.
Fan, C.C. 1996. Economic opportunities and internal migration: A case study of Guangdong province, China. Professional Geographer, 48(1), 28–45.
Fan, L. 1992. Inter-regional migration and economic development in China in the late 1980s. Population Research, 5, 1–6 [in Chinese].
Greenstone, M., Hornbeck, R. and Moretti, E. 2010. Identifying agglomeration spillovers: Evidence from winners and losers of large plant openings, Journal of Political Economy, 118(3), 536–598.
Huang, T. 1993. Regional economic development and opening to the outside in China. Economic Geography, 13(3), 1–8 [in Chinese].
Kline, P. 2010. Place based policies, heterogeneity, and agglomeration. The American Economic Review, 100, 383–387.
Kline, P. and Moretti, E. 2013. Local economic development, agglomeration economies, and the big push: 100 years of evidence from the Tennessee valley authority, No. w19293. Cambridge, MA: National Bureau of Economic Research.
Lao, C. 1993. Recognition on the theory and practice of China's economic regionalization. Economic Geography, 13(3), 9–13 [in Chinese].

Li, S. 1988. The multilateral exploration of regional economy. Economic Research, 11, 78–9 [in Chinese].

Liao, R. 1993. The optimization of structure in regional economic coordinative development. Economic Geography, 13(3), 14–18 [in Chinese].

Lin, J. 1993. On some problems of development areas. Economic Geography, 13(2), 1–4 [in Chinese].

Meng, L. 2013. Evaluating China's poverty alleviation programme: A regression discontinuity approach. Journal of Public Economics, 101, 1–11.

Morduch, J., 2000. Reforming poverty alleviation policies, in A. Krueger (ed.), *Economic Policy Reform: The Second Stage.* Chicago, IL: University of Chicago Press.

Naughton, B. 1988. The Third Front: Defense industrialization in the Chinese interior. The China Quarterly, 115, 351–86.

Naughton, B. 1995. Growing out of the plan: Chinese economic reform, 1978–1993. New York: Cambridge University Press.

Nee, V. 1992. Organizational dynamics of market transition: Hybrid forms, property rights, and mixed economy in China. Administrative Science Quarterly, 37, 1–27.

Neumark, D. and Kolko, J. 2010. Do enterprise zones create jobs? Evidence from California's enterprise zone programme, Journal of Urban Economics, 68(1), 1–19.

Peng, Q. 1991. Regional development study: New trends of Chinese geography. Economic Geography, 11(4), 1–6 [in Chinese].

Ravallion, M., 2008. Evaluating anti-poverty programmes, in T.P. Schultz and J.A. Strauss (eds.), *Handbook of Development Economics, 4.* Amsterdam: North-Holland.

Rosenthal, S.S. and Strange, W.C. 2004. Evidence on the nature and sources of agglomeration economies, *Handbook of regional and urban economics, Vol. 4,* 2119–2171.

Sai, F. and Zhu, M. 1990. On the division of labour in regional industry. Economic Theory and Business Management, 4, 46–51 [in Chinese].

Wang, J., Mo, H. and Wang, F. 2014. Evolution of air transport network of China 1930–2012. Journal of Transport Geography, 40, 145–158.

Wu, F. and Yeh, A.G-O. 1999. Urban spatial structure in a transitional economy. Journal of the American Planning Association, 65(4), 377–394.

Yang, W. 1991. A summary of discussions on some problems of regional economy in recent years in China. Economic Theory and Business Management, 2, 74–9 [in Chinese].

Yang, Y. 1994. Current challenge and strategy of helping the development of the poor. Inquiry into Economic Problems, 8, 48–9 [in Chinese].

Zhang, K. 1992. Issues on China's regional economic movement. Economic Research, 6, 52–7 [in Chinese].

Zhang, W. 1989. On the transformation and selection of regional economic development strategy in China. Economic Research, 10, 71–6 [in Chinese].

Zhu, L. 1992. Ill-balanced regional economic relations: Symptoms, mechanism and remedy strategy. Research on Economics and Management, 2, 5–10 [in Chinese].

5 Planning for urban and regional agglomeration

Introduction

The last two chapters showed how the Chinese national five-year-plans, as in many other transitional socialist countries, provided State intervention and investment in shaping China's economic geography patterns over time. The transformation from Maoist redistributive policies to Deng's development philosophy places planning policies at the core of Chinese theory of urban and regional agglomeration. The planning policies that advocate economic development based on market mechanism are effective means for allocating resources and capital between cities and regions. This chapter looks into the evidence of urban and regional agglomeration, as a complement to understanding the economics of China's planning policies. It focuses on the interaction between spatial agglomerations and planning policies, with a specific focus on the geography of the 'four largest' urban agglomeration belts.

The spatial forms of cities and regions have been changing and displaying substantial disparities across areas. The characteristics of regional inequality have been well discussed in literature (Démurger, 2001; Kanbur and Zhang, 2005; Zhang and Zou, 2012). Planning policies are interspersed with regulations that control the amount and location of infrastructure investment within and between cities and therefore influence distributional patterns of economic activities. One important role of planning policies is to help provide an integrated layout of transportation system so as to promote regional development. But it is not easy to address the problems of spatial economic unevenness, owing to the externality of locational policies, or who will benefit more from local and regional planning policies (Bartik, 1991). At the local level, firms and individuals may take advantage of the external economy and leave the problems related to external diseconomy to planning policymakers. For example, there is clear evidence that local public goods to be capitalized in within-city property markets have puzzling heterogeneous amenity values (Zheng and Kahn, 2008; Wu et al., 2015) and the building of high-speed railways have external effects on wages and housing prices in nearby cities (Zhang and Kahn, 2013). This chapter does not elaborate on these arguments, although it highlights planning implications on shaping the geographic layout of urban agglomeration. As shown in Chapters 2 and 3, China's uneven regional development has a close relationship with the history of planning policies. In the centrally planned economy era, the formulation of planning policies was anchored around national defence and industrial development. These projects have shaped the basic industrial structure of many cities in mainland China. After the economic reform and opening-up in the 1980s, planning policies turned their focus to establishing special economic zones and districts in the coastal region, which gave rise to the formation of mega-metropolitan regions, such as the Yangtze River Delta Metropolitan Region, the Pearl River Delta Metropolitan Region, and so on.

Recent evidence suggests that urban and regional development needs to rely, to a large extent, on the operation of the market mechanism. However, planning policy intervention might also help stimulate urban and regional agglomeration. The rest of this chapter is structured as follows: the following section draws on the previous literature and findings of an evaluation of recent planning policies in developed countries and China, to shed light on the economic consequences of locational planning policies. The second section presents the characteristics of planning policies and their relationship with regional development and spatial agglomeration. The next section describes the formation of urban agglomeration belts and their future visions, as guided by the current planning system, and the final section concludes the chapter and points to future work.

Economic consequences of locational planning policies

Governments are concerned with settling the problem of locational disparities by revitalizing the economic development of declining areas and promoting spatial economic agglomeration between cities and regions. Before looking at the implications of China's planning policies on urban and regional agglomeration, it is first useful to summarize the economic consequences of planning policies, especially place-based policy initiatives learnt from the existing literature.

There is a growing amount of empirical literature that explores various aspects of planning policies, including people-based and place-based policies targeted at firms, households, employment and poverty, among others. In particular, empirical studies have shifted the main method of policy evaluation from the macro-analytical approach to explicit experimental approach by analysing the impacts of the implementation of place-based policies on local economic performance (Erickson and Syms, 1986; Cheshire and Hilber, 2008; Glaeser and Gottlieb, 2008; Gibbons et al., 2011; Cheshire et al., 2015). Earlier studies have predicted the dispersal of public-sector relocation plans (Ashcroft and Swales, 1982a,b; Ashcroft et al., 1988; Jefferson and Trainor, 1996; Larkin, 2010). As suggested by the literature, the rise of job opportunities in the local area can also stimulate economic activities through the spatial multiplier channel at work (Marshall et al., 2005; Moretti 2010; Faggio and Overman, 2014). Recent studies have examined the local impact of the UK relocation programme in the public sector on the service and performance of manufacturing firms, by comparing those in areas close to a relocation site with those in areas further away (Faggio, 2014). In addition, as suggested by the industrial-relocation literature, planning policies for relocating polluting industries should have serious impacts on workers' welfare. For example, while some workers may benefit from industrial-sector relocation, a proportion of less productive workers in treated areas may then lose their jobs, or may endure prolonged unemployment after the implementation of place-based policies (Abraham and Medoff 1984; Gibbons and Katz, 1991; Jacobson et al., 1993; Von Wachter et al., 2009; Walker, 2011). Whereas changes in workers' welfare and firms' productivity tend to be affected by place-based policies, the spillovers in affected areas might also be attributable to the ever-widening spatial economic disparities, or the unintended economic consequence of planning policies. By showing that planning programmes in the Enterprise and Empowerment Zone can create jobs, economic studies have discussed the effectiveness of place-based policies in gentrifying the designated areas through careful examination of the causal relationship (e.g. Neumark and Kolko, 2010; Mayer et al., 2012 Busso et al., 2013). Other place-based policies such as tax incentives have also been evaluated according to evidence from the USA (Papke, 1994). More recent work has attempted to summarize the fundamental causality problems that provide insights into the intended and unintended consequences from the implementation of place-based policies at the local level (Glaeser and Gottlieb, 2008).

First, it is clear that the endogeneity problem has impacted in different ways on answering the questions on which policy causes what. Like anywhere else, China's economic development is not balanced. The intended consequences of China's planning policies, in many cases, are to benefit society and to reduce regional disparities. These would consist of intervening in the infrastructure provisions, and benefiting the spatial economic agglomeration. These planning policies do not, in themselves, predict whether a place will be likely to grow or decline as expected. For example, Zheng and Kahn (2013) documented the positive impact from the implementation of the high-speed railway planning policies on property prices in nearby cities in China. Zheng et al. (2015) evaluated the impact of locational industrial park policies on firm productivity and other economic activities. Faber (2014) found that the planning policies of highway network expansion led to a reduction in GDP growth among non-targeted peripheral counties, and reduced trade cost between urban peripheries and core metropolitan areas. Baum-Snow et al. (2015) found out the significant impacts of ring roads, highways and railways on the decentralization of the urban population and industrial GDP. Their results provide new insights into the economic implications of transport infrastructure for the spatial layout of Chinese cities, although there has been considerable evidence based on data from the USA. For example, Baum-Snow (2007) evaluated the impact of highway expansion on suburbanization in US cities. At best, these findings suggest that planning policies regarding cities, location and infrastructure have not been able to avoid unintended economic consequences. At worst, it is reasonable to suspect that planning policies may not even play a critical role in spurring local economic growth in some areas.

Second, the dynamic effects of the implementation of planning policies make the interpretation of their direct and indirect economic consequences more difficult in practice. Coupled with the locational heterogeneity of cities and regions, there have been serious implications for evaluating the effectiveness of conventional locational investment programmes. Specifically, in China, the connection between urban agglomeration and the regional development mode is complicated further by the fact that planning policies between different five-year-plans may vary greatly. Thus, it is hard to evaluate the dynamic effects of a specific planning policy initiative on targeted areas in the longer term.

The final significant challenge is the changing nature and complexity of planning policies. For example, the post-2013 Chinese Government places great emphasis on the development of the urban agglomeration belt affiliated to the 'Silk Road'. But at the moment, it is difficult to exploit to what extent such planning initiatives are likely to reduce spatial economic disparities, and strengthen agglomeration benefits through infrastructure provisions. Little is known about how much money Government at all levels should invest in eliminating regional disparities and promoting the coordinated regional development for cities along the 'Silk Road' development belt (*si chou zhi lu fa zhan dai*).

In short, for a complete understanding of the economics of planning policies, it is essential to know the locational characteristics of targeted regions, and what works for the economic development of these regions. For policymakers, it is important to know effective ways for internalizing the unintended consequences and externalities in order to intervene better in the economic agglomeration and market integration. The following sections of this chapter draw on recent practices of planning policies in China to highlight the implications on urban and regional agglomeration. This evidence underpins the main focus of this book: the role that institutional planning initiatives play in China's urban and regional transformation, with potential for growth, agglomeration and regeneration.

Planning policy and spatial economic agglomeration

The planning policy imposes direct, indirect and dynamic impacts on spatial economic agglomerations. With the implementation of various local and regional planning policies, China's spatial economic agglomeration has been structured along with the concentration and diffusion of population, industries and infrastructure. Urban agglomeration belts (*dai*) and zones (*qu*) have been integrated into a multilayered urban system for sustaining the country's economic growth and transformation.

Local agglomeration zones form the basis
of spatial economic development

The local agglomeration zone (*di fang ju ji qu;* hereinafter referred to as 'the zone') refers to an area of dense economic activity. Such zones are usually located in regional or national core cities and play a dominant role in terms of political, financial and logistic functions. Integrated transport systems and arteries have been planned and built to connect these zones with surrounding peripheral regions.

A large agglomeration zone can contain several neighbouring subzones that are linked by a transport infrastructure network. The formation and evolution of these agglomeration zones constitute the basis for spatial economic development.

The available evidence suggests that local agglomeration zones at different geographical scales have been shaped by planning policies. In the eastern region, there are substantial empirical studies in demonstrating that the Pearl River Delta, the Yangtze River Delta and the Beijing–Tianjin–Hebei Region, or the three largest agglomeration zones in China, are of great significance to spatial economic development. The emergence of local agglomeration zones, such as Central and Southern Liaoning, the Shandong Peninsula and the West Coast of the Taiwan Strait, has also played a critical role in driving the regional economy. Recently, the Central Plains Zone (centred on Zhengzhou) and the Yangtze River Midstream Zone (centred on Wuhan) have been recognized by the State Council's planning policies as two important agglomeration zones in the central region. Turning to the western region, the Chengdu–Chongqing Zone has become the key economic agglomeration area in western China. In addition to the Chengdu–Chongqing Zone, there is strong evidence about the formation and development of other agglomeration zones in the wider western and north-eastern regions such as the Zones of Changchun-Jilin-Siping, Harbin-Daqing-Qiqihar, Hohhot-Baotou-Erdos, Northern Piedmonts of the Tianshan Mountains, Central Yunnan and Beibu Gulf, among others. In addition to agglomeration zones, the State Council also approved the establishment of several urban districts at national level as the 'core' for leading the economic development in these agglomeration zones. Tables 5.1 and 5.2 summarize the key urban districts and economic agglomeration zones that are of national significance in China. Figures 5.1 and 5.2 show that these agglomeration zones and urban districts have a higher GDP and a larger population compared to peripheral areas (Data source: 2008 Statistics Yearbooks). While the quality and levels of these zones and national urban districts vary substantially, these zones feature spatial concentration of resources, capital, talented workers and other fundamental factors, and are formed as the basis of economic growth.

Agglomeration is the dominant trend in regional development

This section describes the recent agglomeration trend and clarifies the importance of comparative locational advantages as a determinant of agglomeration reinforcement.

China's regional development is influenced by uneven comparative locational advantages. Over the past three decades, the eastern region has achieved the highest economic growth, compared to other regions since China's economic reform and opening-up in the 1980s. This achievement is inseparable from China's economic reform and opening-up policy, as well as from regional planning policies implemented by the State Council that helped with urban agglomeration in the eastern region. Key urban agglomeration areas include the Yangtze River Delta Metropolitan Region, the Pearl River Delta Metropolitan Region, Beijing–Tianjin–Hebei Region, the Shandong Peninsula Metropolitan Region, the West

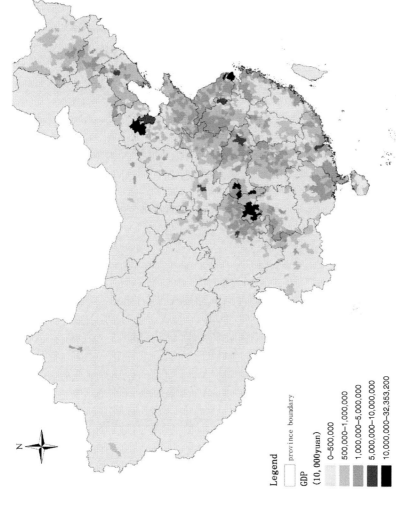

Legend

☐ province boundary

GDP
(10, 000yuan)

0–500,000
500,000–1,000,000
1,000,000–5,000,000
5,000,000–10,000,000
10,000,000–32,353,200

Figure 5.1 Distribution of GDP levels across Chinese counties

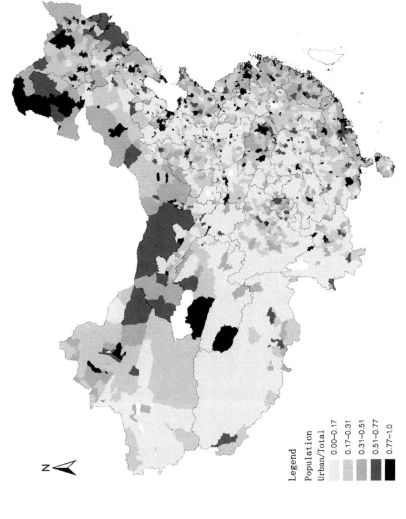

Legend

Population
Urban/Total

0.00–0.17
0.17–0.31
0.31–0.51
0.51–0.77
0.77–1.0

N

Figure 5.2 Distribution of urban population/total population ratio across Chinese counties

Table 5.1 Summary of major new urban districts at national level built during 1990–2015

Name	Province	Region	Establishment Year	Land size (km²)	Population (10,000 person)	Planning policy guidance
Pudong	Shanghai	East	1992	1,210	504	Developing this district as the national experimental field for economic reforms and an international agglomeration centre for finance, trade and shipping businesses.
Binhai	Tianjin	East	2005	2,270	242	Developing this district as Northern China's opening-up gateway, as the base for modern manufacturing and R&D transformations, and as the centre for shipping and international logistics in Northern China.
Liang-jiang	Chongqing	West	2010	1,200	221	Linking to the implementation of the western development strategy; developing this district as the pilot area of urban-rural comprehensive reforms; as the important inland base for advanced manufacturing industries; and as the centre of economic growth and technological innovations in the upstream Yangtze River region.
Zhoushan Islands	Zhejiang	East	2011	1,440 (including 100 1,390 small islands)	221	This is the first national-level new urban district focusing on the marine economy. The planning objectives include developing this district as the important growth pole of the Yangtze River Delta Metropolitan Region; as the national centre of commodity trading and storage; as the important island protection, modern ocean-industry and development demonstration zone, etc.
Lanzhou New district	Gansu	West	2012	806	18.95	Linking to the implementation of the western development strategy; developing this district as the important economic growth pole in the western region, the country's important industrial base, and an important strategic platform to undertake industrial transfer and stimulate the growth of the surrounding areas of Gansu province, as well as the broader western region.
Guangzhou Nansha	Guangdong	East	2012	803	240	Building this district as the comprehensive cooperation demonstration zone to connect with Hong Kong and Macao.

(continued)

Table 5.1 (continued)

Name	Province	Region	Establishment Year	Land size (km²)	Population (10,000 person)	Planning policy guidance
Xi'an–Xianyang	Shanxi	West	2014	882	150	Linking to the implementation of the western development strategy; promoting the Xi'an–Xianyang market integration process; and exploring the new urbanization development strategy in the western region.
Guiyang-Anshun	Guizhou	West	2014	1,795	73	Linking to the implementation of the western development strategy; an important spatial plan to accelerate institutional innovation in the inland area.
Qingdao West coast	Shandong	East	2014	2,096	171	Planning for further promotion of the economic transformation, social transformation, institutional restructuring' policy incentives to achieve the 'three recreating' objectives on the West Coast of Qingdao, namely: recreating an upgraded version of the reconstruction of Qingdao Port; recreating an upgraded version of economic outputs; and urban growth in the city of Qingdao.
Dalian Jin-pu	Liaoning	Northeast	2014	2,299.8	158	To lead the economic development of the Liaoning coastal areas, and the revitalization and development of the north-east region; and to promote the cooperation opportunities with North-east Asian countries
Chengdu Tian-fu	Sichuan	West	2014	1,578	600	Linking to the implementation of the western development strategy; to push forward the new urbanization process in the inland area; and to promote the transformation and upgrading of industries in the inland area.
Xiang-Jiang	Hunan	Central	2015	490	85	This is the first national-level new urban district built in the central region. It aims to link with the implementation of the central-region development strategy and midstream Yangtze River economic development strategy.
Nanjing Jiang-bei	Jiangsu	East	2015	2,438	170	Developing this district as the innovation-driven development and demonstration zone, to promote the modernization and economic growth of southern Jiangsu-section Yangtze River areas.

Data sources: Data are compiled based on the information released from the relevant government reports

Table 5.2 Planning policies and their potential impacts on economic agglomeration zones (EAZ)

	Key Planning Policies	Key Planning Objectives	Spatial Pattern	Core Cities	Infrastructure	Intended Spatial Economic Effects
Yangtze River Delta EAZ	• In September 2008, the 'Guiding Opinions of the State Council Concerning Further Promotion of the Reform and Opening-up and Socioeconomic Development in Yangtze River Delta Area' were issued. • In June 2009, the State Council passed the 'Planning for Development of Coastal Regions in Jiangsu. • In May 2010, the State Council approved the implementation of 'Regional Planning for Yangtze River Delta Area'.	• Construct the zone into a leading zone in terms of reform and innovation, a pioneer zone in terms of modernization and internationalization. • Construct the zone as an important international gateway in Asian-Pacific regions, as a major global centre of modern service industry and advanced manufacturing, and a world-class city agglomeration with strong international competitiveness.	• 'One Core and Nine Belts': with Shanghai as the core, promote coordinated regional development by establishing development belts along Shanghai–Nanjing Railway, Shanghai–Hangzhou–Ningbo Railway, the Yangtze River, the Hangzhou Bay, the sea, Nanjing–Huzhou–Hangzhou Railway, the Taihu Lake, the East Longhai Railway, the Grand Canal, and the Wenzhou–Lishui–Jinhua–Quzhou Railway.	• Core city: Shanghai. • Subcentres: Nanjing, Suzhou, Wuxi, Hangzhou and Ningbo.	• Promote transregional integration of major infrastructure construction, and enhance the co-building, sharing and inter-operability of transportation, energy, water conservation, and other infrastructure. • Improve the construction of traffic channels, accelerate the construction of integrated hubs, promote energy infrastructure, improve water-conservancy infrastructure, and improve the information infrastructure.	• Support the industrial and economic development along the transport systems..

(continued)

Table 5.2 (continued)

	Key Planning Policies	Key Planning Objectives	Spatial Pattern	Core Cities	Infrastructure	Intended Spatial Economic Effects
Pearl River Delta EAZ, plus Hainan EAZ	• In January 2009, the State Council approved the 'Guidelines on the Planning for Reform and Development of Pearl River Delta Area (2008–2020)'. • In January 2010, the 'Several Opinions of the State Council Concerning Promoting the Construction and Development of Hainan International Tourism Island' were issued. • In April, 2010, the 'Framework Agreement on Hong Kong/Guangdong Cooperation' was signed. • In July 2010, the 'Approval of the State Council Concerning the Establishment of the Comprehensive Bonded Zone of Guangzhou Baiyun Airport' was issued.	• Construct the zone as a centre of international shipping, logistics, trade, exhibition, tourism and innovation, as a major economic centre and an important international gateway to widen opening-up in China. • Closely cooperate, integrate and develop with Hong Kong and Macao, and jointly create the most dynamic and internationally competitive urban agglomeration in the Asian-Pacific regions.	• Take the lead in forming a new pattern of urban and rural integrated development by improving and enhancing urban functions in accordance with the integration of urban and rural planning, industrial layout integration, infrastructure integration and integration of public service.	• Core cities: Guangzhou and Shenzhen	• Construct an open and modern integrated transport system, a water-conservancy project system with harmonious relationship between man and water, and an efficient and convenient information network system.	• Stimulate labour and resources moving from the central and western areas to coastal areas and industries from the coastal areas to the central and western areas. • Promote industrial upgrades in the Pearl River Delta region, and southern China in general.

Beijing–Tianjin–Hebei EAZ						
• In 2007, the *'Regional Planning for Beijing–Tianjin–Hebei Metropolitan Area'* was issued. • In April 2015, the *'Guidelines on the Planning for Synergic Development of Beijing, Tianjin and Hebei'* were issued.	• Construct and develop the zone as a 'third pole' of China's economic growth. • With the capital as the core, build a world-class city agglomeration zone, a leading zone in regional synergic development reform. • Build a new engine of nationwide innovation-driven economic growth, and a demonstration area of ecological restoration and environmental improvement.	• Develop the economy in the circum-Bohai-sea region in the pattern of 'One Core and Two Cities' with Beijing-Tianjin-Binhai New Area as the axis, Beijing–Tianjin–Hebei as the core, and Liaoning and Shandong Peninsulas as the wings.	• Core cities: Beijing and Tianjin	• Construct a multinode, grid-like, full-coverage transport network with rail transportation as the backbone, and develop unified and open regional transport market. • Focus on building highly efficient dense rail network, improve the smooth and convenient road network, construct a group of modern ports in Beijing–Tianjin–Hebei Region, create world-class aviation hubs, accelerate the construction of Beijing's new airport, and enhance regional integrated transport services.	• Unlock the diffusion effect of intelligence industry and knowledge-based economy in the whole metropolitan region, where the core cities will serve as a bridge and liaison.

(continued)

Table 5.2 (continued)

	Key Planning Policies	Key Planning Objectives	Spatial Pattern	Core Cities	Infrastructure	Intended Spatial Economic Effects
Western Taiwan Strait EAZ	• In May, 2009, the 'Several Opinions of the State Council Concerning Supporting Fujian Province to Accelerate the Construction of Western Taiwan Strait Economic Zone' were issued. • In March 2011, the 'Planning for Development of Western Taiwan Strait Economic Zone' was issued.	• Construct a pilot area of cooperation and exchange between the people across the Taiwan Strait. • Expand the comprehensive channel for cross-strait cooperation and exchange, build an important base of advanced manufacturing in eastern coastal areas, and forge an important centre of natural and cultural tourism in China.	• Promote regional cooperation between the Fujian and Yangtze River Delta and the Pearl River Delta, and gradually develop a complete development layout along the whole coastline from the circum-Bohai-sea region to the Pearl River Delta.	• Core cities: Fuzhou and Xiamen	• With Xiamen Port and Fuzhou Port as the mainstay, draw a rational pattern of development for ports along the south-east coastline. Construct an expressway network in Western Taiwan Strait Economic Zone. Speed up the construction of Wenzhou–Fuzhou, Fuzhou–Xiamen and Xiamen–Shenzhen railways. Plan and construct Beijing–Fuzhou and Kunming–Xiamen high-speed railways, forming express rail transport channels linking up the Yangtze River Delta, the Pearl River Delta and the central and western regions. Build a group of main and feeder airports on the basis of Fuzhou and Xiamen airports.	• Provide a fast and smooth strategic channel for opening-up to promote the rise of Fujian province. • Set up the frontier platform for national reunification, and become the venue, pioneer and channel for economic cooperation and cultural exchanges across the strait.

Chengdu–Chongqing EAZ	• In 2004, the State Council issued the *'Study on Key Economic Belts in China's Western Development'*. • In 2006, the *'11th Five-Year-Plan'* clearly put forward the construction of *'Chengdu–Chongqing EAZ'*. • In June 2007, the *'the Approval of the Pilot Area of Urban-rural Comprehensive Development Reform in Chongqing Municipality and Chengdu Municipality'* was issued. • In March 2011, the *'Regional Planning for Chengdu–Chongqing EAZ'* was issued.	• Become an important growth pole in the regional development of western China. • Become the core metropolitan area of Yangtze River Upstream Economic Belt, and a pilot area of integrated urban and rural development, and a demonstration area of inland opening-up. • Become the protection zone of national ecological safety, and an important base of advanced equipment manufacturing, modern service industry, high-tech industry and agricultural products.	• Develop 'two cores': Chengdu and Chongqing. Specifically, Chengdu–Chongqing EAZ should feature 'five bases and one barrier' (energy, heavy equipment manufacturing, science and technology industry, IT-oriented high-tech industry of national defence, special agricultural and sideline product-processing and the ecological barrier in Upper Yangtze River.) in regional division of labour and spatial layout of China. • Core cities: Chengdu and Chongqing	• Construct Chongqing–Lichuan, Lanzhou–Chengdu, and Zhengzhou–Chongqing railways. Reconstruct Dazhou–Chengdu, Baoji–Chengdu (the section of Chengdu–Mianyang–Guangyuan), Chengdu–Kunming railways. • Construct national expressways like Chengdu–Chongqing Expressway. Regulate the waterway of the Yangtze River. Renovate and expand Chongqing Jiangbei airport and Chengdu Shuangliu airport. Build a new airport in Leshan. Establish central railway container stations in Chengdu and Chongqing. • Promote construction of main highway hubs in Chengdu and Chongqing, airline hubs in Chengdu and Chongqing, and major river hub ports in Yibin, Chongqing, etc.	• Gather advantageous resources to achieve optimal allocation, and promote the coordinated development of the whole region through the first development in key areas. • Become an important economic growth pole in the western regions, lead and promote the development of the western regions.

(continued)

Table 5.2 (continued)

	Key Planning Policies	Key Planning Objectives	Spatial Pattern	Core Cities	Infrastructure	Intended Spatial Economic Effects
Beibu Gulf EAZ	• In January, 2008, the 'Planning for Development of Beibu Gulf Economic Zone, Guangxi' was issued. • In March 2010, the 'Guidelines on the Planning for Town Clusters in Beibu Gulf EAZ in Guangxi' were issued.	• Serve the South-west and central-southern China regional development, face South-east Asia, give full play to the functions as an important channel connecting multiple regions, a bridge for exchanges, and a platform for cooperation. • Under the opening-up and cooperation framework between China and the ASEAN countries, construct an important international and regional economic cooperation zone serving as a logistics base, business base, manufacturing base and information-exchange centre.	• Develop 'two poles, one axis and one corridor' by constructing the two development poles of 'Nanning and the coastal areas', the axis of 'Nanning-costal urban development', and the 'Yuchong Development Corridor'.	• Core city: Nanning	• Promote integrated development of port operation, and construct Guangxi coastal ports. • Build a group of large-tonnage berths and deep-water channels in the ports along the coastline, build port logistics centres, strengthen energy, iron ore, container transportation system and the collection and distribution supporting system connecting the hinterland, and improve the capacity of coastal ports. Improve the high-grade highway network construction.	• Beibu Gulf EAZ has an advantageous location, strategic position, and huge potential for development. It's the only coastal area in the western China that enjoys coastal opening, and ethnic minority and border areas opening policies. It is also the hub for onshore exchanges between China and ASEAN countries. The economic effect is reflected by the activation of the rapid development of cities along the Xi River region and the Beibu Gulf region.

| Central Plains EAZ | • In March 2011, the *'Guidelines on the Construction of Central Plains EAZ'* were issued.
• In September 2011, the *'Guiding Opinions of the State Council Concerning Supporting Henan Province to Accelerate the Construction of Central Plains EAZ'* were issued.
• In November 2012, the *'Planning for Central Plains EAZ'* was issued. | • Construct a major grain-production and modern agricultural base for the country.
• Build a demonstration area of coordinated development among industrialization, urbanization, information technology and agricultural modernization.
• Construct a strategic pivot for regional coordinated development, an important modern and integrated transport hub, and an area of inheritance and innovation of China's history and civilization. | • In accordance with the principles of 'core-driven, axial development, nodal improvement and surroundings integration', form a radial and networked pattern of development to promote the rapid development of the central region. | • Core city: Zhengzhou
• Subcentre: Luoyang | • Consolidate and promote the status of Zhengzhou as an integrated transport hub. Promote the construction of the large domestic aviation hub in Zhengzhou, and transform Zhengzhou into an important domestic transfer and regional freight-distribution centre. Improve the status and function of Zhengzhou railway hub in the national railway network, and advance the construction and renovation of comprehensive passenger hub.
• Carry forward the integration of air and land transport, and form a modern and integrated transport hub that interacts and develops together with Zhengzhou.
• Form a joint development pattern between cities in this region and develop a new EAZ that can help to sustain economic growth in the central China. |

(continued)

Table 5.2 (continued)

	Key Planning Policies	Key Planning Objectives	Spatial Pattern	Core Cities	Infrastructure	Intended Spatial Economic Effects
Yangtze River Midstream EAZ	• In December 2007, the State Council approved Wuhan City Circle as the 'Pilot Area of Comprehensive Supplementary Reforms of the Construction of National Resource-economical and Environment-friendly Society'. • In December 2013, the 'Regional Planning for Development of Wuhan City Circle' was issued. • In April 2015, the 'Planning for Development of Yangtze River Midstream City Agglomeration' was issued.	• Promote the linking up of the industry and infrastructure, the flow of economic elements, and the unification of markets between key metropolitan regions, including the Yangtze River Delta city agglomeration, Yangtze River Midstream city agglomeration and Chengdu–Chongqing EAZ. • Promote the orderly transfer and convergence of industries, optimize and upgrade the industries, and motivate the agglomeration and development of new towns. • Develop into a new economic growth pole of China, the pioneer in new urbanization in middle and western areas, and the leader and demonstrator of inland opening-up and cooperation.	• Build an axis of interactive development linking up the eastern part of the urban agglomeration and the south-western region, and provide an important channel among the eastern, central and western regions. • Develop and interact with Yangtze River Delta and Chengdu–Chongqing regions, and jointly construct the Yangtze River Economic Belt. Become an important axis linking up Beibu Gulf Economic Zone, Central Plains Economic Zone, Guanzhong–Tianshui Economic Zone, etc. Establish a north-south axis of economic development.	• Core city: Wuhan • Subcentre: Changsha and Nanchang	• Improve the interoperable land transport network. Construct and form an inland waterway system in the middle reaches of the Yangtze River, featuring a smooth main channel and interwoven branch channels, with the Yangtze River waterway as the axis, supplemented by Hanjiang River, Dongting Lake basin, and Poyang Lake basin. • Build an efficient and convenient air transport network. Strengthen the function of Wuhan Tianhe International Airport and Changsha Huanghua International Airport as regional hub, and the function of Nanchang Changbei Airport as main airport by adding international and domestic transport routes. Jointly construct water-conservancy infrastructure system.	Accelerate the formation of the Yangtze River City Agglomeration, and Yangtze River Mega-city Agglomeration, and promote the economic development of cities closing to the Yangtze River.

Coast of the Taiwan Strait Metropolitan Region, as well as the Central and South Liaoning Metropolitan Regions. These urban agglomeration areas have attracted a huge amount of foreign capital, skilled labour and other fundamental production factors to reinforce their continued future growth. The patterns of economic activities in peripheral regions are dominated by core cities such as Beijing, Shanghai, Guangzhou, Nanjing, Hangzhou, Qingdao, Shenyang and Xiamen. In the central and western regions, urban agglomeration areas centre on provincial capital cities and medium-sized towns along main transportation arteries at provincial/ autonomous levels. Based on Christaller's central place location theory,[1] a variety of specialized economic centres are formed in the peripheral regions that can be integrated to sustain the growth of core cities within an orderly arranged urban hierarchical system. With the implementation of railways, highways and airport development programmes during the Eleventh and Twelfth Five-Year-Plans, transport infrastructure improvements constitute a new driver for regional development and this is consistent with findings from economic studies (Démurger, 2001; Glaeser and Kohlhase, 2004). Key nodal cities along the land and air transport network, such as Zhengzhou and Wuhan, have emerged as new metropolitan areas owing to their privileged locations along the Beijing–Guangzhou and Xi'an–Shanghai high-speed railways, and other main transportation arteries.

The rise of economic agglomerations is not a surprising consequence. As indicated by the economic geography literature, there are good reasons for this: first, economic agglomeration zones could have significant effects on optimizing locational layout, making the fundamental infrastructure accessible to core and peripheral areas, and integrating the market mechanism into the national five-year-plan implementation process. This process is achieved mainly through the integration and concentration of markets, trade and industries across regions (Ellison and Glaeser, 1999; Rosenthal and Strange, 2003). As such, the formation and evolution of key economic agglomeration zones have had profound impacts on shifting Chinese economic growth. Second, the rise of economic agglomeration zones strengthens the role of core cities over space. With the persistence of spillover effects, core cities will be blessed with a broader hinterland for influencing the growth of small- and medium-sized towns, and this may lead to the wider economic integration within zones. In addition, this process is grounded on the development of transport infrastructure that can facilitate the movement of labour, goods and resources over space. Coupled with agglomeration and spillover effects, regional disparities are increasing. Airports, railways, highways, telecommunications and other infrastructure have been built to form an integrated 'networked, hub-like and multinode' infrastructure system within and across economic agglomeration zones. These infrastructure establishments are supported by various planning policies and are related to the success of urban and regional agglomeration. In particular, China's unique political regime allows the Government to implement mega-infrastructure projects efficiently. The Chinese Government also has power to successfully implement infrastructure and regional planning policies by providing State-owned land, offering financial incentives and ignoring the possible side effects, such as pollution and other inconveniences.

More generally, economic implications of planning policies can be reflected in the following ways: first, China's planning policies have provided a conceptual foundation for developing the national economy in a comprehensive and coordinated way. The implementation of planning policies over the past three decades has provided strong evidence that the Government's intervention in spatial agglomeration as integrated in the planning system has played a key role in guiding local and regional development. For instance, the national long-term regional development strategy as proposed by the Chinese policymakers is well implemented through the formation of major economic agglomeration zones across the north-eastern, eastern, central and western regions.

Second, there are many planning policies that aim to stimulate the medium-term and long-term economic consequences. The spatial evolution of planning policies, such as the 'Five-Year' national plans and a series of regional and local planning programmes, brings about fundamental impacts on the ever-widening regional inequality. With Deng's development strategy as the basic ideology, the purpose of regional planning policies is to guide the layout of locational agglomeration. Although there are some side effects such as congestion and air pollution to be solved in the evolution of economic agglomeration zones, these issues are likely to be addressed properly through the so-called principle of '*government intervention, market operation, and social participation*'.

Third, China's planning policies have impelled Government at all levels to find a way to support local economic development in a coordinated pathway. Before China's reform and opening-up, local and regional planning strategies were not designed uniformly. The main task of each provincial director was to complete the planned objectives set by Central Government. After the reform and opening-up, with the rapid development of regional economy, provincial governments in different regions were asked to formulate their own regional development plans and to recognize their comparative locational advantages to maximize their economic gains. Meantime, after carrying out in-depth investigation of locational characteristics, Local Government paved the way to the formulation of the national development strategies in subsequent years. In short, China's planning policies have effectively promoted the adjustment of industrial structure, the construction of interprovincial infrastructure, and the formation of a unified transregional market over history.

Finally, the wide adoption of planning policies has transcended the administrative boundaries between different provinces and autonomous regions. The Government is motivated to resolve conflicts that exist among various administrative areas, in accordance with the principles of optimal market-resource allocation and rational provision of infrastructure. By doing so, the planning policy is designed to recognize spatial economic differences between regions and exploit the comparative locational advantages, in order to generate agglomeration benefits for the whole country. For example, there are many planning programmes that have attached great importance to building diversified industrial structures for different regions (Zhang et al., 2009). In particular, with the rising regional disparities in wages and living costs, recent planning policies have focused on gentrifying the depressed regions through infrastructure improvement.

However, it is still important to question to what extent these place-based locational planning policies work to reverse the fate of depressed areas and create employment opportunities for migrants and local residents. Recent studies from the USA have shown that place-based locational policies such as the Enterprise and Empowerment Zone programmes in the USA could spur employment growth by offering financial incentives to businesses that relocate in designated zones (Neumark and Kolko, 2010; Busso et al. 2013). The UK Government has also implemented various locational planning programmes such as the Lyons Review with various objectives, including rearranging Government resources and reducing the disparities in income and employment (Faggio, 2014; Faggio and Overman, 2014). Table 5.2 summarizes recent planning policies with respect to key economic agglomeration zones and their potential economic impacts.

Geography of urban agglomeration belts

China's planning policies and their implications on the formation of spatial agglomerations, presented in the previous section of this chapter, generally describe endeavours made by Government at all levels to intervene in the provision of direct resources and infrastructure in particular geographic areas. If public investment affects production and labour costs in spatial equilibrium, there could be strong implications for optimizing place-based policies and internalizing externalities (Glaeser and Gottlieb, 2008). This section discusses implications of planning policies for shaping the geography of urban agglomeration belts (*dai*).

In contemporary China, most economic activities take place in cities and economic productivity is higher in mega-cities. Centred on mega-cities, urban agglomeration belts have emerged to boast rapid local economic development. Specifically, four urban agglomeration belts have been gradually formed on the basis of the T-model development strategy, as suggested by Chinese scholars (Peng, 1991; Lao, 1993; Chen, 1994). These four belts, namely 'two vertical belts and two horizontal belts' (*liang heng liang zong*), include the Coastal Urban Agglomeration Belt (Figure 5.3), the Beijing–Guangzhou (Jing–Guang) Railway Urban Agglomeration Belt (Figure 5.4), the Yangtze River Urban Agglomeration Belt (Figure 5.5) and the land-based Silk Road Urban Agglomeration Belt (Figure 5.6). With the implementation of recent planning policies issued by the Chinese Government (Table 5.2), these four belts have generated substantial effects in shaping the country's urban system and regional inequality over the past three decades.

Coastal urban agglomeration belt

Located in the most developed regions of China, the Coastal Urban Agglomeration Belt runs from the north to the south (Figure 5.3). This belt includes many metropolitan areas that are of national and international significance, such as the Pearl River Delta Metropolitan Area, Western Taiwan Strait Metropolitan Area, Yangtze River Delta Metropolitan Area, and Beijing–Tianjin–Hebei Metropolitan Area. This belt also included almost all First-tier mega-cities in the country and has become the frontier of China's economic growth and the centre for internationalization.

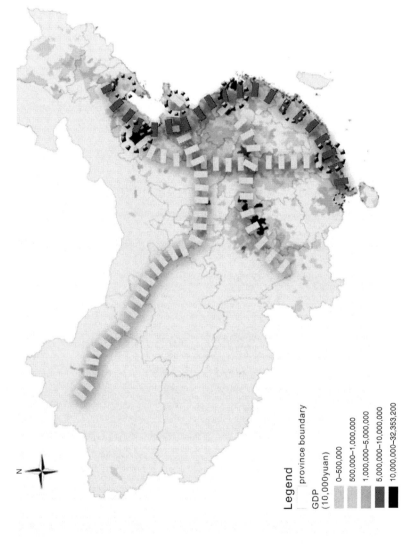

Figure 5.3 Geography of coastal urban agglomeration belt

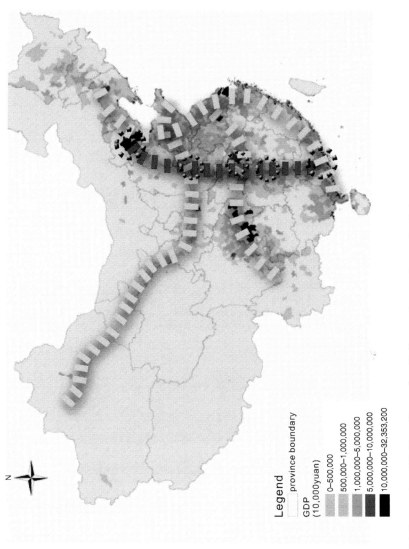

Figure 5.4 Geography of Beijing–Guangzhou Railway urban agglomeration belt

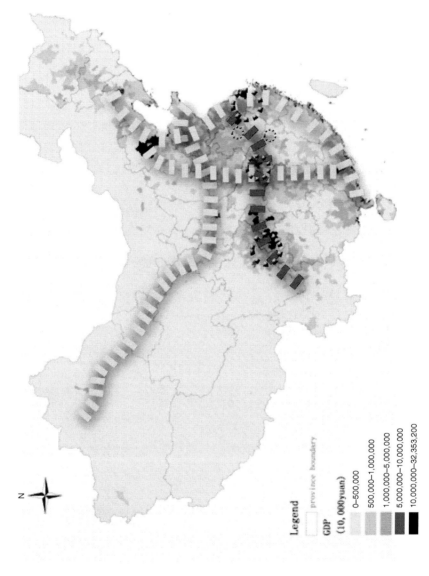

N

Figure 5.5 Geography of Yangtze River urban agglomeration belt

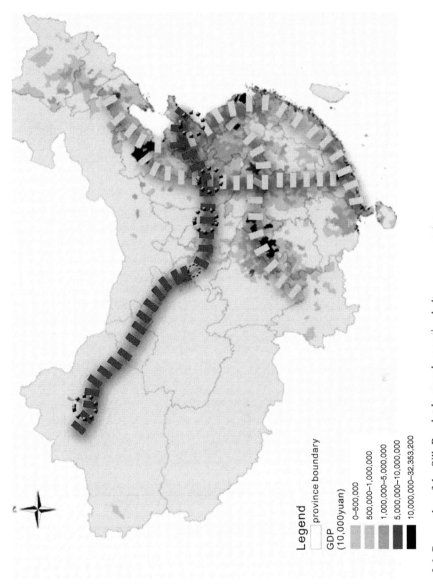

Figure 5.6 Geography of the Silk Road urban agglomeration belt

One fundamental characteristic of this belt is that it has gained competitive locational advantages in terms of a high concentration of skilled workers, science and technology facilities, and transport infrastructure. In particular, public and private investment in science and technology facilities is growing rapidly in this belt, giving birth to a variety of R&D technological innovation centres. These technology and innovation advantages are the key driving force for the urban economic transformation from a labour-intensive economy to a capital and technology-intensive economy in this belt. Meanwhile, some peripheral districts have emerged as new growth poles with favourable port conditions. Examples include, but are not limited to: Bayuquan District close to Huludao and Dalian Metropolitan Areas (Liaoning province), Caofeidian District close to Tangshan (Hebei province), Tianjin Binhai New District (Tianjin), Yantai-Qingdao (Shandong), Hangzhou Bay Areas (Zhejiang province), and the eastern and western wings of the Pearl River Delta Metropolitan Areas in this Coastal Urban Agglomeration Belt.

Acting as the opening-up frontline, cities from this belt have attracted more FDI and foreign enterprises than anywhere else in China. Furthermore, this belt has played an influential role in upgrading the traditional industrial structure, and in supporting the development of advanced manufacturing and modern service industries. In light of comparative locational advantages and infrastructure accessibility, cities in this belt have become the optimal location for businesses and skilled workers, and therefore, the level of economic agglomeration continues to improve in this region, forming the diversified and loosely structured urban agglomeration belt, and connecting cities from the north to the south. The future vision as guided by the current planning system in this region includes:

- The establishment of an advanced industrial structure. This pathway involves the development of world-class industries by focusing on automobile, shipbuilding, electronic information, communications equipment, aerospace, mechanical and electrical integration, and other skill-intensive manufacturing industries.
- The establishment of multilayered central business districts, involving financial, shipping and trade sectors that can generate spillover effects on peripheral cities. This pathway is designed to further reinforce the agglomeration in shaping the regional economic integration and in restructuring the division of labour and resources in the Coastal Urban Agglomeration Belt.
- The infrastructure provided for facilitating the reallocation of labour, capital and other fundamental production factors between core cities in the Coastal Urban Agglomeration Belt.

Beijing–Guangzhou railway urban agglomeration belt

The Beijing–Guangzhou Railway Urban Agglomeration Belt refers to the north-south urban agglomeration corridor, including Beijing and cities in the provinces of Hebei, Henan, Hubei, Hunan and Guangdong, which are distributed along the Beijing–Guangzhou Railway and the Beijing–Zhuhai Expressway (Figure 5.4). It is about 2,300 km in length from north to south. Some major economic agglomeration zones are concentrated in this belt, such as the Beijing–Tianjin–Hebei Agglomeration Zone, Wuhan Agglomeration Zone, Changsha–Zhuzhou–Xiangtan Agglomeration Zone, and the Pearl River Delta Agglomeration Zone, etc. Along the belt, the population is larger and urban density is higher than the national average. The integrated transportation system, involving highways, railways, and civil aviation, offers solid support to the economic agglomeration in this region.

In line of the locational advantages, four core cities – Beijing, Zhengzhou, Wuhan, and Guangzhou – have played a dominant role in this region. Small- and medium-sized cities from Henan, Hubei and Hunan provinces in central China are connected to these core cities through various transport pathways along the Beijing–Guangzhou Railway. On one hand, the cities in the provinces of Henan, Hubei and Hunan are of national significance in terms of agricultural production, leading to a plentiful supply of agricultural output to meet rising demand. On the other hand, the spatial concentration of economic activities in dense industrial clusters surrounding core cities provides supportive evidence of the existence of agglomerations in this region.

The Beijing–Guangzhou Railway Urban Agglomeration Belt is the second largest national urban agglomeration belt in China. The overall mission of this region is to support the market integration from the north to the south along the central provinces of China. The future vision of this belt as guided by the current planning system involves:

- The introduction of the Central Plains Economic Region (CPER) as a prominent policy instrument for promoting the concentration of production factors, economic restructuring, and the development of modern equipment manufacturing, automobile manufacturing and raw-material industrial bases.
- The optimal use of land and water resources for developing a set of high-quality bases for grains, oil and fishery products, and the balanced provision of transport infrastructure to promote the concentration of economic activities in small-and medium-sized cities.
- The transformation from the resource-based economy to the technology, capital and labour-intensive economy, and the transformation from the production of intermediate products to the production of high value-added consumer products.

Yangtze River urban agglomeration belt

The Yangtze River Urban Agglomeration Belt refers to the scattered metropolitan areas located along the Yangtze River Corridor, connecting Chengdu–Chongqing, Nanchang, Changsha, and Wuhan metropolitan regions (Figure 5.5). This region is located close to the golden waterway of the Yangtze River. The completion of the Three Gorges Dam project and associated infrastructure has boasted intercity connections and economic agglomeration and urbanization in this region.

The explicit rationale for the rise of the Yangtze River Urban Agglomeration Belt is that the richness of energy and resources, which include hydropower in the upper and middle streams of the Yangtze River, natural gas and oil fields in the Sichuan Basin and the great potential of raw materials such as nonferrous metals and steel resources in Anhui province, Jiangxi province and Hubei province, has provided a solid foundation for supporting densely distributed manufacturing and high-tech industries. For example, national supersized steel enterprises such as Masteel and Wuhan Iron & Steel, and petrochemical enterprises such as Jinshan Petrochemical, Sinopec Yangzi Petrochemical, Sinopec Zhenhai Petrochemical, Yueyang Petrochemical, and other large enterprises, are concentrated in Wuhan city, Yichang city, Wuhu city, Jiujiang city, Yueyang city, Fuling city and other cities in this region. This has played an important role in the regional economic agglomeration. As guided by the current planning system, this belt is designed to be developed as the base for manufacturing, electronic information, bio-pharmaceuticals, automobiles, motorcycles, precision machinery, electric power, petrochemical and metallurgical industries, energy, and raw materials production among other industries, and to be an important economic agglomeration zone in China. The more specific future vision of this region involves:

- The optimal use of the land-and-water and river-and-sea coordinated transport systems that can attract the agglomeration of economic factors along the golden waterway of the Yangtze River.
- The cooperation and division of infrastructure provisions between cities along the Yangtze River, so that the upstream and the downstream areas can be integrated together.
- The relocation of water-consuming, high-energy consuming and heavy-polluting industries to other regions, to form a set of ecological port-centred industrial clusters.
- The promotion of industrial upgrading and international competitiveness in economic agglomeration zones along the Yangtze River.

Silk Road urban agglomeration belt

The Silk Road Urban Agglomeration Belt starts from Lianyungang in the east, spans all the way through Xuzhou, Kaifeng, Zhengzhou, Luoyang, Xi'an and Baoji to Lanzhou, and then stretches along the Lanxin Railway to the Alataw Pass, passing through the Hexi Corridor and Urumqi. As part of the historical Silk Road, this belt includes key urbanized areas like Northern Jiangsu Urbanized Area, Central Plains Urbanized Area, Guanzhong Urbanized Area and Northern Tianshan-Mountain Urbanized Areas in the central and western regions. It should be noted that there are also alternative Silk Road routes connecting China and other countries, but the land-based route highlighted in Figure 5.6 is an important part of the historical Silk Road. This belt not only plays an essential role in producing agricultural and livestock output to meet the country's demand, but also functions as a major agglomeration zone of energy and raw materials. Resources such as coal, hydropower, oil and gas are relatively abundant in this region. In particular, coal and oil mining that has been concentrated in Xuzhou, Huaibei, Yanzhou, Tengzhou, Pingdingshan, Jiaozuo and Xinmi, can generate sufficient energy power for cities along the Yellow River, and the entire urban agglomeration belt. In this belt, industrial cities like Xuzhou, Xi'an, Baoji, Zhengzhou, Luoyang, Lanzhou and Urumqi have long been developed in the Chinese planning system over the past sixty-five years. As such, this belt is featured as an important manufacturing base in China, with a cluster of construction machinery, electronic information, electrical machinery, aerospace, automobile manufacturing, machine tools and other heavy industries.

The agglomeration pattern here is still in an immature stage owing to substantial differences in terms of locational characteristics between cities within this region. Overall, the eastern wing of this belt is better developed than the western wing. In fact, the spatial agglomeration structure of this belt can be regarded as a miniature China, which consists of a diversified group of cities in terms of economic performance. Nevertheless, this region is of vital importance in linking up economic activities among the eastern, central and western regions. On one hand, the richness of energy, raw materials and natural resources in this region has supported the sustainable economic growth of other regions. On the other hand, this urban agglomeration belt provides a buffer for supporting the knowledge and technology shifts from the developed coastal regions to inland regions. By actively promoting the formation of this urban agglomeration belt through recent planning policies, senior Chinese policymakers aim to boost the economic cooperation along the 'Silk Road', and accelerate the diffusion of production factors among regions.

The future vision of this region involves:

- A transformation from the 'scattered city points' development mode surrounding core cities like Xi'an, and Lanzhou to the 'network-based' development mode that connects all nodes along the main transportation system. Generally speaking, the planning initiative aims to facilitate the diffusion of resources and labour between core cities and peripheral cities in a comprehensive manner.
- The re-orientation of the Silk Road for speeding up the construction of the transportation infrastructure and the development of resources along the Silk Road region. This planning initiative aims to link China to other countries located in the Eurasian Continental Bridge, for a wider range of market integration and economic cooperation.
- The development of modern manufacturing industries in the major urbanized areas, including Zhengzhou–Kaifeng–Luoyang Industrial Corridor, Guanzhong Economic Corridor, Lanzhou–Baiying Corridor and Urumqi-Changqi-Miquan-Fukang Industrial Corridor. This planning initiative aims to make use of the geographical advantages of these spatially clustered corridors to restructure economic agglomeration in this region.

Conclusion

This chapter focuses on discussing recent urban and regional agglomeration in China, and explains how planning policies help guide both the way these uneven patterns play out spatially and the role that infrastructure, location and cities play in reinforcing spatial agglomeration. The explanation for urban and regional agglomeration is shadowed within the national shifts in institutional transitions (for example, economic reform and opening-up), industrialization (for example, shifts from labour-intensive industries towards skill-intensive and low-carbon emission industries) and urbanization (for example, a shift in the regional development strategy towards a sustainable pathway). But it is also important to know that the notion of urban and regional agglomeration is introduced to coordinate regional development, support social production and consumption, make transport infrastructure accessible, and integrate a variety of market channels into the urban and regional transformation.

Whereas some urban agglomeration belts and regional agglomeration zones have been formulated effectively, others may not work well. This highlights another implication of this chapter: policymakers should be more realistic about the feasibility of achieving the development goals when implementing regional planning programmes. Given that trade and industrial disparities largely reflect differences in urban connections, policymakers should particularly highlight the importance of considering fundamental factors such as labour skills, business productivity, infrastructure accessibility and the natural environment as key components of planning policies.

This raises a set of questions about the effectiveness of planning policies, as well as the delivery of the planning programmes discussed above. The evidence of and experience from Chinese planning policies suggest several empirical challenges for shaping the trends and patterns of spatial agglomerations. First, there are reasons to believe that initiatives of regional planning policies can intervene in the means of optimizing locational layout and delivering economic agglomeration benefits. But it is difficult to identify the straightforward positive or negative economic effects in relation to the spatial scope of planning interventions. There is clear evidence that the scale of Government investment matters, and in turn, implementing initiatives of planning policies has exerted heterogeneous effects on reinforcing economic agglomeration in core cities and relative peripheral cities. But this does not make the definitive case that place-based, locational planning policies can work for local economic growth. Conversely, there are also solid grounds for rethinking that applying planning policies to intervene in the natural process of economic agglomeration and market integration might generate a series of unintended consequences. Since the externalities of economic development are likely structured in a nonlinearity manner, welfare benefits achieved from place-based, locational planning policies might be expensive.

Second, there are overlapping issues among different regional planning policies even though the Chinese Government has a clear governance structure. To address this, the Chinese Government[2] issued national-level guidance in 2015, for regulating the decision-making and implementation of various regional planning policies. The rationale behind this is that desired planning goals appear to be subject to area-based financial incentives and infrastructure investment, whereby cities become more productive when they are located in designated regions supported by good infrastructure and other resources. But limited information is released publicly about how Government at all levels has sponsored the targeted areas or specific infrastructure construction projects. It is difficult to know how many planning programmes have been implemented initially in the same region and how these policies have produced economic impacts at the local or regional level. As there is no clear prediction of the spatial economic goals, it is challenging to make robust future visions for urban and regional agglomeration in China. The fact that the economic effect of a specific planning programme for particular regions cannot be predicted accurately is due partly to the spatial-temporal uncertainties involved.

China's evidence and experience of the implementation of planning policies shed light on many aspects of these challenges. The rise of local market potentials (Harris, 1954) has identified some metropolitan areas as key growth poles for economic agglomeration, and has shifted the geography of the core-periphery urban system to be influenced locally by planning policies. Despite empirical challenges, place-based and locational planning policies have produced a new alternative way for rethinking the configuration of China's economic geographic patterns.

In order to achieve the intended spatial economic goals, it is arguable to say that the current planning system needs to develop a more specific data-driven decision-making process, in which the objectives and contents of policies should be different over space, so as to make use of the comparative locational advantages in different regions. Mayors also need to deliver a more explicit 'roadmap' for gaining economic benefits from the implementation of planning policies. The content of this chapter will help to build a clear big picture about planning policies and their relationship to the trend and pattern of urban and regional agglomeration in China. In the following chapters, special topics regarding the economic and geographical implications of planning policies will be discussed, with a specific focus on infrastructure, cities and location. As various regional planning policies are implemented, there is a necessity to involve strictly designed monitoring procedures in guiding public capital spending in infrastructure and regional development, based on cost-benefit assessment of what policies work for structuring the core-periphery urban system and economic agglomeration. One of the most appealing features of recent planning policy practices is the involvement of scientific researchers in helping the Government to assess the effectiveness of public policies. Direct and causal evaluations on the economic impacts of initiatives of large-scale place-based and locational planning policies are still rare in China. Future work is encouraged to provide the evidence on this line of research.

Notes

1 https://en.wikipedia.org/wiki/Central_place_theory
2 http://www.ndrc.gov.cn/zcfb/zcfbtz/201507/W020150720317933777296.pdf

References

Abraham, K.G. and Medoff, J.L. 1984. Length of service and layoffs in union and nonunion work groups, Industrial and Labour Relations Review, 38(1), 87–97.

Ashcroft, B., Holden, D., Smith, J. and Swales, J.K. 1988. ODA dispersal to East Kilbride: An evaluation, Department of Economics, mimeo, Glasgow: University of Strathclyde.

Ashcroft, B. and Swales, J.K. 1982a. The importance of the first round of the multiplier process: The impact of civil service dispersal, Environment and Planning A, 14, 429–444.

Ashcroft, B. and Swales, J.K. 1982b. Estimating the effects of government office dispersal, Regional Science and Urban Economics, 12, 81–98.

Bartik, T.J. 1991. Who benefits from state and local economic development policies? Kalamazoo, MI: W.E. Upjohn Institute for Employment Research.

Baum-Snow, N. 2007. Did highways cause suburbanization? Quarterly Journal of Economics, 122(2), 775–805.

Baum-Snow, N., Brandt, L., Henderson, J.V., Turner, M. and Zhang, Q. 2015. *Roads, Railroads and Decentralization of Chinese Cities*. London: LSE manuscript.

Busso, M., Gregory, J. and Kline, P. 2013. Assessing the incidence and efficiency of a prominent place based policy, American Economic Review, 103(2), 897–947.

Chen, H. 1994. Basic strategy of regional economic development in China in the 1990s. Economic Theory and Business Management, 2, 1–6 [in Chinese].

Cheshire, P.C., Hilber, C. and Kaplanis, I. 2015. Land use regulation and productivity-land matters: Evidence from a UK supermarket chain. Journal of Economic Geography, 15(1), 43–73.

Cheshire, P.C. and Hilber, C.A.L. 2008. Office space supply restrictions in Britain: The political economy of market revenge, Economic Journal, 118(529), F185–221.

Démurger, S. 2001. Infrastructure development and economic growth: An explanation for regional disparities in China. Journal of Comparative Economics, 29, 95–117.

Ellison, G. and Glaeser, E.L. 1999. The geographic concentration of industry: Does natural advantage explain agglomeration? American Economic Review, 89(2), 311–316.

Erickson, R.A. and Syms, P.M. 1986. The effects of enterprise zones on local property markets. Regional Studies, 20(1), 1–14.

Faber, B. 2014. Trade integration, market size, and industrialization: Evidence from China's national trunk highway system, Review of Economic Studies, 81, 1046–1070.

Faggio, G. 2014. Relocation of public sector workers: Evaluating a place-based policy. SERC Discussion Paper No. 155. London School of Economics and Political Science.

Faggio, G. and Overman, H. 2014. The effect of public sector employment on local labour markets, Journal of Urban Economics, 79, 91–107.

Gibbons, R. and Katz, L. 1991. Layoffs and lemons, Journal of Labour Economics, 9(4), 351–380.

Gibbons, S., Overman, H. and Sarvimäki, M. 2011. The impact of subsidising commercial space in deprived neighbourhoods, mimeo, London: LSE.

Glaeser, E.L. and Gottlieb, J.D. 2008. The economics of place-making policies. Brookings Papers on Economic Activity, Spring.

Glaeser, E.L. and Kohlhase, J.E. 2004. Cities, regions and the decline of transport costs. Papers in Regional Science, 83(1), 197–228.

Harris, C. 1954. Market as a factor in the localization of industry in the United States, Annals of the Association of American Geographers, 44(4) 315–348.

Jacobson, L., LaLonde, R. and Sullivan, D. 1993. Earnings losses of displaced workers, American Economic Review, 83, 685–709.

Jefferson, C.W. and Trainor, M. 1996. Public sector relocation and regional development, Urban Studies, 33(1), 37–48.

Kanbur, R. and Zhang, X. 2005. Fifty years of regional inequality in China: A journey through central planning, reform, and openness. Review of Development Economics, 9(1), 87–106.

Lao, C. 1993. Recognition on the theory and practice of China's economic regionalization. Economic Geography,13(3), 9–13 [in Chinese].

Larkin, K., 2010. Public sector relocations. London: Centre for Cities.

Marshall, J.N., Bradley, D., Hodgson, C., Alderman, N. and Richardson, R. 2005. Relocation, relocation and relocation: Assessing the case for public sector dispersal, Regional Studies, 39(6), 767–787.

Mayer, T., Mayneris, F. and Py, L. 2012. The impact of urban enterprise zones on establishments' location decisions: Evidence from French ZFUs, CEPR Discussion Papers 9074, C.E.P.R. Discussion Papers.

Moretti, E. 2010. Local multipliers, American Economic Review: Papers and Proceedings, 100(2), 373–377.

Neumark, D. and Kolko, J. 2010. Do enterprise zones create jobs? Evidence from California's enterprise zone programme, Journal of Urban Economics, 68(1), 1–19.

Papke, L.E. 1994. Tax policy and urban development: Evidence from the Indiana enterprise zone programme. Journal of Public Economics, 54(1), 37–49.

Peng, Q. 1991. Regional development study: New trends of Chinese geography. Economic Geography, 11(4), 1–6 [in Chinese].

Rosenthal, S.S. and Strange, W.C. 2003. Geography, industrial organization, and agglomeration, Review of Economics and Statistics, 85(2), 377–393.

Von Wachter, T., Song, J. and Manchester, J. 2009. Long-Term Earnings Losses due to Job Separation during the 1982 Recession: An Analysis Using Longitudinal Administrative Data from 1974 to 2004, New York: Columbia University Department of Economics Discussion Paper Series 0708–16.

Walker, R. 2011. Environmental regulation and labour reallocation, American Economic Review: Papers and Proceedings, 101(3), 442–47.

Wu, W., Dong, G. and Zhang, W. 2015. The puzzling heterogeneity in amenity capitalization effects on land markets, Papers in Regional Science, online version available. DOI: 10.1111/pirs.12186.

Zhang, Q. and Zou, H. 2012. Regional inequality in contemporary China, Annals of Economics and Finance, 13(1), 113–137.

Zhang, W. et al. (eds.). 2009. *Theory and Practice of Industrial Development and Planning.* Beijing: Science Press [in Chinese].

Zheng S. and Kahn M.E. 2008. Land and residential property markets in a booming economy: new evidence from Beijing. Journal of Urban Economics, 63,743–757.

Zheng, S. and Kahn, M.E. 2013. China's bullet trains facilitate market integration and mitigate the cost of megacity growth. Proceedings of the National Academy of Sciences, 110(14), E1248–E1253.

Zheng, S., Sun, W., Wu, J. and Kahn, M.E. 2015. The birth of edge cities in China, NBER working paper. No. 21378.

Part III

Planning implications

Infrastructure, location and cities

6 Dynamics of urban networks

Evidence from airport infrastructure expansion

Introduction

City growth in large developing countries like China is fuelled by a desire to gain better access to markets. Infrastructure improvements, in particular transport infrastructure expansions that facilitate labour and capital relocation, offer potentially large agglomeration benefits, and have shaped urban networks. The chapters in Part III present alternative ways for thinking structurally about how planning policies might work to influence urban networks and provide evidence to support the claim that China's transport infrastructure configuration is playing this role. Chapters 6 and 7 follow this train of thought, with a specific focus on air and rail-transit transport infrastructure – a lens through which planners and geographers often evaluate the evolution of urban networks from the perspective of infrastructure improvement. A second way is to abstract from the details of specific urban planning policies, and instead ask about the interactions of market reform, land development and urban vibrancy. This is the approach that is applied in Chapter 8, which looks at land-development patterns and the spatial-temporal distribution of human-activity intensity based on mobile phone big data.

To be clear, this chapter is the most technical one in this book.[1] While some of the discussions and evidence, of both the link between airport-network expansion and dynamics in urban networks, might be of more general interest, some of the detailed techniques and quantitative methods might not. Readers interested in the economic implications of transport infrastructure expansion for accessibility and/ or market potentials (Chapter 7), but not in the specific implications for urban networks, can skip this chapter, which discusses the evolution of China's airport-network structure. Readers with no interest in the empirical intercity evidence can skip to Chapter 8, which focuses specifically on intra-city vibrancy and land development

China's airport development

China was known in the post-Cold-War era for its high-speed economic growth and huge investment in its transport infrastructure system. China increased its land-based transport investment (i.e. highways and railways) from below 2%

of GDP in the early 1990s, to around 6% by the 2000s. However, China's airports were widely considered underdeveloped. In fact, China's airport networks became notorious for their overcrowding, poor connectivity conditions and heavy reliance on a few hub cities (see Zhang, 1998; Wang and Jin, 2007).

Much of the airport underdevelopment has been attributed to the institutional environment in post-war China. After the Second World War, Asian countries such as South Korea, Singapore and Indonesia launched planning policies to reconstruct their civil airline services within an industrialization context. China, in a roughly thirty-year isolation from the rest of the world (1949–1978), committed most of its valuable resources to military industry development. The Civil Aviation Administration of China (CAAC) was founded in 1954 as a branch office under the Military Commission, and was responsible for operating airports and airlines. In line with the Soviet aviation system, the air-transportation system was built primarily to link major Chinese cities serving Government officials and military defence. No airport or airline in place was considered to improve productivity and trade.

From the late 1980s, the Central Government launched waves of market-orientated reforms on the air-transportation system and the Civil Aviation Administration of China (CAAC) was removed from military control (see Table 6.1). The first codified State involvement in developing a national civil-aviation system came with the *Civil Aviation Act* of 1995. This legislation instructed the CAAC to formulate a series of plans for reconstructing airline services and managing airport facilities. Owing to the institutional constraints sustained during the 1990s and the early 2000s, air traffic was not widely used by firms or households. Land-based transport methods, like highways and railways, were the main channels for accessing markets and skilled labour. As industrialization and urbanization proceeded, there was a gradual relaxation of air-ticket price restrictions and an enormous amount of private–public partnership mechanisms established to finance new airport facilities. This triggered local government incentives to build their own airports. However, unlike the decentralized civil aviation system in the United States, the construction and expansion of airport facilities were strictly controlled by the CAAC through airport-allocation plans, under the umbrella of the *Five-Year National Socioeconomic Development Plans*.

This chapter makes a critical assessment of the geography and evolution of the main airport network of China (ANC) during the 1980s and the 2000s – a period when the air-transportation system enjoyed rapid growth (Table 6.2) – as a lens for the city network and urban system. This chapter begins by exploring the appropriate related literature, which views urban networks and the urban system through the airport-network expansion. Indeed, the notion of airport cities implies a sort of bottom-up thinking in terms of the urban system. The 'Methods, data and implementation' section generalizes the complex network approaches to test the statistical properties of the network. The spatio-temporal division of network metric plots and visualization maps (see 'Evolution of China's airport city networks' section) lead to the following set of stylized structures:

Table 6.1 China's civil aviation policy reforms and air-transportation expansion

Period	Milestone events regarding air-transportation development and policy reforms	Airport and airline route expansions
Centrally planned economy era (1949–1980)	In the 1950s–1980, civil aviation system in China was underdeveloped and under the control of the Air Force. In February 1980, the Civil Aviation Administration Bureau of China was reformed to become a State-owned enterprise under the control of the State Council. Six regional offices (in Beijing, Shanghai, Chengdu, Shenyang, Guangzhou, Xi'an) were affiliated to this State-owned enterprise.	The first set of national-level civil airline routes was opened on 1 August 1950, including Tianjin–Hankou–Chongqing, Tianjin–Hankou–Guangzhou; The first intra-province-level civil airline route was opened on 5 December 1951, between Chongqing and Xichang; several international airline routes were opened during the 1950s and 1970s, including Beijing–Paris.
Early stages of the reform era (1980–2000)	On 7 January 1985, the State Council approved the Civil Aviation Administration of China's (CAAC) report on the management reform of the civil aviation system. This policy marked the formal transition of the civil-aviation marketization process. Compared to railway and roadway transportation systems, CAAC was the first transportation organization to carry out the marketization reform under the guidance of the State Council. From 1987, market competition modes were gradually allowed in the civil aviation market, and 6 national-level airline companies were established, including China Eastern Airline, China Southern Airline etc.	The first civil airline route to the USA was established: Beijing–Shanghai–San Francisco–New York. More domestic and international airline routes were opened in this period. The domestic routes covered most major Chinese cities.
Contemporary era (2000–2015)	In 2002, the State Council launched 'the issuance of civil aviation reform programme notice'. This is another restructuring process of civil aviation administration levels and airline companies with two key features: first, CAAC will not directly manage State-owned airline companies; and second, business operations of airports were assigned to the local authorities.	On 26 January 2003, the direct flight route between mainland China and Taiwan was opened. Most provincial capital cities opened their international airline routes. In this period, most Chinese cities gained better access to local airports. By 2015, there were 54 civil aviation companies in China, including 40 State-owned companies and 14 privately owned companies. China has become one of the largest civil-aviation markets in the world.

Data source: Information is based on the Civil Aviation Resource website: http://www.carnoc.com/

Table 6.2 Development of China's air transport

Year	1980	1985	1990	1995	2000	2006
Passenger traffic volume (10^4 persons)	343	747	1,660	5,117	6,722	15,968
Turnover volume of passenger traffic (10^6 person. km)	39.6	116.7	230.5	681.3	970.5	2,370.6
Freight traffic (10^4 ton)	8.9	19.5	37.0	101.1	196.7	306.7
Turnover volume of freight traffic (10^4 ton. km)	14,060	41,512	81,824	222,981	502,683	942,753
Total turnover volume of air traffic (10^6 ton. km)	4.3	12.7	25	71.4	122.5	305.7

Data source: Air traffic data obtained from the Civil Aviation Administration of China and the Civil Aviation Resource website: http://www.carnoc.com/

1   national hub-and-spoke patterns surrounding mega-cities
2   regional broker patterns surrounding Kunming and Urumqi
3   local heterogeneous disparity patterns in isolated geographical cities, such as Lhasa, Lijiang, Huangshan, etc.

The penultimate section considers the implications of this study for understanding the likely impact of planning policies.

Airports and urban networks

Increasingly, air-transportation systems are represented by complex topology networks as an analogy for studying their geographical implications on urban and regional development (O'Kelly, 1998). Recent decades have seen the emergence of airport hubs such as London's Heathrow Airport, in the UK, as a principal means for peripheral regions to connect to the public transportation network. Hence, airport-network expansion is often seen as a policy lever to stimulate city connectivity, in the same way that highway and railway expansion improves hub-and-spoke transport systems. This is a particularly important topic today in China, given that the country has become the world's second-largest air-transportation market country since 2000s (Civil Aviation Administration of China, 2006). There is considerable debate over the institutional and network characteristics of the evolution of the airport system in China since the late 1980s (e.g., Zhang, 1998; Zhang and Chen, 2003; Wang and Jin, 2007; Zhang and Round, 2008; Shaw et al., 2009; Lei and O'Connell, 2011; Wang et al., 2011; Lin, 2012). Evaluations of the evolution of airport networks face several empirical challenges, including accurate identification of spatio-temporal network structures.

Most existing research on assessing the evolution of airport networks are focused on US and European countries. Despite the central role of airport-network topology models, these studies concetrate mainly on the network structure formed by the deregulation of the airline industry, the presence of low-cost carriers, and liberalization and other policy reforms (Chou, 1993; Bowen, 2002; Dobruszkes, 2006; Goetz and Vowles, 2009; Ison et al., 2011). There have been few studies on the evolution and efficiency of airline systems in developing countries (Bowen and Leinbach, 1995; O'Connor, 1995; Bowen, 2000), owing largely to a lack of systemic geo-tagged data on air-transportation infrastructure, a lack of clear understanding regarding airport and airline policy arrangements, and the difficulty of tracking flight routes across cities. This section summarizes and highlights existing research that is relevant to this study.

There is a substantial empirical literature on various aspects of China's airport development, many of which are concerned with reforms of China's airport-development policies; an issue that is not directly related to the focus here. Typically, these studies review the market-orientated policy reform process of China's airline industry (Zhang, 1998; Zhang and Chen, 2003; Yang et al., 2008; Zhang and Round, 2008). More recent work has moved away from macro-policy research towards an explicit comparison of State-owned airline companies with private airline companies on their competitive edge, before and after the airline-consolidation policy reform led by the Civil Aviation Administration of China (CAAC) in the early 2000s. It had also shifted its focus away from hard-to-measure policy consolidation variables to the implications for patterns of a contemporary airport network (Shaw et al., 2009). The results vary across studies. Many studies have found that the three largest Chinese airline companies (Air China, Eastern China Airline and Southern China Airline), created by State-led consolidation reforms, tend to use Beijing, Shanghai and Guangzhou as their distinct national hubs, and small airport cities as peripheral areas to balance the structure of airline market competition (Ma and Timberlake, 2008; Lei and O'Connell, 2011). These findings, however, fail to fully capture the spatial characteristics of airport networks. Indeed, it is very likely that the structure of airline market competition may not overlap with the precise spatial structure of airport networks, whose characteristics of concern, such as the topological characteristics of intercity flight linkages, can be measured.

This is also related to a growing body of complex network literature dealing with the statistical, topological and geometric structures of transport systems, including railways (Sen et al., 2003) and airways (Bagler, 2008; Xu and Harriss, 2008). By showing that the worldwide airport network (WAN) had a scale-free property and a small-world structure, Guimerà et al.(2005) provided the most convincing evidence on the hub-and-spoke airport network structure across the globe. The Airport Network of China (ANC), a network much smaller than the WAN, has recently been analysed for its topology and traffic dynamics (Li and Cai, 2004; Zheng et al., 2009; Wang et al., 2011; Lin, 2012). Its topology was found to have small-world network features and a two-regime power-law degree distribution. These studies almost exclusively examined the static network in one year. In general, the fundamental value of the geo-computation in those papers is to compare the statistical distribution of unweighted network metrics. This provides a test to interpret China's aviation networks using statistics at the national scale.

The following assessment of this chapter makes use of a complex network-mining approach. To conduct the analysis, we generalize the unweighted complex network approach developed in the study of Dong et al. (2009) and other recent studies (Wang et al., 2011, 2014). Recent studies such as Dong et al. (2009) have used basic network metrics such as degree and clustering coefficient as a short path for assessing the evolution process of the unweighted topological network in the ANC. In truth, an unweighted network is a special weighted network where all edge weight is the same. In this chapter, we develop this approach further to test the combination of weighted and unweighted network metrics of intercity air flights. In addition, recent studies are concerned with the global network structure at the national level, while this chapter looks at the distribution of hub-and-spoke airport city systems at different geographical scales, as an important complementary inquiry. In addition to documenting the importance of hub-and-spoke patterns, this chapter presents spatially heterogeneous patterns across cities and regions. Conventional core-periphery urban systems are often imposed top-down by governments, while hub-and-spoke airport cities are defined and delineated objectively in a natural air-traffic manner. This natural manner guarantees that we can see a visualized picture of an airport system and its dynamics. This picture is fractal but may partly reflect the generalization of Zipf's law of city distribution by scale (Zipf, 1949), as documented in the existing literature: on one hand, there are more edged airport cities than large ones; and on the other hand, each airport city has an irregular connectivity pattern.

Methods, data and implementation

Modelling indices

For geographers, interest in the network analysis has a long history (Kansky, 1963). Earlier works such as those by Jin et al. (2004, 2005) used traditional network analysis methods to study the evolution of China's network structure from 1980 to 1998, and suggested a hub-and-spoke network in China. With the development of complex network theory over the past decade, there has been a growing body of literature on the topological structure of urban networks in various transport systems, based on a similar set of modelling indices. Thus, it is suitable to apply complex modelling indices based on network theory to study the airport-network structure. Recent applications in China include those of Shaw et al. (2009), Dong et al. (2009), Wang et al. (2011, 2014), Lin (2012), among others. While there are differential focuses among these papers, it seems that commonly used modelling indices fall into the following types: degree, clustering coefficient, betweeness, disparity coefficient and the distribution functions of network metric correlations. And within each of these types, there are particular equations. This section considers each index in turn and highlights the links to our applications of airport networks in China. The interpretations of these indices should overlap with recent studies on the transport system. Again, readers interested in the spatial implications of airport network structure changes, but not in the specific technical details, can skip to the following section, which considers the empirical evolution of China's airport network structure.

To begin with, for any airport network, it comprises nodes (cities) and edges (airline routes). It is reasonable to assume that two nodes are defined to be neighbours if there is a link between them. In this study, the ANC is abstracted as a connected network graph, where $G = \{(V, E) \mid V$ is a set of nodes and E is a set of edges. $E \subseteq V \times V$; an edge $e = (i, j)$ connects two nodes i and j; $i, j \in V, e \in E\}$. This setting is necessary for the calculation of network metrics such as degree, the shortest path, diameter, clustering coefficient as detailed below.

The starting point for evaluating network connectivity is to introduce three basic and important network metrics: degree, the shortest path, and diameter, as shown below (Haggett and Chorley, 1969; Taaffe et al., 1996; Black, 2003):

The degree of a node v in a network, represented as $d(v)$, is the number of connections or edges the node shares with others (Barabási and Albert, 1999). Let $N(v) = \{u \mid (v, u) \in E$ and $v, u \in V\}$, which is a set of the neighbour nodes of v in the graph G. so $d(v)$ is the size of set $N(v)$.

A path in a network is defined as a sequence of nodes $(n_1, \ldots, n_k)$, so from each of its nodes there is an edge to the next node. The path length is the total length of edges in its node sequence. The shortest path between two nodes, i and j, is a minimal length path between them. The shortest path between two nodes is referred to as a *geodesic*. The distance between i and j, noted as $d (i, j)$, is the length of its shortest path. The diameter of the network is the length of the longest path that quantifies how far apart the farthest two nodes in the graph are.

Knowing basic network metrics is not enough to quantify how the node and its neighbours are clustered to be a complete graph. Thus, we calculate the network clustering coefficient. This index was first introduced by Watts and Strogatz (1998) to determine network structure.

The clustering coefficient of node v, noted as C_v, measures the interconnectivity between the neighbours of node v. It is the ratio of the number of edges between the nodes in the direct neighbourhood to the number of edges that could possibly exist among them. C_v can be defined as:

$$C_v = \frac{2 \left| \bigcup_{i,j \in N(v)} e(i,j) \right|}{d(v)(d(v)-1)} : e(i,j) \in E \qquad (1)$$

where $d (v)$ is the degree of node v and $N (v)$ is the set of the neighbour nodes of v. Based on the clustering coefficient of a node, we can define that of a network, which is the average of the clustering coefficient of all nodes in the graph:

$$\overline{C} = \frac{1}{n} \sum_{i=1}^{n} C_i \qquad (2)$$

Centrality is a core concept for the analysis of social networks, and betweenness is one of the most prominent measures of centrality. It was introduced independently by Freeman (1979), and measures the degree to which a node is in the position of geographical centrality (brokerage) by summing up the fractions of shortest paths between other pairs of vertices that pass through it (Borgatti and Everett, 2006). We define the betweenness centrality in a network as follows: let $\sigma(s,t)$ be the length of the shortest path (sometimes referred as *geodesics*) from s to t, and let $\sigma(s,t \,|\, v)$ be the length of the shortest path from s to t, passing through the vertex v other than s or t. If $s = t$, let $\sigma(s,t) = 1$; and if $v \,\varepsilon\, \{s,t\}$, let $\sigma(s,t \,|\, v) = 0$. The betweenness $c_B(v)$ of a vertex v can be defined as:

$$c_B(v) = \sum_{s,t \in V} \frac{\sigma(s,t \,|\, v)}{\sigma(s,t)}$$

(3)

This measure is interpreted as the extent to which a city has control over pair-wise connections between other cities. In the airport network analysis, a city with high betweenness means that it is on the position of geographical centrality (brokerage) between other pairs of cities. Given massive new airport development in China, it is important to identify which cities are acting as geographic brokers in the ANC, and how their dynamics are over time and space. In addition to betweenness centrality, are there any other centrality measures? Of course, yes. Alternative centrality measures such as closeness and straightness could also capture characteristics of transport networks (Ma and Timberlake, 2008). In this study, we only consider the degree centrality and betweenness centrality because degree and betweenness are the most meaningful centrality metrics to quantify different dimensions of network connectivity by geographers.

For transport networks, weighted quantities such as traffic flow and travel distance have recently been applied to investigate the heterogeneity in the intensity of connectivity – measured by weight of edges – between node pairs. In our study, we define the node intensity S_i as follows:

$$S_v = \sum_{j \subset N(v)} w_{vj}$$

(4)

where S_v is the weighted degree of airport city v; w_{vj} is the weight of edges based on the annual traffic flow between two airport cities; and $N(v)$ is a set of neighbour airport cities to airport city v. In addition to the node intensity, we measure the disparity coefficient for each node:

$$Y(v) = \sum_{j \in N(v)} \left(\frac{w_{vj}}{S_v} \right)^2$$

(5)

where $Y(v)$ is the disparity coefficient for airport city v, which reflects the degree of the heterogeneity with respect to the intensity of airport connections.

Empirical implementation

Our first step is to retrieve data from the statistical reports obtained from the Civil Aviation Administration of China (CAAC). We select the approximate ten-year intervals in order to match national development plans and milestones in reforms of China's civil-aviation development policies (Zhang, 1998; Zhang and Round, 2009). For example, 1983 was the year that Boeing 747 and 737 aircrafts first operated in China, indicating the opening of China's airport markets to Western aircraft companies. 1993 was the year that the CAAC was restructured as a direct Government organization under the State Council, which carried out the market-orientated airline management policy reform.[2] 2006 was the year when China became the second-largest airport market in the world and launched a series of new air-transportation policy reforms. We did not select the air traffic information after 2006, partly because the post-2006 high-speed rail development competed with air traffic and influenced the evolution of transport networks (Yang and Zhang, 2012).The data is obtained from the CAAC, which contains detailed information on major airports with regular airline routes on the Chinese mainland, excluding Hong Kong, Macao and Taiwan.

In the second step, we use the Geographical Information System (GIS) technique to match the precise location of flight-route information between airports, and use the annual flight frequency[3] as the edge weight to construct the complex weighted network graph. For further studies, direct and transfer airline routes can be considered and combined in the dataset. The transfer airline routes can be divided into two parts: from the departure city to the transfer city; and then from the transfer city to the destination city. Duplicated airline routes are displayed as one route but are weighted by annual air-flight frequency.

Figure 6.1 maps the location information of airport network nodes and edges. Each dot represents a city node, and each line represents the airline connections between cities, weighted by the annual air-flight frequency. As can be seen from the maps, China's domestic airport network is characterized by regional inequality, but moves towards a more balanced spatial pattern. In 1983, almost all airport city connections occurred on the east side of the famous 'Heihe-Tengchong Line', a hypothesized 'geographic-demographic disparity line' in China (Hu, 1935). Based on the 1980 population census, 93.5% of Chinese residents lived on the east side of this line; however, this figure became 90.8% in the recent 2000 census. When we turn to look at airport network expansion from 1983 to 2006, the dynamic roles of cities are difficult to discern from a purely visual inspection of the data. Thus, we use the complex network-mining approach to make more precise diagnostics about the dynamics of the network structure and the trend of intercity airport connections. By this approach, we set that the Airport Network of China (ANC) comprises domestic airports of China and airlines connecting them. We also let an indirect binary graph be $G = \{(V, E) \mid$, where V represents a set of nodes, and E is a set of edges. $E \subseteq V \times V$, where an edge $e = (i, j)$ connects two nodes i and j, and $i, j \in V$, $e \in E\}$. In the ANC, the nodes of the network

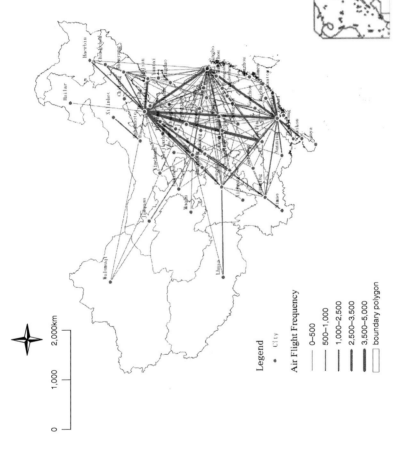

Figure 6.1 Airline frequency flows between airport pairs in China

Source: Wu et al., 2011.

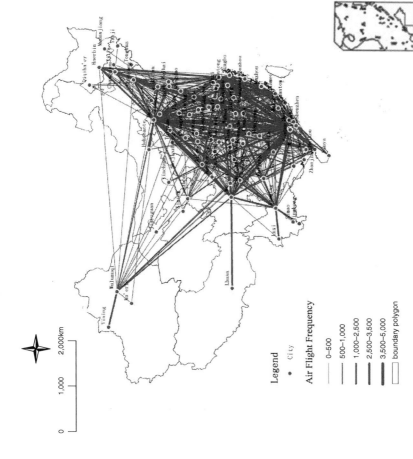

Legend

• City

Air Flight Frequency

— 0–500
— 500–1,000
— 1,000–2,500
— 2,500–3,500
— 3,500–5,000
☐ boundary polygon

0   1,000   2,000km

Figure 6.1 (continued)

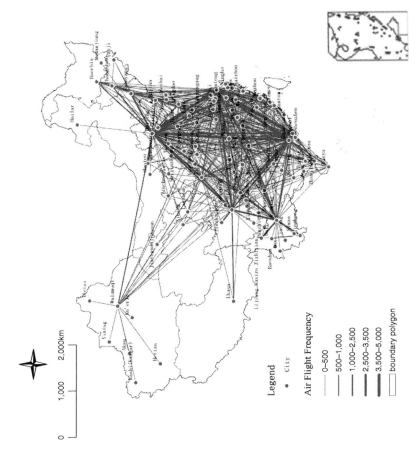

Legend

● City

Air Flight Frequency

— 0–500

— 500–1,000

— 1,000–2,500

— 2,500–3,500

— 3,500–5,000

☐ boundary polygon

Figure 6.1 (continued)

Table 6.3 Basic network characteristics of airport networks in China and other countries and worldwide

Author	Country	Year	Degree ((k))	Path length (L)	Clustering coefficient (C)	Network topology
This study	China	1983	4.47	2.5	0.382	Small world
This study	China	1993	9.95	2.22	0.485	Small world
This study	China	2006	10.11	2.15	0.543	Small world
Bagler (2008)	India	2004	11.52	2.26	0.66	Small world
Guida and Maria (2007)	Italy	1991	12.40	1.98–2.14	0.07–0.1	Small world
Guimerà et al. (2005)	World	2001	13.93	4.4	0.62	Small world

Note: This table shows average values of degree, shortest path length, and clustering coefficient of domestic airport networks of China and other countries as documented in recent literature.

represent the airports, and the edges between the pairs of nodes represent the airlines between the cities.

Evolution of China's airport city networks

Statistical properties of the national airport city network structure

We begin the empirical analysis by looking at the national airport network structure and how it has evolved over the past twenty years. Performing this analysis requires a clear interpretation of network metrics, such as degree, average path length/diameter and the clustering coefficient. Table 6.3 compares the basic network metrics of the ANC with that of other countries, as reported in the existing literature. We find that the average degree, clustering coefficient and path length indicators of the ANC are similar to those of India and Italy, though much smaller than those of the USA. This is not a surprising finding, because the US airport network is much larger than the ANC. In addition, airport networks in developed countries like the USA and Italy are very stable, and remain as mature markets (Xu and Harriss, 2008).

As a second step towards understanding the ANC structure and evolution, we need to know the change in the number of main airport cities, airline routes and the network diameter value over time. The conventional wisdom of these two questions is that: 1) the constant average degree – i.e. the number of airline routes – grows linearly with the number of airport cities; and 2) it is a slowly growing diameter; i.e. as the network grows, the distance between connected cities grows. Perhaps surprisingly, ANC does not follow these two presumptions. As shown by Wu et al. (2011), the ANC's node degree distribution fits the heavy tail distribution law (Clauset et al., 2009) but does not follow the power-law distribution law. This suggests that the ANC is a small-world network but not a typical scale-free network like other airport networks (Guimerà et al., 2005). A credible explanation is that a few large Chinese cities (i.e. Beijing, Shanghai and Guangzhou) connect with almost all other airport nodes in the entire network. As shown by Figure

(a)

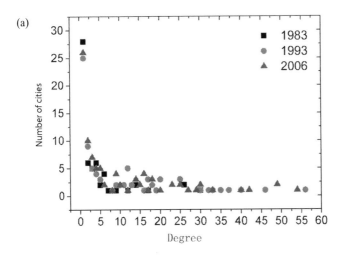

(b)

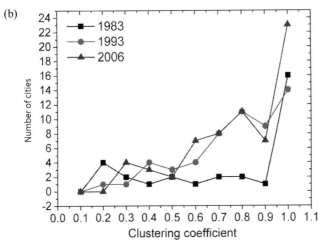

Figure 6.2 (a) Distribution of number of nodes and degree centrality (b) Distribution of
number of nodes and clustering coefficient

Source: Wu et al., 2011.

6.2, there has been a densification trend of intercity airport connections in China.
This is consistent with the decreasing trend of the ANC diameter and the highly
skewed clustering coefficient distribution relative to city node distribution. These
results suggest that intercity airport connections in China are very dense and people can arrive at their destinations with fewer flight transfers.

To illustrate the variations of centrality outcomes in individual airport cities,
we use $\overline{c_B}(k)$ to represent the average betweenness value of airport cities with
the same degree k and plot the distribution as shown in Figure 6.3. The degree

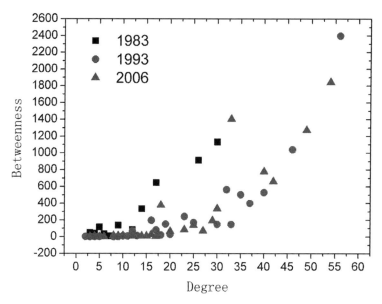

Figure 6.3 Distribution of degree and betweenness centrality
Source: Wu et al., 2011.

betweenness distribution of ANC after scaling following the exponential distribution and the plotted curves can be figured out by the exponential function. This exponential distribution of degree betweenness correlation function suggests that cities with high degree tend to have high betweenness. In light of this tradeoff, our results suggest that the most connected cities are the most central cities in China. This is different from the existing findings in developed countries, where the most connected cities may not necessarily be the most central cities. The underlying reason for this is that the worldwide airport network has multi-community structure, while the ANC is very dense and does not have obvious community structure. The airport cities connecting different communities should have higher value of betweenness. However, all airport cities in China are connected closely and circled around a few hubs, e.g. Beijing, Shanghai and Guangzhou. This provides supportive evidence to the abnormal left-skewed distribution of clustering coefficient given above.

Spatio-temporal breakdown of regional heterogeneity patterns

In this section, we turn to the examination of differences in the evolution of network patterns at the regional scale. As before, we use the degree centrality index to symbolize the connectivity level for each node because it measures the number of airline routes that a city connects with others. We also construct a betweenness centrality to measure the extent to which cities have control over pair-wise connections between other cities in the network.

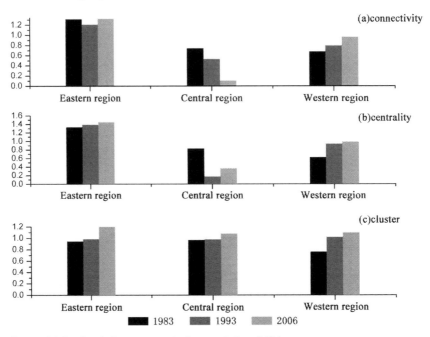

Figure 6.4 Regional airport network characteristics of China

Note: For each region, we computed the standardized change ratio of its average clustering coefficient, betweenness centrality and degree, relative to the national average levels.

Source: Wu et al., 2011.

We begin by assessing the dynamics of the urban network through airport infrastructure expansions across China's three regions (the western, central and eastern regions)[4] from the 1980s to the 2000s. For each region, we computed the standardized change ratio of its average clustering coefficient, betweenness centrality and degree centrality relative to the national average level (see Figure 6.4). We find high values of clustering coefficients across regions, suggesting that Chinese regions have experienced a similar densification over the past twenty years. In terms of degree variations, we find that the flight connectivity of the western region has a much faster growth rate than that of the central and eastern regions. When looking at the betweenness centrality, we find that the western region has experienced the strongest improvement and the eastern region remains at a high and stable level, while the central region has experienced a significant decrease. This heterogeneous pattern may partly reflect the correlation between the uneven population and the economic disparity in China. Also, we know that western and the central regions are less developed than the eastern region.

Spatio-temporal breakdown of network dynamics of airport cities

To reflect geographical implications underlying the above figures, we can identify the most dynamic airport cities in terms of changes in degree connectivity,

Table 6.4 The 35 most dynamic airport cities

		Centrality	
		Better than the average	*Lower than the average*
Connectivity	Better than the average	Beijing; Shanghai; Guangzhou; Chengdu; Xi'an; Shenzhen	Shenyang; Chongqing; Changsha; Wuhan; Xiamen; Qingdao; Hangzhou; Nanjing
	Lower than the average	Kunming; Urumqi	Hefei; Hohhot; Wuxi; Sanya; Tainjin; Guiyang; Fuzhou; Harbin; Guilin; Zhengzhou; Dalian; Ningbo; Haikou; Jinan; Taiyuan; Changchun; Nanchang; Lanzhou; Wenzhou

Source: Wu et al., 2011.

and between-ness centrality relative to national average. Four categories of airport cities are shown in Table 6.4: the first category includes airport cities that have experienced better degree connectivity and betweenness centrality relative to the national average. A potential interpretation for this category is that these airport cities are connected to a large and increasing number of other cities, and have rising centrality roles to play in linking other connections. When looking at specific airport cities that underlie the first category, we find a spatially heterogeneous group of cities, such as Beijing, Shanghai, Guangzhou, Shenzhen, Xi'an and Chengdu, whose network connectivity and centrality roles are strong. This is arguably the First-tier city group in China's urban system that involves either similar demographic characteristics in terms of population size, employment size, and the fraction of education attainment, or similar productivity in terms of GDP, tax revenue and scale of foreign direct investment.

The second category includes airport cities that have improved less in both degree connectivity and betweenness centrality relative to the overall network, such as Hefei, Tianjin, Zhengzhou, and Guiyang. It is likely that these airport cities dispersed their network centrality roles when new airport entrants were added into the network over time. We replicated the exercise, this time for airport cities that have improved more on degree connectivity but less on betweenness centrality relative to the national average. We find that the most dynamic airport cities in this category are: Shenyang, Nanjing, Chongqing, Changsha, Wuhan, Xiamen, Qingdao, and Hangzhou. Airport cities in this category may well be connected with many other cities, however, their centrality roles have been decreasing with the increasing number of new airports and airline routes in China.

Turning to the last category, we focus on airport cities that have higher centrality but lower connectivity relative to national average. Surprisingly, Kunming and Urumqi are the only two cities that meet the criteria in our sample. These two cities are relatively less centralized but have strong tendencies to act as important hubs for airports within their provinces. This is also consistent with the visualized evidence shown in Figure 6.1, where Kunming connected with many nodes such as Zhaotong, Lincang, Simao, and Baoshan etc. with just one degree. These one-degree nodes connect to other nodes in the ANC through Kunming, leading to a high betweeness centrality. Wu et al. (2011) referred to this pattern as the 'Broker' pattern. Urumqi, the capital city of Xinjiang province, is another typical example illustrating the 'Broker' pattern. Airport cities in the province can only be transferred through the Urumqi airport if they want to connect to other places in China. One credible interpretation is the sparsely populated, isolated location and complex landscape constraints in Xinjiang and Yunnan provinces. This is in line with the role of Anchorage as the most central city in Alaska, although it is not the hub of all US cities (Guimerà et al., 2005). In fact, the geographic characterisics of cities like Kunming and Urumqi, and the spatial scale this broker pattern takes place, are certainly supportive of this interpretation.

Disparity patterns in a weighted network

In this section, we use the weighted disparity coefficient to measure the spatial disparity patterns of intercity airport connections; an issue that has not received considerable attention in China. To perform our analysis, we retained the airport cities with at least two degrees of connections in the network, and used the disparity coefficient to measure whether more than 50% of a given airport city's flights are connected with one particular destination city. Panel A of Table 6.5 shows that in 1983, only five airport cities exhibited strong disparity over space: Dalian (88.4% flights from Dalian were connected with Beijing), Qingdao (72.4% flights from Qingdao were connected with Beijing), Nanning (61.5% flights from Nanning were connected with Guangzhou), Lanzhou (52.1% flights from Lanzhou were connected with Beijing) and Xiamen (51.7% flights from Xiamen were connected with Shanghai). Panel B of Table 6.5 suggests that in 1993, there was no clear disparity, aside from the fact that air flights from Huangshan and Hohhot connected mainly with Beijing. In Panel C of Table 6.5, we find that in 2006, four airport cities had significant disparities in connection, specifically: Jiuzhaigou (75.3% flights from Jiuzhaigou were connected with Chengdu), Jinghong (72.3% flights from Jinghong were connected with Kunming), Lhasa (61.5% flights from Lhasa were connected with Chengdu) and Lijiang (53.9% flights from Lijiang were connected with Kunming).

The main finding from here is that most airport cities appeared to have a balanced connectivity. In a small proportion of cases, airport cities tended to be heavily connected with hub cities (e.g. Beijing, Shanghai and Guangzhou). These facts make sense geographically. It is also noteworthy that airport cities with a high disparity coefficient in 1983 and 1993 were not on the list of airport cities with a high disparity coefficient in 2006. This implies that airport cities with a previously high disparity coefficient rebalanced their air-flight connections over time.

Table 6.5 Airport cities with significant disparity coefficients

Panel A: 1983			Panel B: 1993			Panel C: 2006		
Cities	Disparity coefficient	Target destination	Cities	Disparity coefficient	Target destination	Cities	Disparity coefficient	Target destination
Dalian	0.884	Beijing	Hohhot	0.539	Beijing	Jiuzhaigou	0.753	Chengdu
Qingdao	0.724	Beijing	Huang mountain	0.503	Beijing	Jinghong	0.723	Kunming
Nanning	0.615	Guangzhou				Lhasa	0.614	Chengdu
Lanzhou	0.521	Beijing				Lijiang	0.539	Kunming
Xiamen	0.517	Shanghai						

Note. This table reports disparity coefficients for cities if more than 50% of a given city's flights are connected with one particular targeted destination city in the network.

Source: Wu et al., 2011.

These results may also suggest that the tendency for China's airport cities to have (or not have) unbalanced flight destinations is unaffected by the evolution of the global network structure. Although more work is certainly needed, this finding suggests that spatial disparities of airport connections may act as a force to shape urban networks in China.

Implications of this study

The air-traffic network data provide a large amount of significant network metrics for studying dynamics in the urban system. Nowadays, planners and geographers benefit considerably from traffic flow data, with time and locations recorded at different geographical scales. The emerging data from traffic flow and the data intensive GIS computing (Hey et al., 2009) are transforming types of research, from geographical fieldwork analysis into computational virtual modelling approaches (Lazer et al., 2009). In this section, we discuss the profound implications of this study.

There is a growing quantity of literature applying fractal geometry, chaos theory and complexity into geographical analysis (Batty and Longley, 1994; Chen, 2009). The complex network approach adopted in this study, such as long tail distribution, densification mathematical rule and power-law-based statistics can provide useful insights into the evolution of airport city networks and other special networks. The mystery of complex network data-mining is whether it is an effective way to derive a complete understanding of the urban network over time. However, quantitative geographers tend to believe that the diverse and heterogeneous patterns shown by computers are likely to be important complementary evidence for economists and policymakers to understand how cities connect and evolve.

It is important to note that the hub-and-spoke airport city system is biased by not only geopolitical research, but is also driven by disparities in economic growth. Shenzhen is a good example to illustrate this. Geographically speaking, Shenzhen is located close to Guangzhou, one of the three largest mega-cities in China, in terms of physical distance. In 1983, Shenzhen was a small village without access to highways and railways. However, since the Political Leader Deng Xiaoping's famous southern tour visit in 1992, Shenzhen has been transformed into a Special Economic Zone in China (see Wang, 2013, for institutional details), and has experienced dramatic economic growth over the past twenty years. Nowadays, Shenzhen is known as one of four First-tier cities in China, and its airport has played a dominant role in connectivity and centrality in the entire national airport network. The Spearman rank correlation between Shenzhen's GDP growth and air traffic flow growth can be very high and significant. This meets potential economic geography channels at work. The first underlying channel derives from the neoclassical economic theory on increasing returns to scale (Krugman, 1980). Transportation infrastructure investments – like US President Dwight D. Eisenhower's push to pass the *US Federal Highway Act of 1956*, which established the interstate highway system that significantly improved ground-transportation reliability and service – have been a boon for local and regional development. Similarly, intense airport interactions may increase the productivity of cities, whereas sparse air-traffic flows could reflect frictions in the movement of production factors such as labour and capital resources within the core-peripheral urban system.

The second underlying channel is related to the Chinese urban transformation trend as found in the economic literature (Baum-Snow et al., 2015). A key discovery from the literature is that access to transport infrastructure can have significant impacts on shaping the decentralization of Chinese cities and industries. These findings are similar to the interpretation of our presented mapping evidence on the densification law, as reflected by the evolution of airport networks in China. It is likely that changes in airport accessibility could be related to localized economic development as reflected by the improved network centrality. Are there any other socioeconomic factors that can affect a city's airport network? Yes, of course. Testing these mechanisms can provide more direct implications for airport interactions and local economic outcomes. Another concern for our snapshot analysis is that it might not reflect subtle changes when a new airport is created in a particular place. We could, in principle, have sliced the air-traffic flows on a monthly, weekly, or even daily basis, and the observed non-linearity would be even more striking over time. Future works are encouraged to consolidate the economic implications of our study when more useful information is available.

Conclusion

This chapter considered the evolution of China's airport city network in major years between the 1980s and the 2000s. It contributes to the understanding of the likely impact of planning policies in two aspects:

1   National airport hubs, such as Beijing, Shanghai and Guangzhou, have played a central role in the airport network, and the connectivity and centrality of most provincial airport cities need to be strengthened.
2   Empirical evidence suggests that the evolution of China's airport city network meets the densification trend, and such a trend is highly skewed across time and space. This provides supportive evidence for the hierarchical organization of China's urban system (Lin, 2012). However, expansions of air-flight routes and the competition from the land-based transport system may influence the persistence of such disparity patterns.

Abnormally high improvements for a given airport city's network metrics like degree and betweenness centrality can be interpreted as the rising role of that airport city in the whole air-transportation system. One thing to note is that a city's airport network status is likely to be associated with its local economic performance and Government endowments; for example, a cluster of new airline routes and new airports might be more likely to be built in some places than others. However, the evolution of the airport network is compatible with any explanations based on causal effects or Government endowments. It is helpful to explore the dynamics of cities' airport networks when knowing the right mix of causality and Government endowments leading to this pattern. But the fact that airport infrastructure expansion seems to be formed by socioeconomic agglomeration forces points to a natural question about how local economic performance interacts with airport network expansion. To look further into these conjectures, theoretical models and 'casual-sense' estimation will need to be articulated.

Seeing the geographical evolution of urban networks using evidence from airport infrastructure expansions may contribute to recognizing the various sources, including the changing structure of the airport network in the planning system. As outlined in Chapter 5 and in recent studies, there has been an increasing regional inequality trend and profit margins for cities with good airport connectivity, leaving the less-connected cities behind. It is these differences that are leveraged as the spatial manifestation of disparities on economic performance in Chinese urban networks. Planning for new airport allocations and terminal expansion of existing airports in different places seems to have attached more importance to the spatial variations in local economic performance over recent years and in the future. However, this is likely to be a more heterogeneous outcome; that is, planning policies on new airport allocation or terminal expansion of existing airports would be useful to improve local economic performance in certain aspects, and would also be one potential channel for enlarging regional inequality, given that different places may gain differently from airport infrastructure expansion. Thus, even as the airport network continues to expand in Chinese cities to meet the rising demand of speedy transportation, the possible economic importance of such infrastructure planning policies should be clearly predicted and evaluated carefully by scientific analysis rather than by popular narratives and advocates 'baked' by mayors and political houses. The efforts in building new airports and/or expanding existing terminals should aim to help local businesses and improve city connectivity rather than to refurbish the 'face' of the city. But when it comes to the broader implications, it is not clear if it is a more cost-effective way of using airport infrastructure expansion to improve the city connectivity, compared to railway transportation modes. However, at least for a period when the high-speed railway network is not well-developed, the evidence from airport infrastructure expansion can largely reflect the geographical evolution of urban networks and systems in China.

In sum, the general conclusion, with respect to the impact of infrastructure expansions on structures of urban networks and systems, is, therefore, complicated. If the Chinese Government controls for the planning of airport distribution after the economic reform and opening up, and demand for air transportation is increasing, a good design for intercity airport connections would be helpful to improve the airport-allocation strategies and influence the current urban system through infrastructure expansion. But airports are not simple infrastructure and if air transportation is growing – which in the long term is likely to happen – they will not only serve as a way to exchange information and move people and goods, but also a way to improve the spatial agglomeration between cities. As airport cities acquire more flight routes and flight frequencies, planners may want to use the airports to expand the market potential, formulate stronger economic links with other cities and make airport cities more productive. This is not hard to imagine. Improvement in the airport network, in turn, would imply more reachable hinterlands for market integration, and so investment in airport infrastructure is obvious in the absence of high-speed railway competitiveness in the early twenty-first century. Thus, this is a popular place-based, locational infrastructure planning system welcomed by local government, although not all edged airports are profitable in the short term. But with the rapid development of the high-speed railway system since 2008, policymakers tend to favour the economic implications of high-speed rail infrastructure expansion as they have a large traffic capacity. Chapter 7 discusses the impact of the recent rail infrastructure expansion on local market potential.

Notes

1 This chapter draws heavily on SERC Discussion Paper No. 173, London School of Economics and Political Science, co-authored with Zhengbin Dong. His generosity for giving me the permission to recycle our work here is gratefully acknowledged.
2 See original Government policy details in http://www.caac.gov.cn/b1/B6/200612/P020061219658214793463.pdf
3 It is certainly the case that international air-flight information would offer more complete characteristics of airport networks. However, the collection of international air-flight flow data with precise origin-destination location information would be very costly owing to the lack of stable and systemic timetables for different airline companies. Following the convention, this study focuses on the domestic airport network throughout the analysis.
4 Following the convention, researchers and policymakers used to divide mainland China into three regions: Western China includes 12 provinces – Chongqing, Sichuan, Guizhou, Yunnan, Tibet, Shanxi, Gansu, Qinghai, Ningxia, Xinjiang, Guangxi, Inner Mongolia; Central China includes 7 provinces – Shanxi, Anhui, Jiangxi, Henan, Hebei, Hunan, Hubei; Eastern China includes 12 provinces – Beijing, Tianjin, Shanghai, Heilongjiang, Jilin, Liaoning, Shandong, Jiangsu, Zhejiang, Fujian, Guangdong and Hainan.

References

Bagler, G. 2008. Analysis of the airport network of India as a complex weighted network. Physica A, 387, 2972–2980.

Barabási, A.L. and Albert, R. 1999. Emergence of scaling in random networks. Science, 28, 509–512.

Batty M. and Longley P. 1994. *Fractal Cities: A Geometry of Form and Function*. London: Academic Press.

Baum-Snow N., Brandt, L., Henderson, J.V., Turner, M.A. and Zhang, Q. 2015. Roads, railroads and decentralization of Chinese cities. London: LSE Working Paper.

Black, W.R. 2003. *Transportation: A Geographical Analysis*. New York: Guilford Press.

Borgatti, S.P. and Everett, M.G. 2006. A graph-theoretic perspective on centrality. Social Networks, 28, 466–484.

Bowen, J., 2000. Airline hubs in Southeast Asia: National economic development and nodal accessibility. Journal of Transport Geography, 8(1), 25–41.

Bowen, J. 2002. Network change, deregulation and access in the global airline industry. Economic Geography, 78(4), 425–439.

Bowen, J. and Leinbach, T. 1995. The state and liberalization: The airline industry in East Asian NICs. Annals of the Association of American Geographers, 85(3), 468–493.

Brockmann D., Hufnage L. and Geisel T. 2006. The scaling laws of human travel. Nature, 439, 462–465.

Chen Y. 2009. Spatial interaction creates period-doubling bifurcation and chaos of urbanization, Chaos, Solitons & Fractals, 42(3), 1316–1325.

Chou, Y.H. 1993. Airline deregulation and nodal accessibility. Journal of Transport Geography, 1(1), 36–46.

Civil Aviation Authority of China. 2006. *The Eleventh Five-Years Plan of the Chinese Civil Aviation Industry.* Beijing: China Civil Aviation Press.

Clauset, A., Shalizi, C.R. and Newman, M.E.J. 2009. Power-law distributions in empirical data. SIAM Review, 51(4), 661–703.

Dobruszkes, F. 2006. An analysis of European low-cost airlines and their networks. Journal of Transport Geography, 14(4), 249–264.

Dong, Z., Wu, W., Ma, X., Xie, K. and Jin, F. 2009. Mining the structure and evolution of the airport network of China over the past twenty years, in Proceedings of 5th International Conference on Advanced Data Mining and Applications (ADMA 2009). Berlin, Heidelberg: Springer.

Freeman, L.C. 1979. Centrality in social networks: conceptual clarification. Social Networks, 1, 215–239.

Goetz, A.R. and Vowles, T.M. 2009. The good, the bad, and the ugly: 30 years of US airline deregulation. Journal of Transport Geography, 17(4), 251–263.

Guida, M. and Maria, F. 2007. Topology of the Italian airport network: A scale-free small-world network with a fractal structure? Chaos, Solitons Fractals, 31, 527–536.

Guimerà, R., Mossa, S. and Turtschi, A. 2005. The worldwide air transportation network: Anomalous centrality, community structure, and cities' global roles. Proceedings of the National Academy of Sciences of the United States of America, 102, 7794–7799.

Haggett, P. and Chorley, R.J. 1969. *Network Analysis in Geography.* London: Edward Arnold.

Hey T., Tansley S. and Tolle K. 2009. *The Fourth Paradigm: Data Intensive Scientific Discovery.* Redmond, Washington: Microsoft Research.

Hu, H.Y. 1935. The distribution of population in China. Journal of Geographical Society, 2, 33–74 [in Chinese].

Ison, S., Francis, G., Humphreys, I. and Page, R. 2011. UK regional airport commercialization and privatization: 25 years on. Journal of Transport Geography 19(6), 1341–1349.

Jin, F.J., Sun, W. and Shaw, S-L. 2005. China's airlines reorganization and its effects on network structure. Progress in Geography, 24(2), 59–68 [in Chinese].

Jin, F.J., Wang, F.H. and Liu, Y. 2004. Geographic patterns of air passenger transport in China 1980–1998, imprints of economic growth, regional inequality, and network development. The Professional Geographer, 56(4), 471–487.

Kansky, K.J. 1963. Structure of Transportation Networks. Department of Geography Research Paper No. 84, University of Chicago, USA.

Kohl, J.G., 1842. *Transportation and Settlement of People and their Dependence on Surface Terrain (Der Verkehr und die Ansiedlungen der Menschen in ihrer Abhängigkeit von der Gestalt der Erdoberfläche:* in German). London: Chapman and Hall.

Krugman, P. 1980. Scale economies, product differentiation, and the pattern of trade. The American Economic Review, 70(5), 950–959.

Lazer, D., Pentland, A., Adamic, L., Aral, S., Barabási, A.-L., Brewer, D., Christakis, N., Contractor, N., Fowler, J., Gutmann, M., Jebara, T., King, G., Macy, M., Roy, D., and Van Alstyne, M. 2009. Computation social science, Science, 323, 721–724.

Lei, Z. and O'Connell, J.F. 2011. The evolving landscape of Chinese aviation policies and impact of a deregulating environment on Chinese carriers. Journal of Transport Geography, 19(4), 829–839.

Li, W. and Cai, X. 2004. Statistical analysis of airport network of China. Physical Review E, 69, 046106.

Lin, J. (2012). Network analysis of China's aviation system, statistical and spatial structure. Journal of Transport Geography, 22, 109–117.

Ma, X. and Timberlake, M. 2008. Identifying China's leading world city: A network approach. GeoJournal, 71 (1), 19–35.

O'Connor, K., 1995. Airport development in Southeast Asia. Journal of Transport Geography, 3 (4), 269–279.

O'Kelly, M. 1998. A geographer's analysis of hub-and-spoke networks. Journal of Transport Geography, 6(3), 171–185.

Sen, P., Dasgupta, S. and Chatterjee, A. 2003. Small-world properties of the Indian railway network. Physical Review E, 67, 036106.

Shaw, S-L., Lu, F., Chen, J. and Zhou, CH. 2009. China's airline consolidation and its effects on domestic airline networks and competition. Journal of Transport Geography, 17(4), 293–305.

Sui D. and Goodchild M. 2011. The convergence of GIS and social media: challenges for GIScience, International Journal of Geographical Information Science, 25(11), 1737–1748.

Taaffe, E., Gauthuer, H. and O'Kelly, M. 1996. *Geography of Transportation,* Upper Saddle River, NJ: Prentice- Hall.

Wang, J. 2013. The economic impact of Special Economic Zones: Evidence from Chinese municipalities. Journal of Development Economics, 101, 133–147.

Wang, J. and Jin, F.J. 2007. China's air passenger transport: an analysis of recent trends. Eurasian Geography and Economics, 48 (4), 469–480.

Wang, J., Mo, H. and Wang, F. 2014. Evolution of air transport network of China 1930–2012. Journal of Transport Geography, 40, 145–158.

Wang, J., Mo, H.H., Wang, F.H. and Jin, J.F. 2011. Exploring the network structure and nodal centrality of China's air transport network: A complex network approach. Journal of Transport Geography, 19(4), 712–721.

Watts, D.J. and Strogatz, S.H. 1998. Collective dynamics of "small-world" network. Nature, 393, 440–442.

Wu, W., Dong, Z., Zhang, W., Jin, F., Ma, X. and Xie, K. 2011. Spatio-temporal evolution of the China's inter-urban organization network structure, Acta Geographica Sinica, 66(4),435-445 [in Chinese].

Xu, Z. and Harriss, R. 2008. Exploring the structure of the US intercity passenger air transportation network: A weighted complex network approach. GeoJournal, 73, 87–102.

Yang, H. and Zhang, A. 2012. Effects of high-speed rail and air transport competition on prices, profits and welfare. Transportation Research Part B: Methodological, 46(10), 1322–1333.

Yang, X., Tok, S.K. and Su, F. 2008. The privatization and commercialization of China's airports. Journal of Air Transport Management, 14, 243–251.

Zhang, A., 1998. Industrial reform and air transport development in China. Journal of Air Transport Management, 4(3), 155–164.

Zhang, A. and Chen, H. 2003. Evolution of China's air transport development and policy towards international liberalization. Transportation Journal, 42(3), 31–49.

Zhang, A. and Round, D. 2008. China's airline deregulation since 1997 and the driving forces behind the 2002 airline consolidations. Journal of Air Transport Management, 14(3), 130–142.

Zheng, Y. and Zhou, X. 2011. *Computing with Spatial Trajectories,* Berlin: Springer.

Zipf, G.K. 1949. *Human Behavior and the Principles of Least Effort*, Cambridge, MA: Addison Wesley.

7 Geographical evolution of railway network development

Introduction

China's growth is uneven. Political leaders and mayors in China are concerned with tackling the problems of unsustainable and uneven growth through planning policies and place-based, locational investments. Based on Chapter 6, this chapter argues that infrastructure planning policies in China, as in other developing countries, have focused on using Government investment to improve local economic performance. As discussed in Chapter 6, in the past two decades there has been significant regional inequality across airport cities, and infrastructure improvements continue to serve as a potential policy intervention in driving the configuration of the core-periphery urban system. This implies that those planning policies have been able to influence market forces and can improve local economic performance continuously.

This chapter draws on previous chapters, supplemented with findings of rail-transit infrastructure improvement, to quantify the impact of place-based, locational infrastructure planning programmes, particularly those on city connections. By doing so, a market potential function is used to show that transport investments indeed reshape the location's accessibility (Harris, 1954; Gibbons et al., 2012). This evidence underpins the focus of this book: the need to understand the rationale of place-based locational planning policies in China that drive uneven growth, and the channels through which planning policies affect the spatial economic disparities.

Rail system upgrading and expansion have affected the transformation of cities (Cervero and Bernick, 1996; Banister and Berechman, 2000). Japan's Shinkansen project, as the world's first high-speed railway (HSR) connecting Tokyo and Osaka, opened in 1964. Since then, HSR investment has been a boon for local and regional development in Korea, France, Germany and Spain. There are considerable debates on its effectiveness in spurring urban growth. Opponents argued that HSR projects were costly, which might outweigh the economic benefits. Indeed, HSRs are expensive infrastructure to build and run, and there have been unsuccessful cases. Despite the abundance of empirical studies on the relationship between HSR investment and aggregated growth in developed countries, however, there has been relatively little evidence of whether the cost reduction on transportation can reinforce accessibility, or whether it serves to diffuse the traffic flow between core and peripheral regions in large developing countries.

China offers an ideal textbook scenario for tracking these questions. Since 1997, the Chinese Government has spent large amount of money on increasing railway speed and improving HSR infrastructure, as a policy to boost the connectivity between cities and regions. By 2014, China had been the world's largest railway market, with about 19,369.8 kilometres of HSR lines, which carried a large proportion of the world's total HSR passengers. Recent studies suggest that rail-transit network expansion has allowed for falling trade costs and the diffusion of economic activities by saving commuting time (Banerjee et al., 2012; Baum-Snow et al., 2015; Faber, 2014). The evolution of railways may therefore improve economic integration, whereas more efficient use of the transit system can acquire agglomeration benefits over space. This chapter investigates the extent to which railway improvements contribute to the connections between core and peripheral regions, and identifies the evolution of accessibility patterns.

China's railway speed-up and HSR development

China was known during the Second World War for its large population and poor accessibility to railways. By the foundation of the People's Republic of China in 1949, China had only around 23,000 kilometres of railways over space, and these railroads were constructed for national defence and shipping raw industrial materials during the Second World War. Between the 1990s and the 2000s, however, China's railroad constructions were widely considered to be well-funded, with operating rail-transit lines increased to around 66,000 kilometres, connecting all major cities and counties along the railway network. Table 7.1 provides a summary of the implications of railway infrastructure expansion on regional development.

Before the mid-1990s, the rapid economic development in China intensified the 'bottleneck' effect derived from the relationship between the underdeveloped railway system and the growing travel demand between cities. To address this bottleneck concern, it was important to strengthen the railway system. As a result, the Ministry of Railways of China implemented six national strategic planning programmes on railway speed-ups between 1997 and 2007, aimed at increasing average train speed and rail track line capacities (see Table 7.2). These speed-up programmes raised the speed of some main railway lines from 80–100 km/h to 200–250 km/h, decreased travelling times between cities and optimized the railway resource allocation capacity within and between different regions. Such 'time convergence' effect has speeded up the logistics and the flow of people so that network resource allocation has become more rapid and convenient. According to the Ministry of Railways, it was predicted that after the sixth speed-up in 2007,

Table 7.1 Implications of railway infrastructure expansion for regional development

Policy period	Railway infrastructure expansion	Implications for regional development
1949–1959	Built and recovered several important railway lines in the inland areas, including the opening of Cheng–Yu railway line in 1952, the Bao–Cheng railway line in 1958 and other lines.	Built the railway lines to link old industrial cities (Chengdu, Chongqing, Baoji) in the mountainous western region for the first time in history.
1960–1979	Built additional railway lines in the inland areas, including the opening of Cheng–Kun railway line, the Jiao–Liu railway line, Xiang–Yu railway line, Han–Dan railway line, Lanzhou–Urumqi and Guiyang–Chongqing lines.	For the purpose of promoting the industrial productivity and economic activity in inland cities, further expanded the railway network between core industrial cities (including Chengdu, Chongqing, Kunming, Liuzhou, Jiaozuo, Lanzhou, Urumqi, Hankou, Xiangfan and among others) in the inland areas.
1980–1990	Built new railway lines in both of inland areas and coastal regions, with a specific focus on developing railway transportation capacities in mining towns and water ports.	Proposed railway infrastructure expansion strategy towards linking inland areas to the eastern region. Key projects include Datong–Qinhuangdao line, Hengyang–Guangzhou line, and some other lines in the eastern region.
1991–1999	Built Jing-jiu railway line, Guang–Shen semi-high-speed railway line; began to upgrade the speeds of important passenger railway lines.	Expanded the railway infrastructure systems for linking inland areas to coastal regions.
2000–2004	State Council approved the 'national medium-long term railway network planning' in January 2004, with a specific focus on optimizing the national railway network of 'eight horizontal direction railway lines+ eight vertical direction railway lines'.	The railway speed upgrading strategy applied mainly to 'horizontal direction railway lines', such as Longhai railway line, Zhe-gan railway line, to reduce the commuting costs between inland areas and coastal regions.
2005–2010	Opened the Tibet–Qinghai railway line in 2006; the first railway line linking Tibet to the rest of the country. Built high-speed railway lines in core metropolitan regions such as the Beijing–Tianjin, Wuhan–Guangzhou high-speed railway lines and others.	Promoted the development of Qinghai, Tibet areas through the opening of Qinghai–Tibet railway line, and this was consistent with the implementation of the western development planning policy. Promoted the rational adjustment of industrial structures, urbanization and industrialization and modernization process in core metropolitan regions, to achieve the pioneering regional development strategy in the eastern region.
2011–2015	Further expanded the railway networks in the whole country. Key projects include the opening of the Xiamen–Shenzhen coastal railway line in 2013, and the Hainan Island high-speed railway line in 2015, as well as the construction of railway lines in the north-eastern, central and western regions.	Promoted the railway connectivity between cities in four regions: western region, north-eastern region, eastern region, and central region.

Table 7.2 Basic facts of passenger railway speed-ups in China (1997–2007)

No.	Time	Key features and changes
1st	1 April 1997	40 pairs of express train and 64 sunset-departure and sunrise-arrival trains with max speed of 140 km/h were launched.
2nd	1 October 1998	The max speed was increased to 140–160 km/h.
3rd	21 October 2000	Longhai Railway, Lanxin Railway, Beijing–Kowloon Railway and Zhejiang–Jiangxi Railway were speeded up.
4th	21 November 2001	New train diagrams and a nationwide online booking system were put into practice.
5th	18 April 2004	19 pairs of Z-series trains, some at a speed of up to 200 km/h, were initiated between several major cities.
6th	18 April 2007	Railway lines at a speed of 120 km/h and above extended from the original 16,000 km to 22,000 km. The number of passenger and freight trains reached 1,312.5 pairs and 16,656 pairs; an increase of 140.5 pairs and 1,316 pairs, respectively. It was estimated that passenger capacity would be increased by 18% thereafter.

Source: Jin and Wu, 2007

the travel time between major cities would be reduced down by 20–30% and the railway transportation capacity of passengers and goods would be increased by over 18% and 12%, respectively. Table 7.2 summarizes the main characteristics and changes in the six passenger railway speed-ups.

In addition to the railway speed-up programmes, the development of high-speed railways (HSR) at the national scale began with the announcement of the *Mid-Long Term Railway Network Plan* by the State Council in 2005, with the goal of expanding the high-speed railroad length to 100,000 kilometres by the end of 2020. This plan was further revised by the State Council in 2008, to construct 120,000 kilometres of HSR lines by the end of 2020, with a budget of around RMB4,000 billion yuan (State Council, 2008). China's HSR network is structured by three components: upgraded existing rail lines that can run high-speed trains; intercity HSR lines (including the Maglev High-Speed Line) linking large metropolitan areas; and some special passenger dedicated HSR lines (PDLs). The average speed for these HSR trains varies from 200 to 350 km/h, but these lines belong to the HSR system based on global standards. As stated in the Plan, the typical route arrangement for constructing HSR lines is based on the distribution of population demand, natural resources, national defence and environmental protection, as well as the economic geography of each province and region. In terms of financing, the State Government pays over half of the HSR construction cost, while the destination City Governments are expected to pay the remainder, together with some State-owned organizations.[1] Today, China is the world's largest HSR market. By the end of 2012, there were approximately 17,000 kilometres of HSR lines in operation, carrying trains with an average speed of over 200 km/h. Together, these railway speed-up programmes and the rapid expansion of the HSR network mean that there was reduced travel time between cities and substantial changes in the geographical patterns of railroad accessibility in China, on which the following sections carry out some empirical evaluations.

Implications of railway speed-ups on regional development

After six passenger railway speed-ups, there are currently 1,312.5 pairs and 16,656 pairs of systematic passenger and freight trains, respectively. Lines at a speed of 120 km/h and above have reached 22,000 kilometres in length. The speed-ups have covered most provinces and municipalities, marking significant improvements in China's passenger railway speed-ups. These speed-up programmes have concentrated mostly between the core cities and metropolitan areas. For example, 212 pairs of intercity high-speed trains at over 200 km/h have been concentrated within and between: the Circum-Bohai-Sea Metropolitan Region centring on Beijing and Tianjin; the Yangtze River Delta Metropolitan Region centring on Shanghai, Nanjing and Hangzhou; the Pearl River Delta Metropolitan Region, centring on Guangzhou and Shenzhen; the Shandong Peninsula Metropolitan Region centring on Jinan-Qingdao; and the Guanzhong Metropolitan Region centring on Xi'an-Baoji.

These transport improvements have contributed to regional development by promoting the transformation of industrial structures, resource allocation, and urban exchanges in the surrounding areas along main railways. This section describes the potential implications of railway speed-up planning programmes on regional development. The following section applies the market potential function to quantify the evolution of local accessibility derived from transport improvements.

Railway speed-ups are conducive to the formation of metropolitan areas

After six railway speed-ups in recent years, China's railway-based urban network has been strengthened centring on the Circum-Bohai-Sea Metropolitan Region (hub city: Beijing), the Yangtze River Delta Metropolitan Region (hub city: Shanghai) and Pthe earl River Delta Metropolitan Region (hub city: Guangzhou). Table 7.3 summarizes the economy and railway traffic development of several major hub cities in China. In addition, railway speed-ups have shortened travel time between cities in the Central Plains Metropolitan Region centring on Zhengzhou, Wuhan and Changsha, and the North-eastern Metropolitan Region centring on Shenyang, Dalian and Changchun.

These targeted railway speed-up planning interventions have significantly upgraded railway capacities and strengthened urban exchanges. The improved transport accessibility helps to promote the formation of hub cities in the railway network through the agglomeration of industries and travel flows. If Second-tier cities can be connected closely to hub cities through high-speed railways, the list of locations that has access to hub cities can be improved. To strengthen the socioeconomic implications of railway speed-up planning programmes, the Ministry of Railways of China has implemented intensive direct intercity trains within and between large metropolitan areas. These dense intercity express train services have

Table 7.3 Summary of major transport hub cities' economy and railway traffic development in China

City	GDP (hundred million Yuan)	GDP per capita (Yuan)	Passenger capacity (ten thousand people)	Passenger turnover (ten thousand people km)	Freight capacity (ten thousand ton)	Freight turnover (ten thousand ton km)
Beijing	7,720.31	57,431	4,351.8	619,631	2,264	2,409,620
Tianjin	4,337.74	47,972	1,498.0	578,200	4,519	2,280,000
Shanghai	10,296.17	65,473	3,391.0	381,000	6,400	1,180,000
Guangzhou	5,115.75	32,142	5,285.0	2,281,594	4,852	2,284,834
Zhengzhou	1,670.00	25,798	1,570.0	591,180	2,330	1,673,526
Wuhan	2,238.00	25,311	2,611.6	1755000	5824	4330000
Chengdu	2,371.01	20,016	2,896.0	884000	4565	3835800

Data source: *China City Statistical Yearbook*, 2006; *Railway Statistical Bulletin 2006.*

Source: Jin and Wu, 2007.

been initiated to accelerate human mobility, information spread, capital flow and resource movement through the reduction of travel time. In terms of planning implications, these rail transit speed up programmes are conducive to the formation and improvement of large metropolises. The rationale behind this is that, individuals can commute easily from Second-tier cities to hub cities, and therefore people can enjoy the benefits of access to hub cities without paying much to live in the hub cities.

Railway speed-ups promote upgrading and restructuring of regional industry

Railway speed-ups show not only 'time' and 'speed' values, but also stimulate the transformation of productivity layout and industrial structure from the perspective of economic geography research. On the basis of the locational theories, improved rail access can also enlarge the market potentials of cities that have saved a great deal of travel time through the railway network. Railway speed-ups have also lowered transportation cost per hour, which can help labour-intensive manufacturing industries relocate to Second-tier cities with lower labour and land costs.

Railway speed-ups are conductive to coordinated development of eastern, middle and western regions

The railway improvement has played a role in optimizing the resource allocation, such as transporting agricultural and industrial raw materials between regions. For example, as China's important heavy-industry base and major grain-producing region, the north-eastern region transports most of its agricultural and industrial raw materials by means of the railway system. After the implementation of speed-up planning programmes, it has become more convenient for the north-eastern region to interact with other regions in order to improve the efficiency of resource allocation.

In terms of intercity connections, trains have experienced a significant upgrade of travel speed after these railway speed-up planning programmes. The sixth speed-up planning programme has the most significant effect, leading to an average travel-time reduction of 20–30% between major cities (Jin and Wu, 2007). For example, after the speed-up programmes, the travel time from Beijing to major eastern and central cities had been greatly reduced. In addition to Beijing, it is also clear to see substantial travel-time reductions from Shanghai to other cities such as Shanghai-Nanchang and Shanghai-Changsha, where travel time had been reduced by more than 50%. The travel-time reductions have stimulated the reallocation of labour and human capital resources between cities, and thus promoted urban growth and regional integration. Railway speed-ups have also gradually improved the traffic 'bottleneck' from the central and western regions to the coastal region. In total, 52 pairs of long-distance passenger trains were added during the sixth speed-up programme, with 29 pairs of them being allocated to connect to the western region. For example, express trains have reduced the travel time from Beijing and Shanghai to Urumqi by 3–5 hours. The key focus of these railway speed-up planning programmes is to allocate speedy trains to link economically underdeveloped areas such as Jinggangshan to developed areas such as Beijing and Shanghai.

Implications for local accessibility

This section first highlights the relevant literature dealing with the accessibility impacts of rail-network expansion, and then explores the implications of recent HSR development on the evolution of local accessibility patterns in China.

International experience

Although methodological designs vary across studies, existing studies tend to find mixed effects of railways on local and regional development. By evaluating land-based access on roads and railways, and airport networks among 42 major European cities, Bruinsma and Rietveld (1993) documented the relationship between accessibility dynamics and urban growth. Gutiérrez et al. (1996) applied the contour accessibility measures based on daily travel buffers to evaluate the impact of a high-speed link along the Madrid–Barcelona–French border. Recent studies have used not only the macro-location accessibility approach, based on static time, distance or contour measures, but have also used the explicit modelling of accessibility indicators (Gutiérrez et al., 1996; Handy and Niemeier, 1997; Gutiérrez, 2001; Geurs and Van Wee, 2004; Lopez et al., 2008; Vandenbulcke et al., 2009). For example, Sánchez-Mateos and Givoni (2009) evaluated the accessibility effects of the HSR line in England, with a specific focus on analysing whether cities that were directly linked to that line could gain more benefits than comparable areas without HSR linkage. Chang and Lee (2008) examined the impacts of Seoul's HSR lines on accessibility improvements for key metropolitan areas in South Korea. Levinson (2012) summarized and criticized the HSR planning effects on location accessibility in the USA. By applying a market potential function, Donaldson and Hornbeck (2016) investigated the effects of railroad improvements on agricultural land value in the USA. Yet, the growing body of literature on empirical evaluations of transport infrastructure have so far paid little attention to using the market potential function in dealing with the general equilibrium impacts of transport improvements on accessibility dynamics in a large developing country (Hou and Li, 2011; Banerjee et al., 2012; Zheng and Kahn, 2013).

Geography of HSR network expansion

The number of train stations and transit lines has experienced tremendous growth. By 2014, the number of HSR train stations rose up to 426 in 2014, and the spatial coverage of HSR networks had a sharp increase, with 26 provinces (81.25% of the total) being allocated HSR lines.

The spatial distribution of HSR network expansions is not even (Figure 7.1). Provinces with fewer rail improvements are located mostly on the periphery of the network, such as Tibet and Hainan (Figure 7.2). Perhaps more surprisingly, there is a sharp difference between provinces that experienced a high transit length change rate and those that had a high station number change rate, between 2006 and 2014 (Figure 7.2). Provinces in the western region, such as Xinjiang, Qinghai and Inner Mongolia, have improved a lot on the mileage expansion of high-speed railways, whereas Shanghai, Zhejiang, Sichuan, and Fujian have experienced large station number changes with continued network expansion.

Table 7.4 reports the top 20 cities with longest transit mileage and HSR mileage by 2014, as well as relative changes of transit mileage between 2006 and 2014. Hulunbuir city and Chongqing were placed at the top in 2014, in terms of total transit mileage and total HSR mileage, owing largely to their large geographic boundaries. In addition to conventional hub cities, some cities in rapidly developing peripheral regions, such as Kaili, Zhaoqing, Shangrao, Nanping and Chuzhou, also appear in the top-ranked HSR cities. Generally, top-20 cities have occupied a large proportion of the total HSR mileage, and more than half of them are clustered around the emerging metropolitan areas, such as the Greater Wuhan Area, Zhengzhou Metropolitan Area and the Chengdu–Chongqing Metropolitan Regions. In terms of relative changes in transit mileage, cities in heavy mountainous areas such as Guizhou, Fujian, Chongqing and Guangxi provinces improved their railways between 2006 and 2014. These descriptive results suggest that the location of a city within the entire HSR network plays a key role in determining its potential accessibility benefits gained from HSR network expansion. This pattern is also consistent with the pre-planned route-placement policies for stimulating balanced links between developed regions and depressed and/or mountainous regions (Chen, 2012).

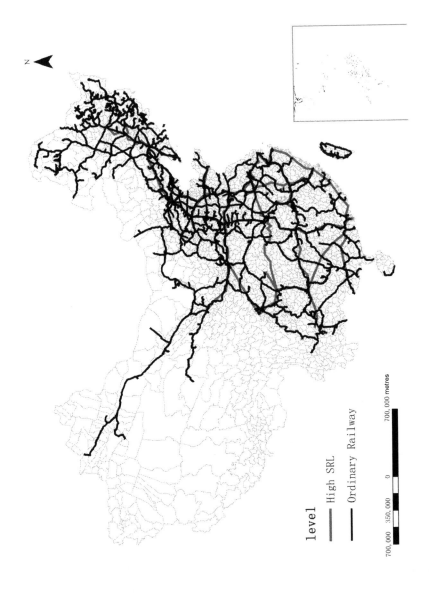

level

High SRL

Ordinary Railway

700,000   350,000   0   700,000 metres

Figure 7.1 Spatial distribution of main railway network by 2014 in China

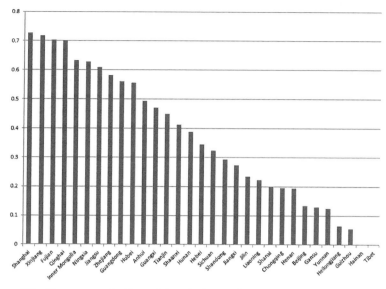

Figure 7.2a Change rate of rail transit lengths by province

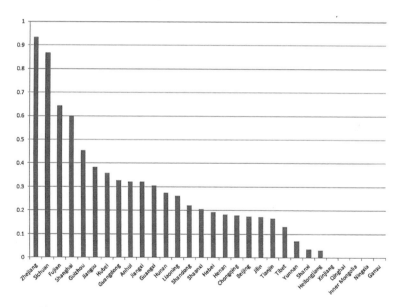

Figure 7.2b Change rate of rail transit station numbers by province

Accessibility patterns and network centralization

On the basis of the market potential function (Harris, 1954), a railway accessibility index can be defined to reflect aggregated impacts of railway connections on local market potentials. In essence, it captures a county's market potentials,

Table 7.4 Top-20 prefecture cities with absolute value and relative changes of lengths of HSR lines in China

Rank	city	2014 Total railway city length (m)	Total railway city	2014 HSR length (m)	HSR length/total railway length ratio	city	Change rate 2006–2014
1	Hulun Buir	2,179,844	Chongqing	343,704.3	0.0207	Wenzhou	4.68
2	Yanji	1,563,256	Kaili City	315,537.9	0.0190	Zhaoqing	3.14
3	Harbin	1,358,729	Shangrao	311,173.4	0.0188	Ningde	2.95
4	Mudanjiang	1,067,965	Zhaoqing	239138.4	0.0144	Chongqing	2.12
5	Yichun	1,061,776	Shijiazhuang	232,415.2	0.0140	Fuzhou	1.92
6	Heihe	888,573.5	Nanping	223,028.6	0.0135	Chaozhou	1.85
7	Beijing	849,792.6	Chuzhou	218,730.6	0.0132	Shaoyang	1.62
8	Xinzhou	840,858.8	Xi'an	202,891.7	0.0122	Shenzhen	1.61
9	Jilin	818,961.5	Hefei	197,125.2	0.0119	Lu'an	1.53
10	Tangshan	776,872.6	Hanzhoung	196,797.2	0.0119	Kaili	1.47
11	Chengde	770,435.9	Changchun	193,985.1	0.0117	Guigang	1.44
12	Baoding	746,776.2	Enshi City	191,508.8	0.0116	Hezhou	1.40
13	Nanping	726,829.8	Mianyang	190,261.5	0.0115	Shangrao	1.37
14	Tongliao	681,292.3	Zhengzhou	185,181.6	0.0112	Tongren	1.34
15	Shijiazhuang	667,250.6	Wuhan	180,646.6	0.0109	Xiamen	1.33
16	Kunming	661,580.5	Chengde	179,872.3	0.0109	Suzhou	1.27
17	Baishan	644,352.5	Shangqiu	179,770.3	0.0108	Ningbo	1.25
18	Jiuquan	640,880.3	Chaoyang	178,100.7	0.0107	Anshun	1.14
19	Huaihua	634,706.7	Yichang	177,904.9	0.0107	Dezhou	1.11
20	Chaoyang	630,843.5	Fuzhou	177,131.6	0.0107	Yichang	1.05

which are connected to other areas by transportation. Its equation can be written as follows:

$$A_{it} = \sum_i P_j \Omega_{ijt}^{-\theta}$$

(1)

where A_{it} is the accessibility index in place i, in year t by railway transportation mode, and Ω_{ijt} is the transportation cost along the minimum travel time route along the rail-transit network from place i to place j in year t. The origin-destination travel-time matrix is constructed based on traffic speed and least-length routes between county pairs. P_j is the population in place j. The parameter θ is the cost-distance spatial decay parameter from the origin i to the destination j. Following the existing literature, the inverse cost-weighting scheme ($\theta=1$) is applied. When one is interpreting the results, it is important to note that over one-third of travel time is likely to be spent elsewhere rather than on the railways. Actually, a lot of time is spent waiting for trains and buses to come, and en route to the stations. Thus, using the shortest path to measure the spatial decay (or more correctly speaking, the time-distance decay) may miss parts of the total travel time in the railway system. Despite these data limitations, it is still useful to formulate the accessibility calculation as a proxy for identifying local market potentials.

Figure 7.3 shows the distribution of the railway accessibility growth rate (in normalized value) across Chinese counties. Areas that are close to the railway lines have gained higher accessibility improvements than areas that are further away from railway lines. In particular, areas with high accessibility improvements are concentrated mainly along the Beijing–Guangzhou main railway line and the Shanghai–Chengdu main railway line. This is consistent with recent findings about the traditional *T*-type regional development model centring on the Beijing, Shanghai and Guangzhou metropolitan regions, proposed by Dadao Lu, an academician at the Chinese Academy of Science. In addition, areas in the south-eastern coastal region and Yunan–Guizhou provinces have also experienced substantial accessibility improvements as a result of recent railway expansion.

The descriptive findings from this figure also suggest that not all counties have benefited equally from rail-network expansion. There are two possible channels which may lead to a slowdown in accessibility improvements in some peripheral regions relative to core regions. First, rail-network expansions may not provide local train services in all affected counties along the transit lines. That is to say, the railway speed-up process and ongoing HSR network expansions could have squeezed out conventional train frequencies in remote locations with sparsely distributed populations, such as the Hanzhong region in the southern Shanxi province, the middle grassland regions of Inner Mongolia, and Xinjiang, compared to other places. As a consequence, the rail accessibility change rate decreased in those counties, suggesting the rise of transportation costs in such remote locations in comparison to other places. This does not mean that these remote locations have not experienced better access to the railway system, but it does imply that benefits from rail-network expansion are not distributed evenly over space. Qin (2016) has verified this channel at work using the train service

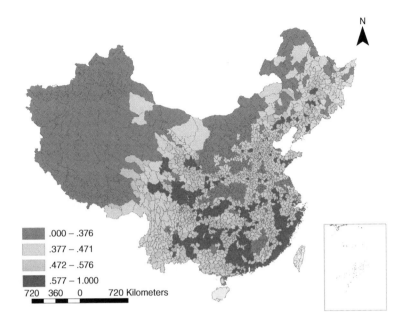

N

.000 – .376
.377 – .471
.472 – .576
.577 – 1.000
720   360   0   720 Kilometers

Figure 7.3 Spatial distribution of county-level rail accessibility change rate

data in China. Second, railway speed-up upgrading and HSR routes are not allocated randomly. Large cities with good economic performance have often been treated as the priority for railway upgrades. This political channel enables large cities to connect with smaller peripheral cities more efficiently through railways. In this situation, it is not surprising to find that core regions such as the Beijing–Tianjin Metropolitan Region, the Yangtze River Delta Metropolitan Region, and the Pearl River Delta Metropolitan Region have gained higher accessibility improvement compared to other regions. A typical example is illustrated in Figure 7.4, which visualizes a conceptual spatial connection model between cities in the Beijing–Tianjin Metropolitan Region. As can be seen, peripheral cities such as Baoding and Langfang have been tightly connected to core cities such as Beijing and Tianjin through various transportation systems. This underlying mechanism also plays an important role in promoting spatial agglomeration spillovers in the core-periphery urban system as suggested by findings in the economic geography literature (Faber, 2014; Qin, 2016).

Network centralization is subject to the spatial variations of accessibility improvements throughout the whole country. In order to uncover spatial variations, a variety of deviations are used to reflect the centralization trend from the accessibility indices. Let us define A_{it} as any of the county's accessibility indices in county i in year t. The most central node (county) in the network is the one with the highest accessibility value; i.e., $A_{MAX} = Max\ \{A_{it}\}$. This centralization index (C_i) in a given year could therefore shed light on how central the most central

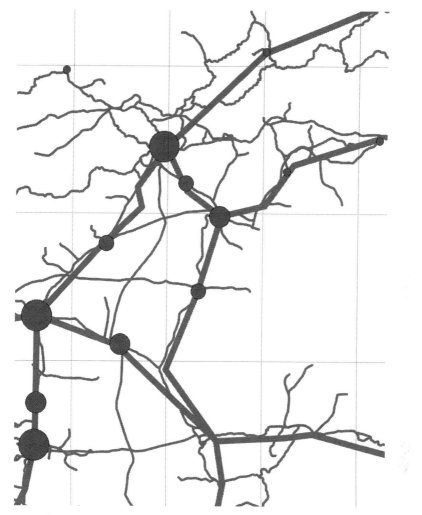

Figure 7.4 Conceptual model for urban connections in Beijing–Tianjin metropolitan region

node in the network is in comparison to other nodes. To simplify the interpretation, this index's function can be written as below, whose value is normalized between 0 and 1:

$$C_i = \frac{\sum_i \left(A_{max} - A_i \right)}{MAX \sum_i \left(A_{max} - A_i \right)}$$

where the numerator sums up the difference of accessibility between the most central county and other counties throughout the country, and the denominator represents the maximum value for the entire county sample (k), computed by the following equations: $\sum_{i=1}^{k-1} \max(A_{max} - A_i)$ i.e. $(k-1)*(A_{max}-A_{min})$. A smaller centralization index indicates a more decentralized network, and a comparison of the centralization index between 2006 and 2014 would allow us to uncover the (de)centralization trend over time. For example, based on the accessibility ($\theta=1$) in the 2006 rail-transit network, Xuchang in Henan province has the highest accessibility value (A_{max}), and some rural counties in the national borders have a very low accessibility value with the minimum value (A_{min}). For the measurement of the centralization index in 2006, the numerator is the sum of the differences of centrality between Xuchang and all other counties, and the denominator equals $(k-1)*(A_{max}-A_{min})$, where $k = 2388$.

Table 7.5 reports the change of the centralization index in different spatial decay parameter scenarios ($\theta=1$ or 4) by provinces. The key pattern that emerged from this analysis is the general centralization trend, as reflected from the improvement in the centralization index across most provinces. One potential explanation is due to the improvements in rail technologies, the building of HSR transit lines as well as the encouragement of market competitions between train lines across regions. On the other side, Henan, Guizhou, Ningxia have experienced the reduction in the centralization index over time, suggesting that the network decentralization pattern did occur in some regions. Overall, the expansions of HSR systems have led to a more diversified network in China, and may collaborate with the recent city decentralization process (Wang et al, 2009; Chen, 2012; Cao et al., 2013).

Channels at work

Rail transportation is known as an important infrastructure to business and trade in developed economies (Gibbons and Machin, 2003; Albalate and Bel, 2012). Hence, planning policies for new HSR lines or upgrading railway capacity are often used as a place-based locational policy instrument that can boost the city-level, regional and national economies. In evaluating whether HSRs are 'indispensable' to the Chinese economy, it is important to go beyond the descriptive evidence to examine the impacts of accessibility changes on local economic growth, and their geographical implications for urban and regional agglomeration. In this section, we discuss the relations of the main findings in the above sections, to explain the economic and planning mechanisms of rail-network expansion that have been highlighted in both the economic geography and planning literature.

First, the evidence provided in this chapter has taken a step back by illustrating the evolution of accessibility patterns, rather than by applying the causal identification strategy for explaining the economic mechanisms. However, there is a large number of literature that investigates various aspects of land-based transport infrastructure investments on economic development. Of these, the most fundamental idea is that firms can benefit from improved transport access to markets for trade, owing to externalities of agglomeration economies (Marshall, 1920). In recent years, there has been a growing interest in evaluating the causal effects

Table 7.5 Changes in centralization index by province

province	centralization index (θ=1)		centralization index (θ=4)	
	2006	2014	2006	2014
Beijing	0.59	0.64	0.83	0.88
Tianjin	0.44	0.53	0.80	0.72
Hebei	0.39	0.38	0.96	0.96
Shanxi	0.51	0.65	0.98	0.98
Inner Mongolia	0.50	0.65	0.98	0.98
Liaoning	0.46	0.49	0.98	0.97
Jilin	0.48	0.54	0.96	0.93
Heilongjiang	0.50	0.58	0.97	0.97
Shanghai	0.60	0.60	0.87	0.85
Jiangsu	0.56	0.62	0.94	0.97
Zhejiang	0.54	0.60	0.96	0.94
Anhui	0.41	0.44	0.95	0.95
Fujian	0.65	0.48	0.98	0.98
Jiangxi	0.50	0.51	0.96	0.96
Shandong	0.43	0.47	0.91	0.94
Henan	0.44	0.41	0.97	0.96
Hubei	0.41	0.42	0.96	0.97
Hunan	0.43	0.59	0.99	0.98
Guangdong	0.53	0.50	0.96	0.97
Guangxi	0.53	0.61	0.99	0.99
Sichuan	0.51	0.38	0.91	0.93
Chongqing	0.37	0.43	0.97	0.97
Guizhou	0.51	0.46	0.99	0.99
Yunnan	0.59	0.63	0.98	0.97
Tibet	0.66	0.65	0.89	0.87
Shaanxi	0.59	0.52	0.91	0.96
Gansu	0.43	0.45	0.85	0.85
Qinghai	0.44	0.52	0.94	0.92
Ningxia	0.67	0.51	0.77	0.77
Xinjiang	0.53	0.62	0.97	0.97

of railroad improvement on economic growth, in both developing and developed countries (Ahlfeldt, 2011; Atack et al., 2010; Banerjee et al., 2012; Gibbons et al., 2012; Donaldson 2016; Zheng and Kahn, 2013; Baum-Snow et al., 2015). Earlier studies focused on examining the aggregated economic impacts from public capital spending on transport infrastructure (see, for example, Aschauer, 1989; Munnell, 1992; Evans and Karras, 1994; Fernald, 1999). The availability of US historical planning data on transportation networks has stimulated a number of economic studies on the impact of road and railroad infrastructure, using careful identification strategies. Baum-Snow (2007) investigated the effect of the US interstate highway system on suburbanization within cities. Michaels (2008) found a strong impact of US interstate highways on trade-related activities and the demand for skilled labour. Duranton and Turner (2011) examined the road-congestion effects and found that the improvement of the road infrastructure was unlikely to relieve congestion. Duranton and Turner (2012) looked at the impacts of US interstate highways on the distribution of employment and population across cities. Duranton et al. (2014) found strong evidence of the role of interstate highways in determining trade and welfare. Donaldson and Hornbeck (2016) used a market-access approach to investigate the effects of railroad improvements on agricultural land value. More recently, some papers have applied similar ideas in EU and developing countries. For example, Ahlfeldt and Wendland (2011) examined the economic effects of railways in Berlin. Donaldson (2016) examined how the configuration of railways in colonial India influenced income and trade over space. For China, Banerjee et al. (2012) and Faber (2014) found that road and railroad infrastructure improvements could reduce trade costs between urban peripheries and large metropolitan areas. Zheng and Kahn (2013) found that HSR expansion exerted positive impacts on wages and housing prices in Chinese cities. Baum-Snow et al. (2015) documented the significant impacts of ring roads, highways and railways on the decentralization of the urban population and industrial GDP in China. The identification strategy employed in these papers is mainly from historical networks or national highway/railway plans to upgrade current roads and railways. Such identification strategies are helpful for assessing the economic impacts of railway expansion in a causal sense rather than based on the claims of mayors and other lobby groups. However, most of these studies in China did not explore changes in the rail accessibility along the network based on the origin-destination transportation matrix calculation, nor identify the evolution of county-level accessibility changes in a large developing country (see Wang et al., 2009). Future work in this line of research could combine modern identification strategies with a conventional origin-to-destination transportation matrix calculation on the economics of rail-network planning in China.

Second, China has experienced phenomenal, but uneven rail-network expansion in the past decade, which has brought great benefits but also great challenges for its sustainable development. This transformation has come alongside massive transportation investment within and between cities that could bring heterogeneous amenity capitalization effects on land markets (Zheng and Kahn, 2008; Wu et al., 2016). This rapid but differential spatial expansion in railway infrastructure also has potential impacts on commuting behaviour that could transform the growth of transit-based commuting activities in Chinese cities for decades to come. The underlying policy target is to mitigate commuting costs, improve a low-carbon environment, reduce pollution in cities and improve the well-being of its citizens (Transportation Research Board, 1997). Kennedy et al. (2005) suggested that new transit infrastructure investment was likely to be ineffective in the sustainable transportation if land use and neighbourhood designs were not supportive of the investment. But there has been relatively little evidence of exploring such relationships in China. The findings presented in the above sections would be useful to inform those involved in the planning of transportation infrastructure and cities, by shedding light on what accessibility responses to expect when new railway lines are built. Future work should evaluate how rail-network expansion would benefit the low-carbon environment and emission policies.

Conclusion

This chapter has shifted its focus from the impact of airport infrastructure expansion on urban networks to the geographical evolution of railway infrastructure expansion. Shifting the focus sheds light on different aspects of place-based locational infrastructure expansion, to improve local and regional development. But this raises the question as to how infrastructure expansion evolves with the changing accessibility pattern. Fortunately, in addition to the measurement of accessibility for a single and isolated places, economic geographers offer a useful theoretical foundation, or a general spatial equilibrium function, to generate the evidence to reflect the impacts of changes in the railway network on changes in accessibility for all places. Recent studies have shown how this function could be applied to transport infrastructure improvement scenarios, and have provided implications for firm productivity, property values and overall economic growth (Gibbons et al., 2012; Donaldson and Hornbeck, 2016; Zheng and Kahn, 2013). From the perspective of changes in market potential, the economic implication of rail-infrastructure improvements is obvious. As the planning objective for the majority of large cities is to be connected by speedy railway systems, there have been winners and losers in terms of the changing distribution of accessibility patterns across places. Thus, it is important for policymakers to rethink the implications of these infrastructure planning policies on the growth of already-growing places, and to rethink the mechanisms that lead to uneven spatial economic performance and the likely consequences.

This chapter has also explained how railway speed-up planning policies advance the trend of regional development. From 1997 to 2007, China implemented six rounds of passenger railway speed-ups. The speed-ups have had broad and deep implications because railway transport has an important position and role in China's socioeconomic development. Recent studies on passenger railway speed-ups have achieved fruitful results, providing valuable references for research on the relative topics (Jin and Wu, 2007; Wang et al., 2009; Chen, 2012; Ding et al., 2013). Existing studies on passenger railway speed-ups in China have focused mostly on exploring changes in the structure of the transportation network, and their impacts on the evolution of accessibility, at both provincial and the prefecture city levels (Cao et al., 2013; Zheng and Kahn, 2013; Jiao et al., 2014). This chapter however, steps back from theoretical concerns and focuses on the stylized facts to be explained. When looking at the pattern, process and mechanism of railway speed-ups and their economic implications on cities in typical regions, it is necessary to have a better understanding of the main features and changes of the six rounds of passenger railway speed-ups. This may help explain the role that these policies play in reducing commuting time between places, promoting labour mobility and influencing the formation of large metropolitan areas.

As China's most important means of transportation, railways can provide the micro-foundation for shifting economic activities. Therefore, railway speed-ups and high-speed rail investments have not only enhanced connections between cities, but also promoted the urban agglomeration by reducing transportation costs and accelerating the industrial restructuring process. From the macro-regional perspective, the improvement of transport conditions can effectively promote the optimization of core-periphery spatial structures and influence regional development patterns.

To summarize, there is evidence that planning programmes of transport infrastructure, which upgrade railway speeds and build high-speed railways, have significant impacts on the configuration of spatial economy. Indeed, as transport investments continue to grow in China, infrastructure planning policymakers face many challenges. What would happen if policymakers ignored the importance of public capital spending on reversing the connectivity of depressed areas and periphery regions? And what would happen if policymakers emphasized the effectiveness of infrastructure investments and the implications for overall economic growth for the whole country? Given that market mechanisms largely affect the distributional effects of improvements on transport infrastructure, perhaps it would be particularly helpful to consider the importance of place-based locational infrastructure planning policies on shaping the local economy. These challenges have been increasingly recognized by planners and policymakers in China, but the Chinese infrastructure planning system is still a centralized system in terms of railway-network expansion. This is partly because public capital expenditures have been allocated centrally, and partly because the railway system has played an important role in China's socioeconomic development. Under this centralized planning system, China has improved the train speed of existing railways while constructing new high-speed railways and increasing train service frequencies between cities. However, there is strong evidence that planning programmes of railway speed-ups and high-speed rail investments, interacting with transportation cost reductions between local counties and cities, could facilitate urban agglomeration by means of differential impacts on market potentials. Therefore, the Chinese infrastructure planning system has intuitively shaped the uneven patterns of urban and regional development. Other possible driving forces of uneven spatial development are well studied (for example, the positive impact of housing market policy reforms on economic development, and the significant impact of migration policy relaxations on urban growth), but they appear to be interlinked with commuting-time savings induced by transport infrastructure improvements.

Successive Chinese planning policies should have attempted to coordinate spatial development patterns by reforming the policy implementation rules. But it is difficult to understand the interaction between planning policies and underlying economic consequences in the complex spatial context, especially when the timely data information are not available for finer geographic scales. For example, intercity-level analysis presented in this chapter along the railway transportation network may veil intra-city variations in the effects of rail-network expansion. Further studies are recommended to uncover the relationship between planning programmes of transport infrastructure and urban growth in the longer term.

Note

1 See details in http://finance.people.com.cn/GB/1037/8743758.html. Chen (2012) reviewed the opportunities and challenges of China's HSR development.

References

Ahlfeldt, G. and Wendland, N. 2011. Fifty years of urban accessibility: The impact of urban railway network on the land gradient in Berlin 1890-1936, Regional Science and Urban Economics, 41(2): 77–88.

Ahlfeldt, G.M. 2011. The train has left the station: Do markets value intracity access to intercity rail connections? German Economic Review, 12, 312–335.

Albalate, D. and Bel, G. 2012. *The Economics and Politics of High-speed Rail: Lessons from Experiences Abroad,* Lanham, MD: Lexington Books.

Aschauer, D. 1989. Is public expenditure productive? Journal of Monetary Economics, 23, 177–200.

Atack, J., Bateman, F., Haines, M. and Margo, R.A. 2010. Did railroads induce or follow economic growth? Urbanization and population growth in the American Midwest, 1850–1860, Social Science History, 34, 171–197.

Banerjee, A., Duflo, E. and Qian, N. 2012. On the road: Access to transportation infrastructure and economic, National Bureau of Economic Research, NBER Working Paper No. 17897.

Banister, D. and Berechman, J. 2000. *Transport Investment and Economic Development,* London and New York: Routledge.

Baum-Snow, N. 2007. Did highways cause suburbanization? Quarterly Journal of Economics, 122(2), 775–805.

Baum-Snow, N., Brandt, L., Henderson, V., Turner, M. and Zhang, Q. 2015. Roads, railroads and decentralization of Chinese cities, London: LSE working paper.

Bruinsma, F. and Rietveld, P. 1993. Urban Agglomerations in European Infrastructure Networks. VU University, Amsterdam: Faculty of Economics, Business Administration and Econometrics.

Cao, J., Liu, X.C., Wang, Y. and Li, Q. 2013. Accessibility impacts of China's high-speed rail network. Journal of Transport Geography, 28, 12–21.

Cervero, R. and Bernick, M. 1996. High-speed rail and development of California's Central Valley: Comparative lessons and public policy considerations, IURD Working Paper 675. Berkeley, CA: University of California.

Chang, J.S. and Lee, J.-H. 2008. Accessibility analysis of Korean high-speed rail: A case study of the Seoul metropolitan area. Transport Reviews: A Transnational Transdisciplinary Journal, 28(1), 87–103.

Chen, C-L. 2012. Reshaping Chinese space-economy through high-speed trains: Opportunities and challenges. Journal of Transport Geography, 22(5), 312–316.

Ding, J., Jin, F., Wang, J. and Liu, D. 2013. Competition game of high-speed rail and civil aviation and its spatial effect: A case study of Beijing–Shanghai high-speed rail. Economic Geography, 33(5), 104–110 [in Chinese].

Donaldson, D. 2016 (forthcoming). Railroads of the Raj: Estimating the impact of transportation infrastructure, American Economic Review.

Donaldson, D. and Hornbeck, R. 2016. Railroads and American economic growth: A 'Market Access' approach, The Quarterly Journal of Economics, 131(2), 799–858.

Duranton, G., Morrow, P.M. and Turner, M.A. 2014. Roads and trade: Evidence from US cities, Review of Economic Studies, 79(4), 1407–1440.

Duranton, G. and Turner M.A. 2011. The Fundamental Law of Road Congestion: Evidence from US cities, American Economic Review, 101, 2616–52.

Duranton, G. and Turner M.A. 2012. Urban Growth and Transportation, Review of Economic Studies, 791407–791440.

Evans, P. and Karras, G. 1994. Are government activities productive? Evidence from a panel of U.S. states, The Review of Economics and Statistics, 76, 1–11.

Faber, B. 2014. Trade integration, market size, and industrialization: Evidence from China's national trunk highway system, Review of Economic Studies, 81, 1046–1070.

Fernald, J. 1999. Roads to prosperity? Assessing the link between public capital and productivity, American Economic Review, 89, 619–638.

Geurs, K.T. and Van Wee, B. 2004. Accessibility evaluation of land-use and transport strategies: Review and research directions. Journal of Transport Geography, 12(2), 127–140.

Gibbons, S., Lyytikäinen, T., Overman, H.G. and Sanchis-Guarner, R. 2012. New road infrastructure: The effects on firms, SERC Discussion Papers, SERCDP00117. London, UK: Spatial Economics Research Centre (SERC), London School of Economics and Political Sciences.

Gibbons, S. and Machin, S. 2003. *Rail Access and House Prices, An Evaluation of the Wider Benefits of Transport Improvements, and Employment and Rail Access, An Evaluation of the Wider Benefits of Transport Improvements*, November 2003. London: Department of Transport Report.

Gutiérrez, J. 2001. Location, economic potential and daily accessibility: an analysis of the accessibility impact of the high-speed line Madrid–Barcelona–French border. Journal of Transport Geography, 9(4), 229–242.

Gutiérrez, J., González, R. and Gómez, G. 1996. The European high-speed train network: Predicted effects on accessibility patterns. Journal of Transport Geography, 4(4), 227–238.

Handy, S.L. and Niemeier, D.A. 1997. Measuring accessibility: An exploration of issues and alternatives. Environment and Planning A, 29(7), 1175–1194.

Hansen, W.G. 1959. How accessibility shapes land use. Journal of the American Institute of Planners, 25(2), 73–76.

Harris, C. 1954. Market as a factor in the localization of industry in the United States, Annals of the Association of American Geographers, 44(4) 315–348.

Hou, Q. and Li, S. 2011. Transport infrastructure development and changing spatial accessibility in the Greater Pearl River Delta, China, 1990–2020. Journal of Transport Geography, 19, 1350–1360.

Jiao, J., Wang J., Jin F. and Dunford, M. 2014. Impacts on accessibility of China's present and future HSR network. Journal of Transport Geography, 40, 123–132.

Jin, F. and Wu, W. 2007. The spatial economic impact of upgrade of railway passenger traffic system in China. Economic Geography, 27(6), 888–895 [in Chinese].

Kennedy, C., Miller, E., Shalaby, A., Maclean, H. and Coleman, J. 2005. The four pillars of sustainable urban transportation. Transport Reviews, 25(4), 393–414.

Levinson, D.M. 2012. Accessibility impacts of high-speed rail. Journal of Transport Geography, 22(5), 288–291.

Lopez, E., Gutiérrez, J. and Gómez, G. 2008. Measuring regional cohesion effects of large-scale transport infrastructure investments: an accessibility approach. European Planning Studies, 16, 277–301.

Marshall, A. 1920. *Principles of Economics*. London: Macmillan.

Michaels, G. 2008. The effect of trade on the demand for skill: Evidence from the Interstate Highway System, Review of Economics and Statistics, 90(4), 683–701.

Munnell, A.H. 1992. Policy watch: Infrastructure investment and economic growth, *Journal of Economic Perspectives*, 6(4), 189–198.

Qin, Y. 2016. 'No county left behind?' The distributional impact of high-speed rail upgrade in China. Journal of Economic Geography, DOI:10.1093/jeg/lbw013.

Reilly, W.J. 1931. *The Law of Retail Gravitation*. New York: Knickerbocker Press.

Sánchez-Mateos, H.S.M. and Givoni, M. 2009. The accessibility impact of a new high-speed rail line in the UK—A preliminary analysis of winners and losers. TSU Working Paper Series, Ref. 1041. Oxford, UK: School of Geography and the Environment.

State Council. 2008. *'zhong chang qi tie lu wang gui hua*, (2008 *nian tiao zheng)'*, http://jtyss.ndrc.gov.cn/fzgh/W020090605632915547512.pdf.

Transportation Research Board. 1997. *Toward a sustainable future: Addressing the long-term effects of motor vehicle transportation on climate and ecology.* Special Report, 251. Washington, DC: National Academy Press.

Vandenbulcke, G., Steenberghen, T. and Thomas, I. 2009. Mapping accessibility in Belgium: A tool for land-use and transport planning? Journal of Transport Geography, 17(1), 39–53.

Vickerman, R.W. 1974. Accessibility, attraction, and potential: A review of some concepts and their use in determining mobility. Environment and Planning A, 6, 675–691.

Wang, J., Jin, F., Mo, H. and Wang, F. 2009. Spatiotemporal evolution of China's railway network in the 20th century: An accessibility approach. Transportation Research Part A: Policy and Practice, 43(8), 765–778.

Wu, W., Dong G. and Zhang, W. 2016. The puzzling heterogeneity in amenity capitalization effects on land markets, Papers in Regional Science, online version available. DOI: 10.1111/pirs.12186

Zheng, S., & Kahn, M.E. 2008. Land and residential property markets in a booming economy: new evidence from Beijing. Journal of Urban Economics, 63, 743–757.

Zheng, S. and Kahn, M.E. 2013. China's bullet trains facilitate market integration and mitigate the cost of megacity growth, Proceedings of the National Academy of Sciences, 110, E1248–E1253.

8 Market reform, land development and urban vibrancy

Introduction

Chapters 6 and 7 showed how the Chinese planning system, as in many other developing countries, stimulates the supply of air-based and land-based transport infrastructure, and how infrastructure expansion, as guided by the planning system, affects the spatial evolution of core-periphery urban networks across regions. Of course planning policies allocate resources not only for infrastructure, but also for all other types of land uses that are relevant to urban development. From the intra-city perspective, this chapter looks at the evidence for market-reform and land-development patterns in Beijing, and exploits the variations of urban-vibrancy patterns from big data on mobile phones.

Planning policies set regulations and development-zoning plans that influence the spatial-temporal variations of land-market structures (Cheshire and Sheppard, 2002, 2004), housing choices (Cheshire et al., 1999) and patterns of human activities. This is consistent with planning policy goals in enhancing urban vibrancy through the balance of social, economic and environmental welfare. There are many urban planning policies that may affect intra-city spatial structures. The first half of this chapter focuses specifically on land and housing-market policy reforms and the spatial-temporal distribution of land supply and land value (Dowall, 1994; Li, 2000; Wu, 2002; Huang, 2004; Wang and Li, 2004; Zheng et al., 2006; Cheshire, 2008; Huang and Jiang, 2009; Wu, 2009; Logan et al., 2010; Wu et al., 2013; Wu and Dong, 2014). From this set of distributional patterns, it is worth looking at the transformation of the urban spatial structure, particularly with regard to land and housing marketization. Discussions within this chapter do not necessarily cover all aspects of the social-spatial implications of market reforms on the transformation of urban structures. Instead, the evidence presented in this chapter tries to provide insights that emerge from land and housing-market reforms, when rethinking through human activity-based vibrancy patterns using big data. There are good reasons to argue that the interaction of human activities and the configuration of land use could shed light on the vibrancy of cities. Among developed countries there have been debates on the value of consumer cities (Glaeser et al., 2001). The economic interpretation of urban vibrancy has focused traditionally on productivity gains from agglomerations, but neglected the temporal-spatial process of human-activity distribution to some extent.

Human-activity distribution is probably an alternative way to reflect the liveliness of cities with potential for influencing the urbanism process. To this end, the second half of this chapter makes use of mobile-phone positioning data to visualize the level, location and patterns of human activities, and provides implications for urban vibrancy based on big data.

Economic implications of land and housing marketization

There is substantial policy interest in land and housing-marketization reforms to influence intra-city spatial structures. Consistent with the national economic transition towards a market-orientated economy, as outlined in Part II, this interest is driven by several economic considerations: first, the need to encourage land and housing-market transactions that drive economic growth in China's reform and opening-up; second, the ineffectiveness of current planning policies for allocating land and housing resources; and third, the importance of reshaping urban spatial structures and enhancing the vibrancy of people and places.

Housing-marketization effects

One important policy, often referred to as 'housing-marketization reforms' or similar terms, plays a key role in spurring property development in most Chinese cities. This section starts by considering the underlying theoretical logic of the impact of housing-marketization reform policies, aimed at ending the State-allocated housing-provision system in China.

Theory suggests that local residents, to maximize utilities, can be hypothesized to choose residential locations, based on their socioeconomic status and their preferred locational specific characteristics. Two underlying perspectives are involved. The spatial sorting perspective, derived from Alonso (1964), Mills (1967) and Muth (1969), suggests that residents make a trade-off between the commuting cost for jobs located in the central business centre (CBD) and housing costs, before choosing their residential location. LeRoy and Sonstelie (1983) developed the Alonso–Mills–Muth model by predicting that the wide use of cars by households with a relatively high income may further attract them to live in the suburbs. The critique of the Alonso's spatial sorting model argues that with improvements in transportation accessibility and the increasing opportunity costs of commuting time for high-income families, households' location choices are likely to reverse, and/or depend on the relative magnitudes between households' income elasticity for housing demand and the income elasticity for transportation costs (Brown, 1985; Anas, 1992; Glaeser et al., 2008). In addition, this classical economic perspective downplays the importance of the allocation of local public goods and services, and heterogeneous characteristics of residents. such as life-cycle effects when choosing residential locations. In contrast, Tiebout's (1956) fiscal sorting sets households' location choices in a wider social and demographic context. From Tiebout's perspective, consumers will shop across communities over space and choose residential locations that offer an attractive package of local public goods and tax rates. However, it is not easy to identify the determinants of residential location choice within the spatial context. A long line of papers have developed Tiebout's design by investigating issues of stratification in residential location choices, associated with differences in income, social mix and public goods provision across communities. Important contributions include works by Glaeser et al. (1996), Nechyba (1997), Epple and Platt (1998), Rosen (2002), Cheshire and Sheppard (1995, 1998), Bayer et al. (2007), and Ioannides and Zabel (2008) among others.

The existing studies have provided a solid basis for understanding how residential locations can shape residents' activities in different social and spatial contexts. The Chinese housing-marketization reform (as discussed below), which transformed the socialist provisional system for the marketization system, offers a good opportunity to see the determinants of residential location choices in a transitional housing-market country, where both institutional and market forces can contribute to property development and indirectly affect the evolution of urban spatial structures.

Before the housing-market reform, housing was treated as an item of no market value provided by local government or employers (*Danwei*), and its allocation was based on institutional factors in terms of the residents' political status, working age and family size (Huang and Clark, 2002). Coupled with the absence of an explicit labour market, residents used to have limited freedom in choosing their residential locations in the centrally planned economy era. To end this socialist housing system, housing-market reform was first experimented in 1988, and reinforced further in 1998. Since then, housing has been treated as a commodity with flexible market prices, according to its quality and locational specific characteristics. Local residents, who used to have no chance of choosing their housing in the socialist era, now have the freedom to make housing choices in terms of tenure, dwelling size and location (Logan et al., 2010). However, although the market is beginning to function well, socialist institutional factors such as '*Hukou*'[1] continue to play essential roles in housing consumption during the sorting process. There is a substantial group of literature in dealing with various aspects of Chinese housing-marketization reform (Li, 2000; Wu, 2002; Huang, 2004; Wang and Li, 2004; Zheng et al., 2006; Huang and Jiang, 2009). A general argument is that the residential location choice for different groups of people is complex. In particular, residents with *Hukou* and workers of State-owned enterprises in large Chinese cities are the potential 'winners' in this housing-market transition era (Logan et al., 2010). The following discussions will focus specifically on the *Hukou* and occupation dimensions, with Beijing as the study case.

The primary, institutionalized discrimination associated with *Hukou* is the unequal opportunity for residents in gaining access to local public amenities. For example, primary schools and middle schools in Beijing may prefer to accept children from households with Beijing *Hukou*. Another potential *Hukou* discrimination is that only those residents with the host city's *Hukou* can apply for affordable housing provided by City Governments. Note that households that qualify for affordable-housing applications may not be genuine low-income residents, such as poor migrant workers. In many cases, affordable-housing applicants are selected based on their overall socio-political characteristics, not just on their income levels. Although the spatial concentration of affordable housing does not derive from severe poverty concentrations, like that in developed countries, neighbourhoods with affordable-housing projects are seen as special types of 'institutional communities' in the housing-marketization reform era. For example, te Beijing Government completed several extra-large affordable-housing projects (*jing ji shi yong fang*), including Huilongguan and Tiantongyuan during the period from 1999 to 2009. To define the urbanized areas of Beijing, and similar to the term 'zone' (No.1 to No.6) used in London, the Beijing Government and previous researchers often use the term 'ring roads' (No.2 to No.6), which circle the CBD[2] in every direction. As can be seen from Figure 8.1, most affordable-housing projects were distributed in suburban areas of Beijing outside the 3rd ring road. Thus, residents who would like to buy affordable-housing units in these neighbourhoods would endure very long commutes to work, and there is evidence of a lack of demand for affordable-housing projects located in remote suburban areas, where access to rail transport was relatively poor. This situation became better when public transportation systems such as new subway lines were built in these places. That is to say, despite affordable-housing provision, there was evidence of household preferences to buy commodity housing (*shang pin fang*) with good access to local public goods and services (Zhang et al., 2006).

Aside from the *Hukou* issues, impacts of housing-market reform on residential segregations have largely been untested. For example, in Beijing, most State-owned work units (*Danwei*) continued to provide heavily subsidized housing through the 'internal housing market' after the housing-marketization reform (Huang and Clark, 2002; Logan et al., 2010). This subsidized housing followed both the social welfare rules in terms of discounted prices, and the market rules in terms of location[3] and dwelling size (Sato, 2006). On one hand, residents working for private companies could not obtain such housing welfare, and were forced to sort and stratify themselves into neighbourhoods that matched their housing affordability and preferences. On the other hand, the massive construction of a newly built commodity market housing made the housing supply very elastic in Beijing, and in many other Chinese cities. Therefore, it is arguable that residential location choice patterns varied between people living in the *Danwei* (units) housing and the commodity market housing (*Shang pin fang*). Within the housing-marketization context, the difference between *Danwei* housing and the commodity market housing (*Shang pin fang*) had at least two serious implications for the restructuring process of social and regional segregations in Beijing and other Chinese cities. First, communities based on local *Danwei* housing pushed up the matching patterns of job and housing, since people who lived in a *Danwei* community might enjoy reduced commuting costs to work, which is good news if one works in the same *Danwei* (unit). Second, a larger proportion of *Danwei* (units) and communities based on *Danwei* housing in Beijing attracted skilled workers to live, work and play within a relatively limited spatial range, who would otherwise perform different types of daily activities in a broader spatial range. This would help to explain the rhythms of human-activity-based vibrancy patterns in the urban space. More work is needed on the role of residential sorting in restructuring the spatial distribution of labour market activities in Beijing and other Chinese cities.

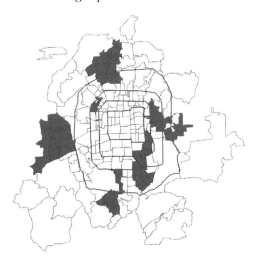

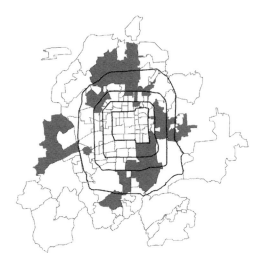

Figure 8.1 Distribution of affordable housing projects at neighbourhood (*jiedao*) level in
       Beijing (1999–2009)

Land-marketization effects

From a spatial perspective, Chinese policymakers have made use of land supply
and marketization reform policies to improve city structures in urbanized areas,
which may be influenced indirectly by land supply and land-value patterns. There
are two ways of structuring the insights into, and evidence of, the likely land-
marketization effects in urban structures.

The first viewpoint sees land-marketization effects as one fundamental part of the national economic transition process. In essence, land-marketization reforms make the price signal gradually effective in Chinese urban land markets (Cheshire and Sheppard, 2005; Cheshire, 2008). Compared with the abrupt and shocking transitions in Eastern-European countries, the market-orientated transition in China is a mild environment (Nee, 1992). As one fundamental part of this transition, urban land reform was first launched in 1987, through the initial practical experiment of the land leasehold system in Shenzhen city – the first special economic zone in China. Since then, most Chinese cities have experienced dramatic transformation of their land-use system, from free allocation towards a leasehold system, as the Government has reinstated the land value from a social welfare to a commodity.

After the reform, urban lands are still owned by the State. But property developers can purchase the leasehold right from the State Government. In urban China, the land-leasing terms are 70 years for residential land use, 40 years for commercial land use and 50 years for industrial and institutional use. The beginning of land-market reform in Beijing started officially in 1992, through the sale of the first long-term land-leasing parcel. Since then, by providing basic road access and public facilities and services, Beijing's Municipal Government has gradually auctioned land-leasing parcels on the market. From 1992 to 1998, the major way to lease land was through Government regulations. However, since 1999, the conventional way to lease land was through negotiation and after 2004, the Chinese Government required that all land leases must be privatized through an open auction process. This switch represents the evolutionary process of constructing a market-orientated economy in China. That is to say, those who bid the highest price can obtain the land parcel. As a result, Chinese land marketization can be divided into three reform periods. During the first two periods, the coexistence of institutional forces and the market mechanism made the price signal ineffective in fully adjusting the land demand and supply. It was unclear to what extent the land parcels bid for by developers could meet the standard market criteria in terms of price, quality and location. Fortunately, since 2004, the Chinese Government has used the open auction transaction method, which is recognized as a well-functioning land-market system. A sketched framework for describing the likely economic impact of the land-marketization process on urban spatial structures is shown in Table 8.1. This unique land-marketization transitional process has provided a good opportunity to investigate spatial variations of land-price attributes in this emerging land market (Wu and Yeh, 1997; Cheshire, 2008; Zheng and Kahn, 2008).

A good case in point was Beijing's residential land-market development from 1992 to 2009. Beijing, as the capital city of China, has experienced fast urban transformation over the past two decades. Such rapid urban transformation parallels land marketization.

From the temporal perspective, Figure 8.2 shows the evolution of land supply and transaction prices from 1992 to 2009. The evidence here focuses specifically on the residential sector since it is the largest sector in urban land markets. As can

Table 8.1 Spatial-temporal interpretation of changes in urban spatial structures in land-marketization contexts

	1992–1997	*1998–2003*	*After 2004*
Institutional factors	Initiated the leasehold pricing system for land use at the early stage of economic reforms and opening-up in the country	Initiated the reforms of urban housing-provision system, and gradually established the land and housing markets	Maximized the market mechanisms in the urban governance of land and housing markets
Rationale of land development	Improve the quality of the urban living environment, and the living space per capita for local residents	The coexistence of a variety of investment mechanisms to stimulate the property-market activity, as guided by urban planning policies	Market demand and supply become the main force in driving land development
Behavioural agents in the land markets	Local government, and State-owned *Danwei* units	Local government, private property developers and State-owned *Danwei* units	Local government, private property developers and State-owned *Danwei* units
City structure features	Formulated the monocentric city structure, with *Danwei* units and *Danwei*-based communities scattered in the city centre and inner suburban areas	The rise of land prices in city-centre locations and prime suburban locations; many city subcentres emerged	The rise of land development in edge towns; transformation from monocentric city structure to polycentric city structure

be seen, land prices have experienced dramatic changes, and there is a general consistency between changes in land-marketization reform policies and changes in land prices over time. Since the establishment of the Beijing land market in 1992, there was an increase in residential land transactions between 1992 and 1993, but this dropped sharply between 1994 and 1998, probably as a result of the spillover effects of the bursting of property bubbles in some southern Chinese provinces (Guangxi and Hainan etc.) in this time period. The 1998 housing-market reform provided good investment opportunities in land development but land transaction prices remained relatively stable during 1998 and the early years of the twenty-first century. Since 2004, with the emergence of open auctions based on the land leasehold system, the Chinese land-marketization reforms have reached maturity. As price signals become increasingly effective in coordinating activities for land-market development, there is clear evidence of a steady land-price boom trend, owing to the rapid urbanization and infrastructure expansion in Beijing and other large Chinese cities. On the land supply side, there was a stable growing trend of land

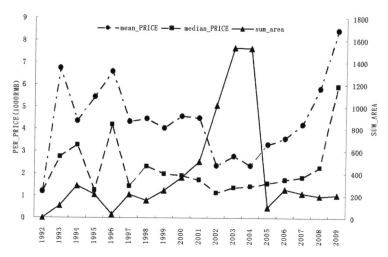

Figure 8.2 Temporal pattern of residential land market in Beijing from 1992 to 2009
Source: Beijing Land Resource Authority.

supply from 1992 to 2006. But with the implementation of a series of national property control policies since 2006, Beijing's residential land supply has shown a clear downward trend. The headline story from here is that land-marketization reforms and policies have exerted significant impacts on land development over time.

The second viewpoint with regard to the interaction of land-market and city structures, is to consider the changing land-development pattern as a way of reshaping city structure. These distributional patterns of land supply and prices provide more subtle and complex evidence when one wants to understand the transformation of city structures. Taking Beijing as a typical example, neighbourhood land-development intensities are much higher in the north-east and north-west parts of the city than in other parts, as evidenced by higher transaction prices and larger amounts of land supply. Rather than formulating a more complicated equation, the land-development intensity index is measured by a simple function: $Intensity_i = \dfrac{I_i - I_{min}}{I_{max} - I_{min}}$, where $Intensity_i$ is a standardized value for the median level of transaction prices (land-price intensity) or the supply of land-parcel sizes (land supply intensity) at the neighbourhood level, in a given time period. I_i indicates the actual median levels of transaction prices, or the supply of land-parcel sizes in a given neighbourhood. I_{max} and I_{min} indicate the maximum and minimum values of transaction prices, or the maximum and minimum supply sizes of land parcels, respectively.

The evidence in Figure 8.3 shows the spatial differentiation of land-development patterns. Data were obtained from the Beijing Land Authority through the Institute of Geographical Science and Natural Resource Research at the Chinese Academy of Science. In general, there is evidence of high land supply intensities in the central locations of the city, such as Guang-an-men,

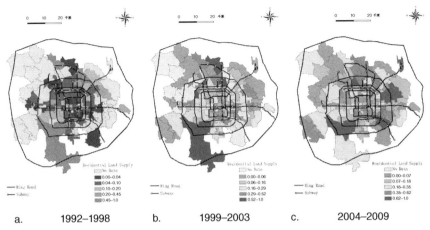

a.   1992–1998   b.   1999–2003   c.   2004–2009

Figure 8.3 Spatial patterns of land supply intensities in Beijing from 1992 to 2009

Gong-zhu-fen, Jian-guo-men-wai and other areas surrounding the 3rd ring road over time. Among suburban areas, the supply of residential land parcels is located mainly in Huangcun, Tiantongyuan, Huilongguan Laiguangying and other regenerated neighbourhoods. More recently, the supply of residential land parcels is concentrated mostly around the Dongba area and the Olympic Park area in the northern part of the city, as well as the Sihui-Fatou area in the eastern part of the city, probably because of relatively improved access, from 2004 to 2009, to public goods and services, such as subway stations.

One of the basic insights from traditional land rent theory is that land prices are likely to be informative for understanding the distribution of local property-development potentials in the urban space. This means that when an area has experienced high land-price intensities, it will be likely to have high comparative locational advantages. For example, when it comes to Beijing's residential land market, interesting patterns emerge. As shown in Figure 8.4, there was strong evidence of high land-price intensities in central locations of the city from 1992 to 2009. But during the early stage of the land-marketization reform, places in the northern suburban neighbourhoods such as Huilongguan also experienced high land-price intensities, owing to the provision of a large amount of low-priced affordable housing. With the emergence of new employment centres in Zhong-guan-cun, and Wang-jing, among others, several new residential central districts (RCD), such as Zhong-guan-cun RCD, Wang-jing RCD, and Da-hong-men RCD, were subsequently formed in the inner suburban areas. To some extent, the formation of new residential central districts (RCD) in the land market has contributed to the transformation from a monocentric city structure to a polycentric city structure in Beijing.

Another version of spatial manifestation used interpolation tools based on the ArcGIS software to visualize continuous land-price distribution in differential spatial directions. To simplify the analysis, the urban space has been divided into

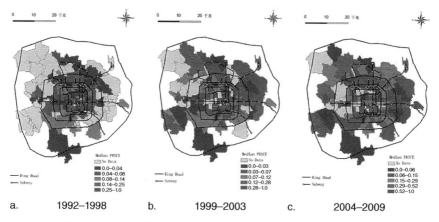

Figure 8.4 Spatial patterns of land-price intensities in Beijing from 1992 to 2009

eight quadrant-based geographic zones. Figure 8.5 shows the attempt to view the heterogeneity of land-price gradients across different geographic zones over time periods. In general, price gradients tend to fade with their distance away from the traditional central business district (CBD), although many differential patterns emerge. Of course, the rise of polycentric city structures in Beijing could help explain these differential patterns, but rigorous assessments of driving forces of these differential patterns should be grounded in the localized socioeconomic and locational specific characteristics at stake. In short, while there is reasonable evidence of the interaction of city structures and land-marketization reforms, not much is known about what role the configuration of local land use might play in affecting urban growth and gentrification (see Wu and Yeh, 1997; Zheng and Kahn, 2013). Furthermore, even less evidence has focused on outcomes for human activity at finer spatial-temporal scales. As will be shown in the following parts of this chapter, the spatial-temporal distribution of human activities is useful to help explain the urban vibrancy over time and space.

Urban vibrancy pattern in a modern-day Chinese city

The planning system imposes both explicit (e.g. market potential) and implicit (e.g. vibrancy of cities through human activity) impacts on urban development. In this section, we focus on examining the vibrancy of cities by tracking the spatial-temporal distribution of human activities in Beijing, based on mobile-phone positioning data.

The city of Beijing, entailing significant geographical disparities in human activities and land development, serves as a textbook case for empirical analysis. A big-data approach is applied to overlay the urban-vibrancy patterns through the distribution of human activities on an hourly basis, twenty-four hours a day. The purpose is to identify the distribution of intensity changes in human activities at the grid unit level in Beijing's main metropolitan area.

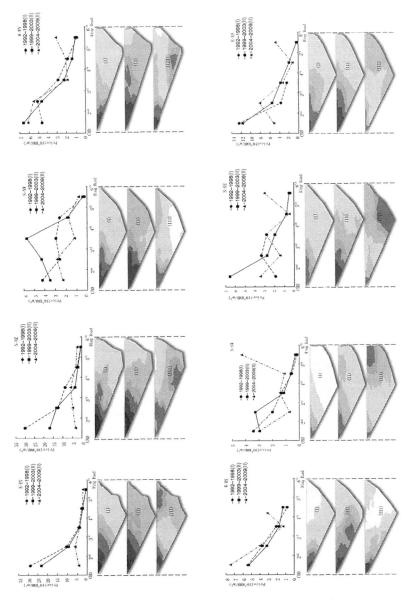

Figure 8.5 Spatial patterns of land-price gradients in Beijing from 1992 to 2009

Source: Wu et al., 2011.

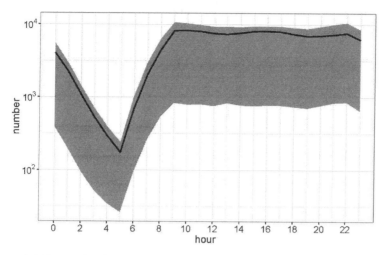

Figure 8.6 Temporal variation of mobile-phone positioning numbers (in log) over a 24-hour day

Note: The grey areas indicate 75 and 25 percentile ranges, and the solid line indicates average distribution.

The big-data source applied here is individual mobile-phone positioning data in Beijing over two weeks in June 2015.[4] The information was obtained from the Tencent social media platform (providing social media applications such as QQ, WeChat on mobile phones). These mobile-phone positioning data are geographically referenced because Tencent social media services make it possible to track users' locations with high accuracy (Deville et al., 2014; Louail et al., 2014; Blondel et al., 2015; Liu and Wang, 2015; Wu et al., 2016a). But, it is not possible to access to mobile-phone users' socioeconomic information because it relates to personal privacy. As a baseline, location-based mobile-phone data provide a new and alternative way for understanding the evolution of urban-vibrancy patterns (Jacobs-Crisioni et al., 2014).

This section considers two implications for the rhythms of urban-vibrancy patterns. The first is the spatial-temporal intensity of various human activities. The temporal distribution of human-activity patterns in Figure 8.6 shows the rhythms of urban-vibrancy processes on an hourly basis. Figure 8.7 shows that human-activity intensities tend to decay in a non-linear manner with the distance from the city centre, although such patterns are not distributed evenly at different time periods. Dividing the whole mobile-phone data sample into weekdays and weekends yields similar results. Focusing specifically on the spatial-temporal variations in the distribution of human activities, Figure 8.7 shows that areas with high intensity of activities are located not only in the centre of the city but also in some peripheral areas of the city, such as the Zhong-Guan-Cun and Olympic zones. This reflects the uneven association between the proximity to the city centre and human-activity intensities. An initial viewpoint is that there are many population flows that would drive the changing patterns of human activity. This largely holds in Chinese cities, where cities are much denser than US and European cities. It is

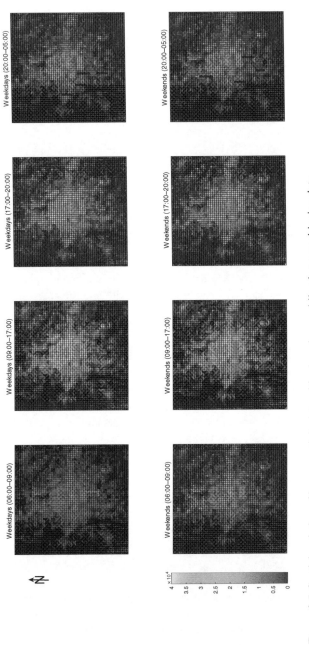

Figure 8.7 Spatial variation of human-activity intensities based on mobile-phone positioning data

Note: *x*-axis and *y*-axis indicate longitude and latitude directions, respectively. *Colour bar* indicates human-activity intensities (1,000 persons per grid unit)

also possible to interpret the extent to which human activities are evolving with urban spatial structures over time, implying an increased consumption demand for not only residential land development but also diversified land use.

The second implication pointing to the importance of urban vibrancy is the rise of human activities in suburban areas. According to traditional monocentric city structure theories, higher activity levels are expected in the city centre during daytime hours and lower activity levels in suburban areas at this time period, on the assumption that people mostly work in the city centre and live in areas away from the city centre, in order to save rent. However, little is known whether this is the case in Chinese cities from a big-data perspective.

Table 8.2 shows the increase in human-activity intensities in Beijing suburban areas. According to convention, Beijing metropolitan areas are divided into two groups: city-centre areas (areas within the 3rd ring road); and suburban areas (areas outside the 3rd ring road). The suburban areas can be further stratified into two subcategories: inner-suburb areas (areas between 3rd ring road and 5th ring road); and edged towns (areas outside the 5th ring road). Under the 500-metre grid unit level, the intensity of daily activities in suburban areas increased by 29.069% per hour during daytime (06:00–19:00), and increased by 17.087% on a 24-hour basis. The proportion of edged towns, despite lower activity intensities, maintained a 27.376% growth rate during the daytime, and a 16.981% growth rate on a 24-hour basis. Meanwhile, there has been a substantial increase in human-activity intensities in inner-suburb areas. Of course, the intensity of daily activities in urban areas is high and also increases quickly, reflecting the compactness of city-centre areas. The results are robust to changes in the area unit levels (see the results using the 2 km grid unit level in the lower panel of Table 8.2). Although one cannot pin down precise individuals' travel behaviour, the evidence presented here may imply the plausible vibrancy of suburban areas. That is to say, inner-suburb areas and edged towns may not be just 'bedroom' areas for commuters to sleep, but are mostly vibrant neighbourhoods with prolonged human activity. It is reasonable to suspect that these human-activity patterns reflected from the big-data perspective are only a small part of the general rise of edged towns as places for people to work, live and play. One serious concern is that local public goods are capitalized into land and housing value, and that human activities might therefore be affected by local land and housing markets. Thus, even if one knows the mobile-phone positioning data on an hourly basis, further studies should take housing rent and land value into consideration.

In sum, city mayors may view vibrancy as necessary for sustainable growth, but when such growth is centred mostly on measuring economic performance, substantial variations in human activities arise. If human activities are declining in booming cities in China, aggregated economic growth may not fully reflect the success of cities in terms of improvements on the vibrancy of human activities. The emergence of big data in the urban context facilitates a list of options for geographers and planners to identify city vibrancy, by using precise time and location information on tracking individuals' daily activities.

Table 8.2 Distribution of aggregated human activity among city centre, suburbs and edge towns

	Daytime average (06:00–19:00)		24-hour average	
	Mean (s.d)	Hourly change rate	Mean (s.d)	Hourly change rate
	500m grid unit			
City centre	7.927 (6.883)	31.538%	6.359 (5.497)	17.239%
Suburb	1.546 (2.614)	29.069%	1.258 (2.047)	17.087%
Inner suburb	4.513 (4.076)	31.140%	3.601 (3.054)	17.318%
Edge towns	0.907 (1.557)	27.376%	0.753 (1.283)	16.981%
	2km grid unit			
City centre	138.478 (58.425)	31.994%	109.905 (46.943)	17.176%
Suburb	24.641 (33.135)	29.242%	20.007 (25.887)	17.093%
Inner suburb	71.405 (44.395)	31.480%	56.808 (33.189)	17.350%
Edge towns	14.515 (18.202)	27.443%	12.039 (14.800)	16.966%

Note: This table reports the mean and standard deviations of activity intensities across urban and suburban areas (in 1,000 persons per unit).

Mechanisms

This section follows the above section and is structured as follows: the first subsection proposes a conceptual model of urban vibrancy from the big-data perspective. The second subsection examines the potential institutional and market forces at work.

Conceptualizing a model of city structures from the big-data perspective

This subsection exploits a conceptual model of city structures in Beijing (see Figure 8.8). The model generalizes and highlights the fundamental characteristics of urban-vibrancy patterns. It can be applied to other fast-growing cities by incorporating human activity with specific locational characteristics.

The mobile-phone positioning data suggest that human activities are evolving from the city centre to the spatially dispersed metropolitan areas. Overall, Beijing is a highly compact city. Human activities are almost all concentrated in the central-city areas throughout the day, and the density of human activities is declining sharply along with the distance from the CBD. In the past, only a small proportion of human activities were concentrated in self-inclusive industrial sites (such as *Shou Gang*) and affordable residential communities (such as *Hui Long Guan*,

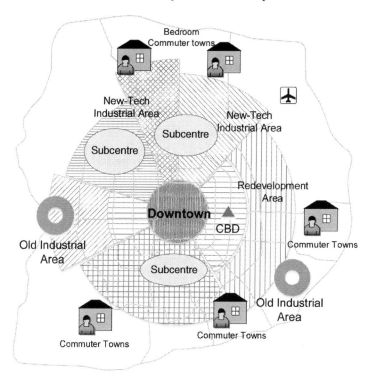

Figure 8.8 Conceptual model of city structures

and Tian Tong Yuan) in the scattered edged towns. This was a typical urban spatial structure in China as a by-product of planning cities in the centrally planned
economy era, when investment in rail-transit infrastructure was underdeveloped in
connecting core areas to peripheral areas. Commuting distances were limited owing
to the self-inclusive State-owned enterprise community development (*Danwei Da
Yuan*), and residents' daily activities were strictly constrained by the *Danwei* (units)
for access to local public goods, private goods, leisure services and public transportation (Shen, 1998; Wu and Yeh, 1999; Wang and Chai, 2009). As a result of
limited vacant land parcels available in city-centre areas, large industrial sites and
affordable residential communities were allocated in suburban areas, which were
connected to the city-centre areas through a few main expressways.

The new urban spatial structure in Beijing is characterized by vibrant human-
activity patterns in both traditional city-centre areas and sprawling suburban
areas. Through recent improvement schemes for public infrastructure (e.g. hospitals, schools, and parks) and transport network expansion, affordable residential
communities and industrial sites in edged towns are more closely linked with
city-centre areas, and employment centres have been gradually dispersed from the
traditional CBD to the suburban CBD urban fringe areas, such as *Zhong-Guan-
Cun* and the Olympic park. Unlike before, people now living in suburban areas

have good access to a diverse set of private goods and leisure services without needing to go downtown for shopping or to go to the theatre. Suburban areas used to be 'bedrooms' or 'ghost' towns with a low density of human activities, but now human activities in suburban areas have begun to be vibrant. The following section will elaborate on the institutional and market forces at work in more detail.

Institutional and market forces

Changes in the distribution of human activities can be easily detected in Figure 8.7, from the big-data perspective, but fully understanding their implications for city structures entails understanding the underlying institutional and market forces at work.

Most economic geographers and planners view the configuration of land use as a necessity to stimulate social engagement and strengthen the intensity of human activities. The evolution of planning practice and theories follows a trajectory from describing the concrete configuration of land use to theorizing considerations about city vibrancy (Jacobs, 1961; Ganderton, 1994; Glaeser et al., 2001). For example, whether, and to what extent, is the configuration of land use associated with the intensity of human activities? The existing empirical knowledge on this question in China is relatively limited. In fact, experiments should be carried out to analyse the role that human activities play in the development of vibrant cities, with the potential to be connected to land use for housing and to consumption amenities on micro-geographical scales (Wu et al., 2016b). The following parts of this section will describe some of these aspects of Beijing in detail, to provide the context for the above conceptual model.

In the Chinese urban system there are substantial variations in urban spatial structures and vibrancy patterns across cities, although Beijing's scenario is the typical one. The contemporary Beijing city structure involves a combination of traditional *Danwei* (units) and emerging private-sector companies as key non-residential land users, as well as a combination of socialist *Danwei* housing and market-based housing, as key actors for residential land. Before the land and housing-market reforms, *Danwei* (units) provided local residents with housing and other public goods and services in the vicinity of *Danwei* (Gaubatz, 1999). The *Danwei* system therefore directly affected Beijing's land-use patterns through its dominant role in housing provision and in the configuration of land use (Wang and Murie, 1999). This *Danwei* system was actually an institutional tool to restrict human activities to a limited area, to achieve a balance of job and housing and the planning objectives of compact cities. The mobile-phone positioning big data show that in contemporary Beijing, *Danwei* (units) also seem to support the planning objective of retaining human activities in the city centre to promote urban vibrancy. A major intended objective of land and housing-market reforms has been to stimulate private investment in market-based land and housing development, so as to gradually eliminate the influence of the *Danwei* system on the configuration of land use and vibrancy patterns.

After the *Danwei*-based land and housing-provision system was phased out, most human activities in large Chinese cities such as Beijing were still compacted in urbanized areas. This consequence was driven by several factors. First, workers from the same *Danwei* (unit) did not necessarily live together in the same community. Like most US and UK cities, spatial disparity patterns between job locations and residential locations were emerging in Beijing, leading to a prolonged and diversified intensity distribution of human activities over time and across space. As a result, market forces and heterogeneous residential sorting preferences played important roles in shifting the transformation of Beijing's spatial structure from a typical monocentric model to an emerging polycentric one. This also linked to the driving force generated by benefits from firm agglomeration. In order to gain agglomeration benefits, firms tended to locate near the central business district (such as *Guomao* in Beijing) and subcentres (such as the *Zhong-Guan-Cun* and Olympic zones in Beijing), leading to high land prices in these areas. When residents cannot afford to buy or rent properties near these areas, speedy transportation facilities are required to support the prolonged commute from the suburbs and edged towns with cheaper land prices to downtown areas with a high concentration of job opportunities. As a result of these underlying mechanisms, it is not surprising to observe spatial-temporal variations of human activities between urban areas and suburban areas from the mobile-phone positioning data perspective. In this regard, the urban transformation resulting from changing the land-use and housing-provision system may spur the challenge of achieving vibrancy in the Chinese cities. Policymakers may need to look at the relationship between the configuration of land-use and human-activity patterns to retain vibrant neighbourhoods, avoid 'ghost' towns and improve social harmony.

Since the market-based mechanism plays a dominant role in the configuration of contemporary land use, this conceptual model supports the view that a less balanced job–housing relationship may lead to not only longer commutes but also much more diversified activity patterns between people and places, 24 hours a day. Of course, the present conceptual model is among the first attempts to highlight the institutional and market driving forces of the urban-vibrancy patterns over time and space. Further studies are needed to substantiate the visualization of vibrancy patterns over a longer time span, and examine the sensitivity of the visualized patterns to changes in data resources. More generally, what we may learn is probably beyond the spatial structure identification of city vibrancy, and the proposed conceptual model framework suggests the possibility of examining the relationship between the intensity of human activities and the distribution of local land use.

Planning approaches for influencing urban vibrancy have attached great importance to considering the levels and patterns of human activities in the urban space. The above section attempts to balance the generalization of urban vibrancy with the empirical evidence of human activities and detailed case evaluations on which speculation relies. Generally, the theoretical discussions noted in the literature and recent policy debates are related to three interlinked dimensions of urban vibrancy: human activity; the configuration of land use; and city structure. To avoid a broad inquiry, this section views the formation of city structure as a contextual constraint in which spatial intensity disparities of human activities occur through the configuration of land use in urban space. The whole human-activity process can also be influenced by the wider political economy. This perspective entails the necessity of understanding how city structures and the configuration of land use are organized in China. Most existing research into the causes and consequences of urban planning policies have focused on specific sectors, such as housing and land markets (Zhu, 1994; Zhou and Logan, 1996; Wang and Murie, 1996; Zheng and Kahn, 2008; Wu, 2015), local amenities and infrastructure (Cheshire and Sheppard, 1995; Wu and Dong, 2014; Wu et al., 2015). There is also evidence to suggest significant differences in the land-use distribution in the Chinese cities before and after the political economic reforms since the 1980s. For example, Wu and Yeh (1997, 1999) examined the patterns of the changing spatial distribution and modes of land development in Guangzhou, and discovered the decentralization of city structures after the transition from a centrally planned economy to a socialist market economy. Zheng and Kahn (2008) found significant local public goods capitalization effects after the re-establishment of Beijing's housing and land markets. Within the land and housing marketization, seeing urban-vibrancy patterns through changes in human activities, resulting from the reduced importance of traditional *Danwei* in non-residential and residential land provision, has not been given enough attention by policymakers.

As outlined before, *Danwei* is a socialist-legacy term indicating the working place in China (Bray, 2005), which can provide employees with an attractive mix of land use within a given areal unit, including residential areas, working areas and leisure areas (Chai, 1996). In the centrally planned economy era, *Danwei* was the fundamental unit of China's urban activity patterns in which working, living and other social engagements were all integrated together (Björklund, 1986; Bray, 2005; Wang and Li, 2004). Within the *Danwei* system, employees were allocated housing units based on their occupation rank and their *Danwei* service time span (Wang and Murie, 1999; Wang and Li, 2004). Land parcels were allocated by local government through land-use plans to *Danwei* (units) to construct residential buildings and non-residential buildings that could meet the working and living needs of employees.

Before the economic transition reform from the 1980s, land-use patterns in Chinese cities were *Danwei*-based patterns with distinctive residential and non-residential zones (Wang and Murie, 1999). This *Danwei* system left employees' activities limited to a small buffer area, because their affiliated *Danwei* could virtually provide all public and private goods and services, from houses, factories, shops to schools, hospitals and restaurants (Chai, 1996). This *Danwei* system also contributed to the formation of a compact city structure in most Chinese cities, where almost all human activities could occur within the compact urban areas. After the economic transitional reform, people could freely choose their residential locations and job locations. The transition to the market-economic system thus resulted in the reduced importance of the *Danwei* legacy, mostly through housing and land-market reforms. In the post-reform era, *Danwei* could not gain freely allocated land parcels from the Government, and therefore could not allocate housing units to their employees as a package of social welfare, whereas private developers could directly develop land and housing, while people could trade these apartments on the market.

In addition to the property-market reforms, China has also experienced substantial changes in the labour and company markets. New types of employment organizations, including private enterprise and corporations, have emerged. This means that State-affiliated *Danwei* (units) are no longer the only employers, and people can choose their jobs in the labour market. In sum, economic transitions of the property and labour market in China have influenced not only the allocation of houses but also the location choice for houses (Wang and Li, 2004; Wu et al., 2013). Building on the land-price gradient theory, property-development companies can bid for land parcels at auctions, to develop residential and non-residential estates. As a result, the levels, patterns and locations of human activities are hypothesized to be associated with the configuration of land use in a modern-day Chinese city.

The changing urban-vibrancy process in Beijing can be summarized as follows: before the economic reform in the 1980s, the main actors in the urban space were State-affiliated *Danwei* (units) and their employees. The fundamental characteristic was the predominant role of State-affiliated *Danwei* and Government plans in allocating public resources, including housing, through the land-use provision system. Under this system, people could not choose residential and working locations and their daily activities were constrained surrounding their *Danwei*, leading to evenly distributed urban-vibrancy patterns in the urbanized areas. Local territorial planning with respect to urban sprawl through mixed land-use development programmes was rare. During the process, citywide land was bargained between *Danwei,* to jointly provide infrastructure and public services. A land-use plan could then be translated as a lens for reflecting sectoral resource allocations, rather than a means of promoting urban vibrancy through increased social interactions between people and places. In this *Danwei*-based city structure in the centrally planned economy era, the following characteristics can be identified:

- Land use was not determined by any market mechanism.
- The configuration of land use was mainly set within the Government allocation system rather than in line with market demands.
- Human-activity processes at the area unit level were determined from top-down in that the *Danwei* played a very important role in influencing the levels, patterns and locations of human-activity intensities.

In the post-reform era, the decentralization of Chinese cities including Beijing transformed urban-vibrancy patterns. The land-marketization policy introduced a new land-use mechanism, allowing not just State-affiliated *Danwei*, but also the private sector to participate in the configuration of land use by bidding for land parcels for residential and non-residential development. The price signal gradually became important in coordinating urban land-use allocation, and residents could choose where to live, work and play. Private entrepreneurs and migrant workers as emerging social classes could turn to the property market to buy or rent housing, while State-affiliated *Danwei* workers still relied on their *Danwei* for housing. Public goods and facilities were no longer provided by *Danwei*, but were organized by the municipal City Governments through different planning programmes. At the centre of this process was the transformation of the evenly distributed intensity of human activities in the centrally planned economy era to spatial-temporal intensity variations of human activities within the metropolitan area in a modern-day Chinese city. Three fundamental changes can be identified:

- A market mechanism has been established for guiding the configuration of land-use and urban development. In the centrally planned economic system, Government commands played a dominant role in influencing human activities and the allocation of public resources, including land and housing. In the new market mechanism, the Government used indirect interventions such as planning for land use to balance urban development patterns.
- Human-activity processes at the area unit level were from bottom to top rather than top-down in that the activities of employees, their patterns and locations were influenced by not just *Danwei*, but also by a wide range of factors such as local public goods, leisure and private services available to the general public.
- The planning initiative of land development has changed from being *Danwei*-specific or place-specific to being people-specific, involving considerations of a flourishing urban vibrancy. The new city structure has shifted to become a by-product of planning policies and human activities in both residential and non-residential areas.

While various aspects of urban development in China's transitional economy have been examined, there is relatively limited evidence of how urban-vibrancy patterns are associated with the configuration of land use on an hourly basis, 24 hours a day. This warrants further empirical study. However, big-data analysis by planners to enhance city vibrancy seems to be useful. Housing and consumption amenities are indispensable in cities. Trying to plan isolated and unique land use is probably pointless, and the scarcity of amenities owing to undesired land use would possibly even be harmful to gentrifying vibrant neighbourhoods. The future success of city planning relies on how to attract and retain activities with good human capital. This suggests that providing facilities for work, living and play, as well as for transportation, would be a particularly effective policy tool to enhance city vibrancy in a sustainable way.

Conclusion

This chapter shed light on several aspects of intra-city spatial structure transformation. First of all, evidence suggests that planning policies that reform the land and housing markets in Chinese cities have significant economic implications for the transformation of city structure. This chapter then proposed a conceptual framework that combines theoretical thinking with big data, to examine urban-vibrancy patterns and the potential channels at work. This hybrid type of empirical analysis should have a promising future by providing solutions for policymakers when they want to quantify evidence on the spatial-temporal integration of human activities and land use.

Given the emergence of big data, it is now possible for planners to identify the information about human activities that can be fine-scaled from the spatial-temporal perspective, and to consider more subtle changes in local areas, to help explain the uncertain geographic context in urban settings (Kwan, 2012). In light of these newly available big data, what would then be the new focus of planning policies in tracking the intensity diffusion of human activities, and the configuration of land use? In practice, the focus should be on encouraging human activities in declining places and edged towns, and dealing with overheated activity intensities in the city centres, to allow for social interactions related to work, play and living across the urban space. Given that the vibrancy of cities depends largely on the intensity of human activities, it is reasonable to argue that the planning approaches need to focus on investing in infrastructure, and mixed land-use patterns for more social engagement and higher productivity. More broadly speaking, this will provide useful insights into many other problems to be solved through planning approaches, including traffic congestion and inappropriately long distances between the working place and home.

To summarize, there is evidence that planning systems that affect the configuration of land use have significant impacts on urban-vibrancy patterns. Such effects have not drawn the sufficient attention of planners and policymakers but will need to be considered when evaluating the implicit socioeconomic benefits and costs associated with planning policies. This is an emerging challenge that has already recognized in large developing countries. However, the Chinese planning system is in a unique position, partly because of the coexistence of non-market and market mechanisms in terms of land provision, and partly because of the diversified distribution of human activities across cities. It has transformed from a socialist land-allocation system on a *Danwei* basis into a market-orientated land-use system on a project basis, where developers can bid for land parcels at auction. In addition, there is evidence that planning approaches on the configuration of land use interact significantly with the intensity of human activities between urban and suburban areas, leading to a rise of edged towns and subcentres. Finally, this human-activity process provides an alternative way to analyse the transformation of city-vibrancy patterns by urban planning approaches in the big-data era.

Other possible implicit impacts of the planning policies are not well understood (for example, the impact on residents' subjective well-being, or the dynamic effects on neighbourhood gentrification), but they appear to be substantial. Successive Chinese city-planning policies should attempt to address these problems by shifting from place-based planning approaches to people-based planning approaches. The recent set of liveability city-planning initiatives introduced in 2005, were increasingly supported by the Beijing Government to focus on city vibrancy by analysing the dynamics of human activities, and people's perceived living experiences as imposed by the planning system (Zhang et al., 2006).

An important implication of this work is to question the extent to which the dynamic patterns of activity intensity are associated with the spatial distribution of land and housing prices over space. The demand for residential and non-residential land use for business, leisure and residential activities is indispensable in cities. In the presence of comparative locational advantages and the high intensity of human activities could be capitalized into land and housing prices, while areas with a consistently low intensity of human activities could be seen as depressed neighbourhoods of low property-development value. In cases where this is true, mayors and planners should design effective planning instruments to promote the areas' vibrancy by analysing human activities and consumption behaviour.

The future success of city planning is likely to be dependent on the extent to which urban-vibrancy patterns will be sustainable. This springs from Jacobs' (1961) proposition that dense and mixed land use could be a prominent tool in enhancing the intensity of human activities and enriching the life of cities. However, it is helpful for future city-planning policymakers to consider the association between human activities and the configuration of land use, even if motivations of human activities are difficult to measure precisely from the big-data perspective. Basically, there is a growing body of literature arguing the importance of applying big-data information to guide urban planning policies and practices. But any useful big data in the urban context should try to rigorously and quantitatively measure the implicit impacts of the planning system, which includes the relationship configuration of land use and various aspects of urban-vibrancy patterns. There may also be multiplier effects of the planning system on local people's quality of life associated with human activities, but our existing empirical knowledge on this topic is limited. It will be interesting to see more innovative use of urban big data in this line of research, which will help to improve the design for effective planning policies.

Notes

1 *Hukou*, like the passport, defines the extent to which a person can obtain access to social welfare benefits in China, which segregates urban residents into two major groups: permanent residents with the host city's *Hukou*; and migrants who live or work in the host city but do not have the host city's *Hukou*. Only those non-migrants with the host city's *Hukou* can buy affordable housing in this transitional housing system.
2 The CBD in Beijing is located to the east of the world-famous *Tiananmen* Square, called '*Guomao*', and has a cluster of high-rise office buildings and many international company headquarters.
3 In order to attract elite employees, most work units choose to build this subsidized housing in places adjacent to their workplaces and have high neighbourhood quality.
4 I am indebted to Jianghao Wang for providing the mobile-phone positioning data.

References

Alonso, W. 1964. *Location and Land Use*. Cambridge, MA: Harvard University Press.
Anas, A. 1992. *Residential Location Markets and Urban Transportation*. New York: Academic Press.

Bayer, P., Ferreira, F. and McMillan, R. 2007. A unified framework for measuring preferences for schools and neighborhoods. Journal of Political Economy 115(4), 588–638.

Björklund, E.M. 1986. The Danwei: Sociospatial characteristics of work units in China's urban society. Economic Geography, 62(1), 19–29.

Blondel, V., Decuyper, A. and Krings, G. 2015. A survey of results on mobile phone data-sets analysis. EPJ Data Science, 4(1), 10.

Bray, D. 2005. *Social Space and Governance in Urban China: The Danwei System from Origins to Reform.* Stanford, CA: Stanford University Press.

Brown, B. 1985. Location and Housing Demand. Journal of Urban Economics 17, 30–41.

Cervero R. 1996. Mixed land-uses and commuting: Evidence from the American housing survey. Transportation Research Part A: Policy and Practice, 30, 361–377.

Chai, Y., 1996. Danwei-centered activity space in Chinese cities: A case study of Lanzhou. Geography Research, 15(1), 30–38 [in Chinese].

Cheshire, P.C. 2008. Introduction of price signals into land use planning: Are they applicable in China? in Song, Yang and Ding, Chengri, (eds.) *Urbanization in China: Critical Issues in an Era of Rapid Growth.* Cambridge, MA: Lincoln Institute of Land Policy.

Cheshire, P.C. and Hilber, C. 2008. Office space supply restrictions in Britain: The political economy of market revenge. Economic Journal, 118, F185–F221.

Cheshire, P.C., Marlee, I. and Sheppard, S. 1999. Development of a microsimulation model for analysing the effects of the planning system housing choices: Final Report, London: Department of Geography and Environment, London School of Economics.

Cheshire, P.C. and Sheppard, S. 1995. On the price of land and the value of amenities, Economica, 62, 247–267.

Cheshire, P.C. and Sheppard, S. 1998. Estimating Demand for Housing, Land, and Neighbourhood Characteristics, Oxford Bulletin of Economics and Statistics, 60, 357–382.

Cheshire, P.C. and Sheppard, S. 2002. Welfare economics of land use regulation. Journal of Urban Economics, 52, 242–269.

Cheshire, P.C. and Sheppard, S. 2004. Land markets and land market regulation: Progress towards understanding. Regional Science and Urban Economics, 34, 619–637.

Cheshire, P.C. and Sheppard, S. 2005. The introduction of price signals into land use planning decision-making: A proposal. Urban Studies, 42, 647–663.

Deville, P., Linard, C., Martin, S., Gilbert, M., Stevens, F.R. and Gaughan, A.E. 2014. Dynamic population mapping using mobile phone data. Proceedings of the National Academy of Sciences of the United States of America, 111(45), 15888–15893.

Dowall, D.E. 1994. Urban residential redevelopment in the People's Republic of China. Urban Studies, 31, 1497–1516.

Epple, D. and Platt, G.J. 1998. Equilibrium and local redistribution in an urban economy when households differ in both preferences and income, Journal of Urban Economics, 43, 23–51.

Ganderton, P. 1994. Modelling the land conversion process: A realist perspective. Environment and Planning A, 26, 803–819.

Gaubatz, P. 1999. China's urban transformation: Patterns and processes of morphological change in Beijing, Shanghai and Guangzhou. Urban Studies, 36(9), 1451–1521.

Glaeser, E.L., Kahn, M.E. and Rappaport, J.M. 2008. Why do the poor live in cities? The role of public transportation. Journal of Urban Economics 63(1), 1–24.

Glaeser, E.L., Kolko, J. and Saiz, A. 2001. Consumer city. Journal of Economic Geography, 1(1), 27–50.

Glaeser, E.L. Sacerdote, B. and Scheinkman, J.A. 1996. Crime and social interactions. Quarterly Journal of Economics 111(2), 507–548.

Huang, Y.Q. 2004. Housing stock, housing market and government behavior: A case study of three cities in China. Environment and Planning A, 36, 45–68.

Huang, Y.Q and Clark, W.A.V. 2002. Housing tenure choice in transitional urban China: A multilevel analysis. Urban Studies, 39, 7–23.

Huang, Y.Q. and Jiang, L.W. 2009. Housing inequality in transitional Beijing. International Journal of Urban and Regional Research, 33(4), 936–956.

Ioannides, Y.M. and Zabel, J.E. 2008. Interactions, neighborhood selection and housing demand, Journal of Urban Economics 63, 229–252.

Jacobs, J. 1961. *The Death and Life of Great American Cities*. New York: Random House.

Jacobs-Crisioni, C., Rietveld, P., Koomen, E. and Tranos, E. 2014. Evaluating the impact of land-use density and mix on spatiotemporal urban activity patterns: An exploratory study using mobile phone data. Environment and Planning A, 46(11), 2769–2785.

Kwan, M.-P. 2012. The uncertain geographic context problem. Annals of the Association of American Geographers 102 (5), 958–968.

LeRoy, S.F. and Sonstelie, J. 1983. Paradise lost and regained: Transport innovation, income, and residential location. Journal of Urban Economics 13, 67–89.

Li, S.M. 2000. Housing consumption in urban China: A comparative study of Beijing and Guangzhou, Environment and Planning A, 32, 1115–1134.

Liu, X. and J. Wang, 2015. The geography of Weibo. Environment and Planning A, 47(6), 1231–1234.

Logan, J.R., Zhang, W.W. and Xu, H.W. 2010. The winners in China's urban housing reform. Housing Studies, 25(1), 101–118.

Louail, T., Lenormand, M., Cantu Ros, O.G., Picornell, M., Herranz, R., Frias-Martinez, E., Ramasco, J. and Barthelemy, M. 2014. From mobile phone data to the spatial structure of cities. Scientific Reports, 4, 52–76.

Mills, E.S. 1967. An aggregative model of resource allocation in a metropolitan area. American Economics Review 57, 197–210.

Muth, R.F. 1969. *Cities and Housing*. Chicago: University of Chicago Press.

Nechyba, T.J. 1997. Existence of equilibrium and stratification in local and hierarchical Tiebout economies with property taxes and voting. Economic Theory 10, 277–304.

Nee, V. 1992. Organizational dynamics of market transition: Hybrid forms, property rights, and mixed economy in China. Administrative Science Quarterly, 37, 1–27.

Rosen, S. 2002. Markets and diversity. American Economic Review, 92(1), 1–15.

Sato, H. 2006. Housing inequality and housing poverty in urban China in the late 1990s. China Economic Review, 17, 37–50.

Shen, Q. 1998. Location characteristics of inner-city neighborhoods and employment accessibility of low-wage workers. Environment and Planning B: Planning and Design, 25(3), 345–365.

Tiebout, C.M. 1956. A pure theory of local expenditures. Journal of Political Economy 64, 416–424.

Wang, D. and Chai, Y. 2009. The jobs-housing relationship and commuting in Beijing, China: The legacy of Danwei. Journal of Transport Geography, 17(1), 30–38.

Wang, D.G. and Li, S.M. 2004, Housing preferences in a transitional housing system: the case of Beijing, China. Environment and Planning A, 36, 69–87.

Wang, D. and Li, S.M. 2004. Housing choice in a transitional economy: the case of Beijing, China. Environment and Planning A, 36(1), 69–87.

Wang, Y.P. and Murie, A. 1996. The process of commercialisation of urban housing in China. Urban Studies, 33, 971–989.

Wang, Y.P. and Murie, A. 1999. Commercial housing development in urban China. Urban Studies, 36(9), 1475–1494.

Wu, F. 2002. Socio-spatial differentiation in urban China: Evidence from Shanghai's real estate markets. Environment and Planning A, 34, 1591–615.

Wu, F. 2009. Land development, inequality and urban villages in China. International Journal of Urban and Regional Research, 33, 885–889.

Wu, F. 2015. *Planning for Growth: Urban and Regional Planning in China.* London: Routledge.

Wu, F.L. and Yeh, A.G. 1997.Changing spatial distribution and determinants of land development in Chinese cities in the transition from a centrally planned economy to a socialist market economy: A case study of Guangzhou. Urban Studies, 34, 1851–1879.

Wu, F.L. and Yeh, A.G. 1999. Urban spatial structure in a transitional economy. Journal of the American Planning Association, 65(4), 377–394.

Wu, W. and Dong, G. 2014. Valuing green amenities in a spatial context. Journal of Regional Science 54, 569–585.

Wu, W., Dong, G. and Wang, B. 2015. Does planning matter? Effects on land markets. Journal of Real Estate Finance and Economics, 50, 242–269.

Wu, W., Wang, J. and Dai, T. 2016a. The geography of cultural ties and human mobility: Big data in urban contexts. Annals of the Association of American Geographers, 106(3), 612–630.

Wu, W., Wang, J., Li, C. and Wang, X. 2016b. *The Geography of City Liveliness and Land-use Configurations: Evidence from Location-Based Big Data in Beijing.* SERC Discussion Paper No.201. London: London School of Economics and Political Science.

Wu, W., Zhang, W. and Dong, G. 2011. Spatial Variation of Residential Land Bid-rent Curves in Transitional Beijing City. Scientia Geographica Sinica, 31(5), 520–527 [in Chinese].

Wu, W., Zhang, W. and Dong, G. 2013. Determinant of residential location choice in a transitional housing market: Evidence based on micro survey from Beijing. Habitat International, 39, 16–24.

Zhang, W., Yin, W., Zhang, J. et al. 2006. *A study of livable cities in China (Beijing).* Beijing: Social Sciences Academic Press (China) [in Chinese].

Zheng, S., Fu, Y.M. and Liu, H.Y. 2006. Housing-choice hindrances and urban spatial structure: Evidence from matched location and location-preference data in Chinese cities. Journal of Urban Economics, 60, 535–557.

Zheng, S. and Kahn, M.E. 2008. Land and residential property markets in a booming economy: New evidence from Beijing. Journal of Urban Economics, 63, 743–757.

Zheng, S. and Kahn, M.E. 2013. Does government investment in local public goods spur gentrification? Evidence from Beijing. Real Estate Economics, 41(1), 1–28.

Zhou, M. and Logan, J.R. 1996. Market transition and the commodification of housing in urban China. International Journal of Urban and Regional Research, 20, 400–421.

Zhu, J. 1994. Changing land policy and its impact on local growth: The experience of the Shenzhen Special Economic Zone, China, in the 1980s. Urban Studies, 31, 1611–1623.

Part IV

Conclusions

9   Concluding remarks

The significance of planning policies in driving the diffusion and agglomeration of labour, capital and infrastructure resources makes understanding their spatial economic implications important. This is also important for shaping China's urban and regional development. And the rules and guidelines of Chinese planning systems have changed dramatically over the past sixty-five years, owing to the transformation from a centrally planned economy era to a market-orientated economy era. Assessment of the spatial economic consequences of this transformation is difficult as there are many potential stages of institutional change and causal impacts for evaluation.

This is a challenging and meaningful task when the objectives of planning policies are likely to reduce spatial disparities and improve economic performance locally and regionally. But there are potentially useful track records and differential timing of planning programmes' implementation – including a series of Five-Year-Plans and major regional development plans – to aid in identifying and documenting plausible implications for the spatial agglomeration of cities and regions; an issue that is highly sensitive in China. This book focuses mainly on the implications of planning policies on the spatial-temporal evolution of China's urban and regional development. There has been a fundamental shift in planning-policy philosophy and a change in focus from promoting uneven spatial development to enhancing the coordinated development of the spatial economy. Over the past sixty years, most Chinese cities have seen massive transport infrastructure planning which has reshaped their internal urban spatial structures and their external access to markets in other cities. The rapidly growing air- and rail-transportation system can alleviate the pressure of road traffic, change the way people travel and contribute to neighbourhood gentrification and the formation of urban systems and hierarchies. The importance of planning policies in enhancing the spatial economic performance is well recognized in China. In terms of temporal variation, it is concentrated in both the market-orientated economy era (1980–present) and in the centrally planned economy era (1950s–1980s), coupled with the implementation of various planning programmes that spring from economic agglomeration in transporting fundamental production factors such as labour, capital and other resources between cities and regions. In terms of spatial variation, cities in the coastal region have gained better access to markets than inland cities, and most old mining towns and industrial cities have not performed as well as administrative mega-cities such as Beijing and Shanghai, or new cities such as Shenzhen.

That is to say, China's economic growth is not evenly distributed, just like anywhere else. The quality and stages of industrialization and urbanization vary substantially within and across regions. Some of the major cities and urban agglomeration belts have more skilled labour, more investment opportunities and better infrastructure accessibility. In general, cities in the coastal regions have outperformed those in the western regions, in terms of economic output and innovation in the market-orientated economy era. Cities in the very mountainous areas and the north-eastern region have 'outperformed' those in the coastal regions, as a result of plentiful Government investment and restrictions on the distribution of labour, private capital and other resources during the centrally planned economy era. While some old mining towns and industrial cities such as Karamay have performed well, most old mining towns and industrial cities have 'underperformed' compared to those with comparative locational advantages and good market potential, such as Anshan, Fushun and other cities in the north-eastern region.

With these implications and in a more detailed interpretation, Chapter 2 explained the fundamentals of China's planning policies with respect to the rationale, principles, main content and way they played a role in the configuration of the spatial economy. In fact, cities, location and infrastructure are not isolated geographic objects. Instead, what have been implemented by the planning system regarding infrastructure, cities and location are critical determinants for influencing the variation in economic output over space. So it is important to understand what works for shaping and enhancing the spatial economic performance before policymakers apply planning policies to intervene in the distribution and re-allocation of economic activities within and across regions.

The history of economic growth in the People's Republic of China's is not long but is vitally important. As discussed in Part II, the formation of regional inequality was influenced largely by the evolution of planning policies (e.g. Third-tier construction, and old industrial city regeneration etc.). But individual cities do not exist in isolation, and intercity connections via air and rail transportation are crucial determinants of national geographic economic patterns and urban systems. Thus it is important to understand the transport connections between cities and how these networks shape the urban development and agglomeration. These effects have fascinated economists and geographers alike. Despite the central role of cities and infrastructure in theoretical models, more evidence is needed to shed light on the economic impacts of planning policies in China. With the new availability of micro-geographical data, recent researchers have begun to evaluate the effectiveness of these planning policies on promoting local economic growth in a causal sense. The lesson emerging from Chapter 5 further indicates the significant heterogeneity of spatial disparities of agglomerations. The evidence suggests that disparities between regions appear to occur when the Central Government carefully intervenes in urban and regional development. When looking at differences across cities and regions, the evidence of spatial disparities can be partly explained by either historical or contemporary planning policies. But researchers are increasingly concerned with whether China is intervening with the right governance toolkits to influence national economic layout, where disparities between cities are generated spatially in the economy. While many argue for more investment in cities and regions where the economic performance is lagging behind, the counter-scenario evidence is that planning policies facilitating the connection between cities can generate multiplier benefits for larger cities and wealthier places. This relates to another central dimension of this book: how transport-infrastructure expansion affects the evolution of urban networks (Chapters 6 and 7). It is self-evident that the new transport infrastructure facilitates links among people, firms and markets and saves commuting time. The time saved is then converted into a measurement of economic benefits from transport improvement, based on the market potential function that has been used elsewhere in the literature. Here the evidence suggests that mega-cities are highly connected cities, and disparities of benefits gained from transport improvement between mega-cities and peripheral cities are also obvious. Thus proponents who argue that transport improvement is a cost-effective way for growth should be treated with caution in the spatial context. On the basis of this kind of 'uneven' pattern evidence, policymakers should balance China's locational planning policies between declining cities and growing cities, where economic and transport demand is booming.

All in all, it is clear that the levels and clustering patterns of industrialization and urbanization are important for local and regional development. The pre-1950 structure of industrial activities has influenced how planning policies respond to the selection of targeted cities and regions for industrial development, leading to widening spatial economic disparities. Policymakers in China have recognized the importance of access to transport infrastructure in shaping interregional connections and economic exchanges. But the expansion and construction of transport infrastructure are not assigned randomly over space. The gain and loss of comparative locational advantages for cities with better access to markets and the transport system are important drivers in the rise, decline and regeneration of cities. The variation in agglomeration economics provides another possible explanation for the uneven spatial economic performance of cities and regions. In addition, wealthier and bigger cities could attract more skilled labour, but it appears that the cost of living is high in these cities. Further studies are encouraged to examine the spatial trends of human and capital flow from First-tier cities, such as Beijing and Shanghai, to Second-tier cities. The re-allocation of labour and other fundamental production factors between places can help reinforce urban and regional agglomeration. This is related to one focus of the literature: how planning policies shape urban and regional agglomerations through the combination of market mechanisms and planning instruments. As shown in Chapter 5, recent regional planning policies push forward the formation of urban and regional agglomerations as the strategic priority for sustaining China's economic growth. The uneven spatial economic performance of cities and regions can be explained largely by differences in locational characteristics and infrastructure, as directly and indirectly affected by the current planning system.

At the intra-city level, the transformation of city growth is also not straightforward. Yet the ultimate success of planning approaches relies on the vibrancy of cities, which is centred mainly on measuring human activities rather than measuring economic performance. If human activities are declining in booming cities, then the success of cities regarding the well-being of their citizens may be overestimated when only considering aggregated economic growth. The emergence of big data in the urban context facilitates the list of options for planners to track individuals' daily activity with precise time and position information, and provides opportunities to use mobile-phone positioning data as a proxy to assess urban-vibrancy patterns. The evidence presented in Chapter 8 on 'ebbs and flows' of the human-activity process supports this claim, but land-use configuration of residential and non-residential land use may influence the dynamics of human-activity levels and patterns, in which the same area can exert differential contextual influences using different spatial and temporal dimensions. As a policy option it is expected that the future success of cities relies on planning approaches for dense and mixed-land uses that can facilitate human-activity levels.

Policymakers are concerned with ways of improving spatial economic development, in order to meet planning objectives, such as achieving coordinated regional development, optimizing the spatial layout of infrastructure and the urban system and promoting the overall growth and welfare of the whole country etc. As discussed in this book, interventions of planning policies may have ignored the market mechanism in the centrally planned economy era. Whereas recent studies have suggested that place-based planning policies may not be effective in revitalizing declining areas and balancing spatial disparities in developed countries, they may still play an important role in enhancing spatial economic development. This, to some extent, relies on China's unique political structure that allows policymakers to implement planning programmes effectively, especially regarding the allocation of public spending budgets, infrastructure construction and the provision of State land resources, among other financial incentives. But in the market-orientated economy era, Chinese policymakers are more likely to achieve planning objectives through a more complete understanding of the market channels at work that drive spatial agglomeration, and eventually make clear what works for sustainable economic growth.

General lessons from this book mainly shed light on the importance of planning policies in influencing the spatially uneven economy in China. The above discussion summarizes two central points stressed by this book: at the regional level, the need to understand the rationale of planning policies that drive the uneven economic development, and the roles of planning policies in affecting the formation and evolution of urban system and regional agglomeration; and at the intra-city level, the importance of focusing on geographic uncertainties of urban vibrancy for people. It seems clear that the implications are seeking to shape China's planning policies regarding urban and regional development for decades to come. Some of these implications are highlighted below.

Transformation of Chinese cities in politically biased urban hierarchies

China's urban transformation has been phenomenal and has changed the shape of the national economic geography. Within China, there is an ongoing process of vast urbanization and intelligent, place-based planning policies, which not only affect city growth but also influence the more than one billion people there. China's unique centralized governance structure suggests that policy attention has focused heavily on cities with high political administration. Evidence of public investment in politically centred cities shows this clearly, hinging on the expectation that the successful growth of politically centred cities is of significant value to stimulate the transformation of nearby cities.

Interventions of planning policies to directly shape urban systems and hierarchies are essential in China. The evidence of planning good access to transport links and high-quality industrial parks in politically centred cities is strong. These locational planning programmes can directly influence the composition of industries within and between cities. More politically centred cities have better access to markets. Certainly, when a city is made more accessible, it can become more attractive to firms and people. The logic follows the available evidence that demand for markets in the politically centred cities increases, and thus new area-based investment programmes through planning policies in the form of industrial parks and transport infrastructure provisions could promote the transformation of cities in the politically biased urban hierarchies. This inequality is likely to be strengthened when agglomeration forces outweigh the diffusion forces in transferring fundamental production factors, such as skilled labour, capital and resources, between politically centred cities and peripheral cities with low political administrative ranks.

This is to say that planning policies need to focus on not only politically centred cities but also on fast-growing peripheral cities, to meet the demands of market integration. Improving the spatial reorganization of urban hierarchies seems important, as cities of various political administrative rank will benefit from agglomeration economies and dense urban systems for higher productivity. This is a key issue that will continue to challenge policymakers in China. It is even more important as the Chinese Government has recently faced slower development in the overall economy.

Cities are perhaps the greatest invention of human society (Glaeser, 2011). Careful research and analysis of planning policies have a crucial role to play in understanding how cities work, and how transport infrastructure systems work, whereas policymakers with a good sense of what works can improve the effectiveness of interventions and locational public investment (Cheshire et al., 2014; Gibbons, 2015). China's planning policies in urban and regional development have experienced dramatic changes every five years over the past six decades. This makes it difficult to make a consistent evaluation of the effectiveness of planning policies over time. Theoretical discussions and the evidence presented in this book aim to help policymakers and researchers gain a better understanding of the economic implications of China's planning policies on cities, location and infrastructure. But one practical problem associated with the evaluation of planning policies is the lack of clearly stated planning control thresholds and outcomes, and therefore evaluations of such policies are generally not possible by rigorous experiments. Recent good examples in this line of research include, but are not limited to Zheng and Kahn (2013), Faber (2014) and Baum-Snow et al. (2015).

China's planning policies that relate to urbanization and industrialization do influence the rise, decline and regeneration of cities. In the politically biased urban hierarchy, there exists the ongoing twelfth national planning programme, where cities gain and lose comparative locational advantages in different ways. It is useful to see what works and what doesn't work for planning policies in supporting urban growth. Planners should work hard to provide solutions for policymakers by participating in evaluations of policy effectiveness.

Planning for spatial agglomeration

The planning policies and strategies for reinforcing and sustaining urban and regional agglomeration should work alongside the market mechanism. In the centrally planned economy era without market mechanism, local governments' endeavours to establish industrial bases in specific locations and to relocate labour and resources from other places to specific locations, as guided by historical planning systems, seemed reasonable, but these efforts were not always very effective in sustaining economic agglomerations in the long term. After the economic reform and opening-up, the evidence from China suggests that the existence and persistence of agglomeration economies will reinforce the urban and regional agglomeration when the market mechanism and price signals become effective in coordinating the allocation of labour, capital and resources, and when policymakers relax the restrictions on the movement of these fundamental production factors between cities and regions. Any locational planning programmes aimed at influencing this spatial agglomeration process should fully understand how policy intervention could work together with the market mechanism. This is one important implication of the evidence presented in this book.

The Chinese evidence offers some insights into other transitional socialist and fast-urbanizing countries for shaping urban and regional agglomeration. First, locational effects such as wages, industrial productivity and population density are key determinants for the development of urban and regional agglomerations. The spillovers from these determinants are the spatial manifestation of agglomeration economies that are essential to the understanding of the economic, social and environmental-pollution inequalities between cities and regions. This is likely to be the same case in other transitional socialist and fast-urbanizing countries. Second, the Chinese planning system suggests the important role of planning policies in balancing spatial economic agglomeration in both the centrally planned economy era and the market-orientated economy era. In this regard, China's economic transitions have not changed the substantial impacts of planning policies on guiding economic development. They imply the presence of strong political power in guiding the implementation of planning policies to improve the formation and evolution of spatial agglomerations. Thus, there is still room for improving the effectiveness of China's planning policies, such as infrastructure development policies that could further influence the spatial disparities between core and peripheral cities in terms of economic performance. Basically, evidence and experience make China a special case for studying the transformation from a planning system which controls the economic performance used in many socialist countries to the market-orientated system applied in contemporary China. This is arguably the fundamental implication; that it is worthwhile to encourage future work on debating and evaluating China's planning policies.

Planning for infrastructure development

One important element of planning policies is improving the urban and regional development through investment in transport infrastructure. Economic studies have well documented the significant impacts of transport improvement on productivity and economic performance, locally and globally. There are several ways of rethinking the likely economic impact of transport-infrastructure expansion. The first way of rethinking infrastructure investment as a policy intervention for stimulating intercity connections suggests the evolution of the urban system and market potential. More than RMB one trillion (US$130 billion) has been invested recently through various planning programmes in expressways, airports and high-speed railways at the intercity level. Since the Eleventh Five-Year-Plan period, China has been the world's largest railway-transportation market and the second largest air-transportation market (just behind the US market). As explained in Chapter 6, there is clear evidence that the building of new airports and the expansion of airport networks matter a lot in influencing the dynamics of hub-spoke urban systems and hierarchies between regions. Another case in point is the expansion of the railway network in recent years (Chapter 7), because when a place gains better access to railway infrastructure, it may have greater local market potential. This will eventually influence spatial disparities in terms of productivity and other economic outcomes.

The second way of rethinking this rapid but differential spatial expansion in transport infrastructure suggests that investing in infrastructure in places with low connectivity will be an alternative to providing incentives for attracting private-capital investment, and will thereby influence the location and growth of economic activity. But infrastructure expansion is driven by decisions of Central Government regarding where to invest, both in physical and social infrastructure, in a context where land resources can be supplied by local government, and construction projects are under strict Government regulation. One of the basic implications of this non-random, distributed planning strategy on infrastructure is that public investment in infrastructure is likely to generate new evidence of the foundation that underlies economic geography theories. Traditional theory suggests that transport systems play a key role in the formation of urban systems and urban growth by facilitating the movements of goods, labour and other resources. Planning for intercity transport infrastructure expansion would therefore affect the spatial layout and structure of urban and regional agglomerations, by moving labour and resources from the edged places to the core places, facilitating industrialization and urbanization towards spatial directions, and offering low mobility costs for the movement of people and firms into different places to live, or to operate their businesses. These economic implications of transport improvements lead to a solid evidence base of predictions regarding the effect of transport-infrastructure expansion on subsequent economic growth. China's recent planning policies of transport-infrastructure investment provide a textbook scenario for studying the economic implications on cities and regions. Future work will focus on offering empirical assessment evidence to provide the precise mechanisms for how planning for infrastructure evolves with urban transformation.

Planning for city vibrancy

The evidence presented in this book indicates that policymakers concerned with urban economic growth should also consider locational planning approaches for stimulating the vibrancy of cities. This implies the importance of focusing on the vibrancy of human activities, rather than the general growth of productivity. This involves the examination of human activities' decline, resilience and recovery during both daytime and night-time hours. Chapter 8 aimed to characterize these patterns in terms of human activity, as reflected from new big-data sources. These patterns could be early warnings for areas that are in danger of decline, and thus help policymakers come to more informed decisions on how cities can be vibrant, and how planning interventions (for example, controls for mixed-land uses) can be managed to support the vibrancy of the city.

The most obvious planning implication pointing to the importance of city vibrancy is the rise of human-activity patterns in suburban areas. Under the traditional theory of a monocentric city structure, one would expect to see a higher level of activity in the city centre in the daytime compared with that in the edged city, on the assumption that people mostly work in the city centre and live in areas with lower rent, away from the city centre. However, the existing knowledge about whether this is the case in China is limited. The evidence suggests that human-activity intensities have grown fast in suburban areas, although one cannot pin down the precise activity from the usage data from social media or on mobile phones. But as a baseline, the implication is twofold. First, local residents are pushing activities towards areas with amenities that are valued by them. Second, areas with similar configurations of amenities can exert differential contextual impacts on human-activity levels between day and night, and between urban and suburban areas. The interpretation is that constraints on human mobility have decreased substantially, owing to public transport innovations, and that the planning of cities must cater to residents' working, living and leisure needs.

In the case of China, planning policies have a major impact on helping cities grow and prosper. The focus of this book is the economics of planning policies because of this concern. There is good evidence of the political support for locational infrastructure investment as a way of supporting city growth, as well as of mapping city vibrancy through mobile-phone big-data perspectives. The fundamental challenge to conventional wisdom is the application of a 'hybrid' approach that combines modern planning policies for stimulating city growth and approaches for stimulating city vibrancy. Addressing this challenge is crucial to the understanding of the processes behind the formation of cities, individual well-being and social harmony, as well as to the empirical evaluation of market reform, land development and urban vibrancy.

Planning for reshaping the economic geography

Tracking the economic implications of Chinese planning policy is an increasingly important and controversial topic. Before ending this conclusion, however, it is important to go beyond the traditional economic thinking and to assess more profound implications for reshaping economic geography in China. In a large developing country like China, differences in economic performance across cities reflect the interaction of planning policies and market mechanisms. While looking at spatial disparities in terms of economic outcomes it is useful for understanding how planning policies work locally and globally. This is indeed the case in China. Over the past six decades, China's economic activities have been concentrated mostly on cities located on the east side of the 'Heihe–Tengchong Line'; a hypothetical 'geographic-demographic disparity line', as proposed by a famous Chinese geographer, Huanyong Hu (1935). Of course, this does not mean that there is no contribution to national economic growth from cities on the west side of the "Heihe–Tengchong Line'. However, there are good reasons to think that a place may become more productive in an economy with fewer geographic constraints and fewer concerns about environmental protection. For example, some places such as grassland and forestry areas in Inner Mongolia, Tibet and Xinjiang are not suitable for rapid urbanization and industrialization, so planning policy interventions should focusd on developing low-carbon emission industries and tourism, rather than building bigger cities and large factories in these places.

Over history, Chinese planning systems have evolved with dramatic transformations, and there have been innovations in the design and implementation of planning policies from the First to the latest Five-Year-Plan period. Recognizing the fact that not all cities are suitable for rapid industrial development is not a straightforward process. From this perspective, it appears that the unevenness of spatial economic performance is a natural evolution process. Thus, policies need to be tailored to meet the needs of the socioeconomic and geographical forces at stake, rather than simply balance economic growth between regions. Fortunately, recent planning policies, such as the *Main Functional Area Plan,* have recognized the inequality of geographical characteristics across Chinese counties, and offered a solid guide to assessing the overall effects of planning policies on reshaping economic geography in China. These policies are sound planning initiatives, and if they work well in practice, there will be more hope to achieve sustainable development.

References

Baum-Snow, N., Brandt, L., Henderson, J.V., Turner, M. and Zhang, Q. 2015. *Roads, Railways and the Decentralization of Chinese Cities,* London: LSE manuscript.

Cheshire, P., Nathan, M. and Overman, H.G. 2014. *Urban Economics and Urban Policy: Challenging Conventional Policy Wisdom*, London: Edward Elgar.

Faber, B. 2014. Trade integration, market size, and industrialization: Evidence from China's national trunk highway system, Review of Economic Studies, 81, 1046–1070.

Gibbons, S. 2015. *Planes, Trains and Automobiles: The Economic Impact of Transport Infrastructure*, London: LSE Spatial Economics Research Centre Policy Paper No. SERC PP013

Glaser, E. 2011. *The Triumph of the City*. London: Pan Macmillan.

Hu, H.Y. 1935. The distribution of population in China. Journal of Geographical Society (*di li xue bao*), 2, 33–74 [in Chinese].

Zheng, S. and Kahn, M.E. (2013). China's bullet trains facilitate market integration and mitigate the cost of megacity growth, Proceedings of the National Academy of Sciences, 110(14), 1248–1253.

Index